Pocket Book of
British Ceramic Marks

Also by J. P. Cushion
(in collaboration with W. B. Honey)

HANDBOOK OF POTTERY AND
PORCELAIN MARKS

Pocket Book of
British
Ceramic Marks

★

including

Index to Registered Designs

1842–83

★

compiled by

J. P. CUSHION

*lately Senior Research Assistant of the
Department of Ceramics
Victoria and Albert Museum, London*

FABER AND FABER

3 Queen Square

London

First published in 1959
by Faber and Faber Limited
as Pocket Book of English Ceramic Marks
Second edition 1965
Second impression 1967
Third impression 1969
Fourth impression 1970
Fifth impression 1972
Third enlarged edition, revised and reset 1976
Printed in Great Britain at
the Alden Press, Oxford
All rights reserved

ISBN 0 571 04869 2

Acknowledgements

The author wishes to express his gratitude to the many officers and colleagues at the Victoria and Albert Museum, numerous collectors, English Ceramic Circle members and ceramic dealers, all of whom have assisted him in the recording of elusive marks for the guidance of future seekers.

Thanks are also recorded to Mr. Murray Fieldhouse, editor of *Pottery Quarterly*, and to the members of The Craftsmen Potters Association, who have assisted him in the collection of the marks and particulars of the present-day studio potters. The author is indebted to Mr. Geoffrey Godden for information concerning the dates of nineteenth-century factories and potters.

Thanks for information concerning recently established factories, closures, take-overs etc. are due to the proprietors of *Tableware International* (formerly *Pottery Gazette and Glass Trade Review*, established 1877), and to Mr. Terence Woolliscroft of Milton, Stoke-on-Trent, who so generously carried out the research concerning the recent, and often very complicated, changes of proprietorship of many Staffordshire factories. Mr. Woolliscroft noted that by January 1972 only one hundred and forty-four factories (individual producing units) remained in the Stoke area, employing thirty-four thousand workers.

Contents

Preface: Scope and Arrangement
of the Book

This pocket-book of ceramic marks has been produced especially to answer the requirements of the collector and dealer who has long needed such a guide when on 'pot-hunting' expeditions. In order to restrict the bulk of this volume the marks shown here have been confined to those of Great Britain and Ireland; Continental and Far Eastern marks are dealt with in the *Handbook of Pottery and Porcelain Marks*.

The marks recorded here are restricted to true factory marks and those others which by their frequent occurrence, or in other ways are of actual use in helping to identify the place and period of manufacture of a piece.

The arrangement is in alphabetical order of towns, subdivided into names of factories or owners, again alphabetically. The pottery centre of Staffordshire is treated in a separate section from the rest of England.

As far as practicable the marks are shown in facsimile (space has not permitted full-scale reproduction in all cases), the chief exception being those numerous modern marks consisting of the names or initials of the maker, or of the place of manufacture, which are reproduced by using printers' type, as has so often been done in the marks themselves on the actual wares.

The scope of this book has been extended to include many nineteenth- and twentieth-century marks not hitherto recorded, and brought right up-to-date by showing the marks of modern studio-potters.

To help the enquirer, an approximate date or period

is given for every mark together with the name of the principal proprietor where of interest, and a word or so of description of the type of ware on which the mark is generally found.

*   *   *

This enlarged and revised new edition of the *Pocket Book of English Ceramic Marks*, includes that part of the Class IV Design Index which relates to pottery and porcelain (Appendix B, page 288). It is included by the kind permission of the Public Record Office and will enable readers not only to date their wares by using the tables on pages 284–287, but also to determine the name of the manufacturer or person or firm, who initially registered the design to protect it from 'piracy' for a period of three years, by consulting the Index (i.e. Appendix B).

Historical Note and Methods
of Marking

The practice of marking ceramic wares as a guide to the manufacturer is a very old one and was carried out by the Romans on their red-wares, but it is not until the sixteenth century in Europe that the soft-paste Italian 'Medici' porcelain appears with a fully developed factory-mark, i.e. the sketch of the dome of Florence Cathedral in underglaze blue.

It was not until 1723 that the Meissen (Dresden) factory in Saxony adopted as a regular factory-mark the crossed swords of the arms of Saxony; this mark was invariably painted in underglaze blue on the base of the article in the Chinese manner. Other European porcelain and faience factories quickly followed the lead of Meissen and in 1766 the porcelain makers of France were required by law to use a mark which had been previously registered with the police authorities.

The practice of marking was never regularized throughout the eighteenth century with the result that factories which were proud of their reputation used a recognized mark, whilst the less important factories either left their wares unmarked in the hope that they would be mistaken for those factories whose style they were copying, or alternatively, used a mark similar enough to a famous one to be mistaken for genuine. The crossed swords of Meissen were used on numerous imitations and quite openly copied on Bow, Derby, Worcester and Lowestoft.

Many of the marks encountered on ceramics are

merely those of painters or workmen and are not a sure guide to the place of manufacture even when identified, for these people were of a very nomadic nature and often worked in many different factories in the course of their career. The throwers and 'repairers' (a term used for the workers who assembled the various parts of figures, etc.) invariably used a mark scratched in the body prior to the biscuit firing. These marks when under the glaze can safely be treated as genuine, but otherwise they should be closely examined for the burr or raised edge which is unavoidable when scratching soft clay, to ensure the mark has not been ground in after firing in order to deceive.

Painters and gilders generally used one of the colours in their palette or gilt, to mark the wares upon which they worked, this information was probably solely for the benefit of the management and for purposes of payment, which was often on a piecework basis.

Not to be confused with the names of potters are those of London dealers, who during the eighteenth and nineteenth centuries had goods made and decorated to their specific orders.

The marks used on English wares were applied in several different ways, including the incising (or scratching) on the unfired clay we have mentioned above. The other marks impressed in the body at this stage are also a reliable guide and usually were names of the factory, place or proprietor, made up of printers' type and stamped in one operation.

Painting or transfer-printing under the glaze in blue (also in green after 1850) was a most common method of marking wares and may be accepted as genuine, at least as far as knowing the piece was marked at the time of manufacture.

The practice of marking by painting, transfer-printing, or stencilling over the glaze in enamel-colours, are methods which are always liable to be fraudulent, as it is possible to add these type of marks at any time after the piece has been made.

The beginner should approach all marks with caution and it is important to learn to detect the difference between the various materials, (i.e. earthenware, hard-paste porcelain, soft-paste porcelain and bone-china, etc.); this would enable him to immediately realize that a neat gold anchor on a Chelsea-type figure cannot possibly be of that factory if the body is a hard continental paste and not the soft-paste as used at Chelsea. Finally do remember that many nineteenth-century factories include the date of their establishment in their mark and those early dates do not signify that the piece in question was made at that date, and also, that grandmother, who died at the ripe old age of one hundred and one, did not necessarily acquire the piece of china she has passed down to you at her birth.

Notes on Wares Made in Great Britain and Ireland

The English late-medieval wares are not only of great artistic interest, but historically important as the direct ancestors of the Staffordshire wares. Little is known of the places of their production, the finer specimens perhaps being made in monasteries, and though of coarse materials the jugs and pitchers are often of great beauty of form and bear simple but effective decoration.

In the fifteenth and sixteenth centuries smaller neater jugs appear with a rich copper-green glaze together with a hard red pottery with dark brown or black glaze sometimes decorated with trailed white slip or with applied pads of white clay.

A rare and distinct class of sixteenth-century English pottery comprises cisterns, stove-tiles and candle-brackets finely moulded in relief and covered with a green or yellow glaze.

English pottery tradition before the industrial period was rooted in the medieval use of lead-glazed earthenware. The sixteenth-century Cistercian pottery was the immediate forerunner of the Tickenhall and Staffordshire slip-wares, and the tradition of the last in turn gave vitality to the 'Astbury' and 'Whieldon' wares made in the same district in the eighteenth century.

The impulse towards refinement, which had been inspired by the Elers brothers (who made fine red wares in the Chinese style) and by the vogue of porcelain, also led to the making of a fine white salt-glazed stoneware in Staffordshire, where the industrializing process was finally carried through by Josiah Wedgwood. His cream-coloured ware was immediately imitated at numerous neighbouring potteries as well as at Leeds, Liverpool, Bristol, Swansea, Sunderland, Newcastle, Portobello and elsewhere, quickly securing a world-wide market.

Aside from the main English tradition are the decorative stonewares of Wedgwood, products of the neo-Classical enthusiasm.

Tin-glazed ware, largely inspired by Italian, Dutch and Chinese models, was made at London, Bristol, Liverpool, Dublin and Glasgow, but had little effect on the main current of the English tradition as represented by the wares of Staffordshire, where delftware (as this is called) was never made. English delftware was painted in high-temperature colours; overglaze enamels were used only on very rare examples and were probably the work of Dutch independent enamellers.

The seventeenth-century stoneware of Fulham, inspired at first by the Rhenish and Chinese wares, produced the isolated phenomenon of Dwight's admirable figures; that of Nottingham, though typically English, was of minor importance, reflecting latterly something of the Staffordshire style.

English porcelain of the eighteenth century is remarkable for its variety of composition. Soft-pastes of French type ware made at Chelsea, Derby and Longton Hall; soapstone pastes at Worcester, Caughley and Liverpool; and hard-paste at Plymouth and Bristol. From about 1750 onwards for several decades Derby was a most productive factory and a large proportion of the surviving English porcelain figures were made there. At Bow the use of bone-ash from 1747 heralded the type of porcelain which towards the end of the eighteenth century became and still remains the English standard

17

body; this last was a hybrid porcelain in which some part of the kaolin was replaced by bone-ash. At Nantgarw and Swansea a belated soft-paste was made in the period 1813–22.

None of the factories enjoyed royal or princely protection or subsidy and most were short-lived. Chelsea, and possibly Worcester, alone reached the standard set by the chief manufacturers of France or the many establishments supported by the rulers of small states in Germany; the porcelain of the first-named, however, ranks with the best ever made in Europe. The unsophisticated charm of Bow and Lowestoft is of a different order and typically English.

From the absence of marks, the English porcelains are difficult to identify. The chief factories were those named above, but other early manufacturers may have existed in Limehouse, Lambeth, Kentish Town, Vauxhall and Greenwich.

The ceramic art of the nineteenth century suffered no less than others from misdirected effort and mistaken enthusiasms. While the early part of the century lived largely on the artistic capital of the preceding period, the later part was chiefly occupied with the deliberate revival of former styles.

Yet in spite of unfavourable conditions the native genius of the English potters did succeed in producing wares which are both beautiful and of permanent value; the simple 'cottage china' and lustre wares of the New Hall type and its kindred earthenware; Worcester, Derby, Spode, Coalport and other porcelains which were its opulent contemporaries and successors, the charming blue-printed ware, and the entirely English brown stonewares of the Midlands and Lambeth. A singular use of glazed Parian is to be noted in the wares of Belleek in Co. Fermanagh, Ireland, where a pottery was started in 1863. Vases in naturalistic shell-forms were especially characteristic.

At the end of the century the revival of handicraft makes its appearance with De Morgan and the Martin Brothers, heralding the studio pottery of the present day.

AMESBURY (Wiltshire)
  Zillwood, W., late 18th-
  early 19th centuries
  pottery

W.Z.
incised

ASHBY-DE-LA-ZOUCH
(Leicestershire)
  Thompson, J., *c.* 1815–56
  general pottery

JOSEPH THOMPSON
WOODEN BOX
POTTERY
DERBYSHIRE
impressed
and other printed marks

Wilson & Proudman
Coleorton Pottery
1835–42, general pottery

WILSON &
PROUDMAN
impressed

ASHTEAD (Surrey)
  Ashtead Potters Ltd.
  1926–36, earthenware

AYLBURTON (Gloucestershire)
  Leach, Margaret, 1946–56
  Taena Community, 1951–56
  and Upton St. Leonards, Glos.
  where L. A. Groves also
  used mark. Studio-pottery

impressed

BARNSTAPLE (Devon)
  Baron, W. L., 1899–1939
  Rolle Quay Pottery
  earthenware

BARON. BARNSTAPLE
incised

Brannam, Ltd., C. H.,   C. H. BRANNAM
Litchdon Pottery, 1879–   BARUM
earthenwares   incised

     as from 1913–   C. H. BRANNAM LTD.
     impressed

printed or impressed, 1929–

impressed, 1930–   C. H. BRANNAM
     BARUM DEVON

BELPER (Derbyshire)   BELPER
     Belper Pottery 1809–34   impressed
     stonewares
     (transferred to Denby 1834)

BENTHALL (Salop)   W. PIERCE & CO.
     Pierce & Co., W., *c.* 1800–18
     earthenwares

     Salopian Art Pottery Co.   SALOPIAN
     1882–*c.* 1912 earthenwares,   impressed

BILLINGHAM (Cleveland) and
elsewhere
     Dunn, Constance, 1924–
     studio-pottery

     incised

BIRKENHEAD (Merseyside)
  Della Robbia Co. Ltd.
  earthenwares, *c.* 1894–1901

  top initial that of decorator

DELLA ROBBIA
impressed or incised

BISHOPS WALTHAM
(Hampshire)
  Bishops Waltham Pottery
  decorative earthenwares
  only from 1866–7 in
  Greek revival form

BISHOPS
WALTHAM
printed

BOVEY TRACEY (Devon)
  Bovey Tracey Pottery Co.
  earthenwares, 1842–94
  Bovey Pottery Co. Ltd.
  1894–1957
  also
  'Blue Waters Pottery'
  c. 1954–57

B.T.P. CO.
printed or impressed

c. 1937–49   1949–56

  Devonshire Potteries Ltd.
  earthenwares. 1947–
  also
  'Trentham Art Wares'
  1959–

MADE IN ENGLAND
TRENTHAM
ART WARE

Ehlers, A. W. G.
  Lowerdown Cross, 1946–55
  studio-potter

incised or painted

Leach, David, 1956–
(also at St. Ives *c.* 1932–56)
   'LD' for Lowerdown
   Pottery

impressed

BOW (London)
  (Stratford High St., Essex)
  c. 1747– *c.* 1776
  soft-paste porcelain
    early marks, *c.* 1750

incised

    presumably 'repairers'
    marks 1750–60

incised

impressed **B**

    probably mark of
    'repairer'
    Mr. Tebo (Thibaud?)   impressed
    marks on blue-painted
    wares 1750–70

underglaze blue

on figures and other late pieces
and
'anchor and dagger'
period, *c.* 1762–76

in red

in underglaze
blue and red

23

in red

in underglaze blue

in underglaze   in underglaze
blue and red   blue

on blue-and-white
cups, in underglaze
blue

in underglaze blue

BRADFORD (W. Yorkshire)   F.B.
   Booth, Frederick, *c.* 1881
   earthenware

BRAMPTON (Derbyshire)   KNOWLES
   Knowles & Son, Matthew
   stonewares, *c.* 1835–1911

   Oldfield & Co., *c.* 1838–88   J. OLDFIELD
   earthenware

                OLDFIELD & CO.
                impressed

   Pearson Ltd., James   J.P. LTD.
   Oldfield and London   impressed or printed
   Potteries. stonewares   from 1907
   19th century—1939
   1920–

Bramfield Ware

BRAUNTON (N. Devon)
Braunton Pottery Co. Ltd.
earthenwares, 1910–
    mark of *c.* 1947–
(moved or finished by 1972)

BRAUNTON
POTTERY
DEVON
printed or impressed

BRISTOL (Avon)
(Lund & Miller's factory)
soft-paste (soapstone)
porcelain 1748–52, then
transferred to Worcester

BRISTOL
BRISTOLL
in relief

(Cookworthy & Champion's factory)
hard-past porcelain
1770–81, transferred
from Plymouth

4
underglaze blue,
blue enamel, red or
gold

early mark during
Cookworthy's
ownership (also used
at Plymouth)

X   6
    X
in blue enamel

underglaze blue
and blue enamel

+ x   x B

blue
enamel

tin-glazed earthenware
(delftware) *c.* 1650–

mark of John Bowen,
painter, apprenticed
1734

yf. 1ˢᵗ: Sept.ᵗ
1761
Bowen – fecit,

in blue

25

initials of Michael Edkins, delft-painter and his wife on plate dated 1760

M E ·B·
J7 60
in blue

Bristol Pottery
c. 1785–1825
earthenwares

BRISTOL POTTERY
impressed or painted

Coombes, a china-mender
c. 1775–1805
in pale brown lustre

Coombes
Queen St
Bristol

Fifield, William (*b.* 1777, *d.* 1857) painter on Bristol pottery
c. 1810–55

W. F.

W.F.B.

W. FIFIELD

Pardoe, Thomas (*d.* 1823) painter at Derby, Worcester, Cambrian Pottery, Swansea, factories, independent decorator of pottery and porcelain in Bristol
c. 1809–20

Pardoe
28 Bath St.,
Bristol
Warranted

Pardoe, Bristol
painted

Pardoe, William Henry (son), decorator at Cardiff and elsewhere
c. 1820–35

PARDOE, CARDIFF

Patience, Thomas
18th century stoneware

PATIENCE
impressed

Pountney & Allies	P.
Bristol Pottery *c.* 1816–	P. & A. P.A.
35, earthenware	B.P.
printed, impressed or	P.A.
painted	BRISTOL POTTERY
impressed	
Pountney & Goldney	POUNTNEY & GOLDNEY
Bristol Pottery, 1836–49	(or as above)
impressed	BRISTOL POTTERY
Pountney & Co., 1849–	P. & CO.
Bristol Victoria Pottery	
1849–89	POUNTNEY & CO.
1889–	POUNTNEY & CO. LTD.

c. 1954–
now Cauldon Bristol
Potteries Ltd.

Bristol founded in 1652 England

Powell, William (& Sons)
Temple Gate Pottery
c. 1830–1906, stoneware

POWELL BRISTOL

impressed c. 1830–

BRISTOL TEMPLE
GATE POTTERY

Ring, Joseph 1785– (*d.* 1788), cream coloured earthenware continued by partners until 1812	RING & CO. impressed

BROSELEY (Salop)
Maw & Co. Ltd., 1850–
tiles and art pottery
from *c.* 1875
    c. 1880–

MAW & CO.

FLOREAT MAW
SALOPIA

BURTON-ON-TRENT (Derbyshire)
Bretby Art Pottery, Woodville
Tooth & Ault 1883–87
Tooth & Co. 1887–
earthenwares
    Henry Tooth *c.* 1883–1900

    c. 1914–

CLANTA
WARE

Woodward, James
Swadlincote Pottery
'Majolica' earthenware
1859–88

printed or impressed

CASTLE HEDINGHAM (Essex)
Hedingham Art Pottery
Bingham, Edward
1864–1901
reproduction of medieval
and Tudor type wares

applied in relief

28

incised signature
1864–1901

E. BINGHAM
CASTLE HEDINGAM
ESSEX

early 20th century

ROYAL ESSEX ART
POTTERY WORKS

CASTLEFORD (W. Yorkshire)
Clokie & Masterson
earthenware, 1872–81

C. & M.
CLOKIE &
MASTERMAN
printed or impressed

Clokie & Co., 1888–1961
earthenware
(Ltd. after 1940)
printed

Dunderdale & Co., David
Castleford Pottery,
c. 1790–1820
earthenware and
stoneware

D.D. & CO.

D.D. & CO.
CASTLEFORD

Gill, William (& Sons)
Providence Pottery
1880–1932

printed

Hartley's (Castleford)
Ltd., Phillips Pottery
c. 1898–1960
stoneware and earthenware;
decorative art wares
from 1953

HARTROX

Nicholson & Co., Thomas earthenware, *c.* 1854–71	T.N. & CO. printed with name of pattern
Robinson Bros. Castleford & Allerton Potteries stoneware, 1897–1904	R.B. printed or impressed
Robinson & Son, John stoneware, 1905–33	J.R. & S. impressed

CAUGHLEY (Salop)
  Turner, Thomas
  c. 1772–1799 (then taken over by John Rose
  of Coalport factory)
  soft-paste porcelain and   SALOPIAN
  black basaltes   Salopian
  (*see also* 'Benthall')   impressed

      printed or painted in $\mathcal{S}$ $\mathcal{S}_x$
      underglaze blue *c.* 1772–95
                                          $\mathcal{S}_o$

      printed or painted $\mathbb{C}$ $\mathbb{C}$
      c. 1772–95

      printed mark usually
      Worcester   ☾   ☽
      open printed crescent
      also on Coalport   printed

Chinese type mark

CHEAM (Surrey)
Clark, Henry, 1869–80
earthenware

HENRY CLARK
CHEAM POTTERY
impressed or incised

CHELSEA (London)
c. 1745–1784 soft-paste porcelain
(1770–84 known as 'Chelsea-Derby'
period under William Duesbury)

rare incised mark on
'triangle' period
1745–c. 1749

usual triangle mark

incised

rare mark of 'crown
and trident', 1745–c.
1750 in underglaze blue

'raised-anchor' mark
c. 1749–52, latterly
picked out in red

in applied relief

'red-anchor' mark
1752–c. 1758
occasionally painted in
blue or purple

painted in red

c. 1750–56 painted in underglaze blue	
'gold anchor' mark *c.* 1756–69 (also seen on Chelsea- Derby wares as late as 1775)	 in gold
rare 'repairers' mark (not Roubiliac)	 impressed
Chelsea Pottery, 1952– (Rawnsley Academy Ltd.) impressed or incised, 1952–	CHELSEA POTTERY incised
Vyse, Charles, 1919–*c.* 63 studio-potter	C.V. C.V. CHELSEA
painted mark with year-date added	19 ⩒ 34 CHELSEA

CHESTERFIELD
(Derbyshire)
   Pearson & Co., 1805–
   Whittington Moor
   Potteries
   1805–*c.* 1880
	P. & CO.
	
	PEARSON & CO.
	WHITTINGTON
	MOOR
	impressed

1880–

from *c.* 1925 renamed as
Pearson & Co. (Chesterfield) Ltd.

Barker Pottery Co.
1887–1957
stoneware
  printed or impressed
  mark 1928–1957

CHURCH GRESLEY (Derbyshire)
  Green & Co. Ltd., T.G.
  c. 1864– earthenware
and stoneware
  printed mark *c.* 1888–

GRESLEY

  mark of *c.* 1930, numerous
  other late marks all
  include 'T. G. Green
  & Co., Ltd.'

CLEVEDON (Avon)   1879–1920
  Elton, Sir Edmund
  Sunflower Pottery
  1879–1930   1920–30

Elton

Holland, William Fishley   *W J Holland*
studio-potter, 1921–
earthenware

WJH   **FH**

incised

33

Holland, Isabel Fishley pottery figures, 1929–42	I. HOLLAND
Holland, George Fishley earthenware, 1955–	

CLIFTON JUNCTION
(nr. Manchester)
   Pilkington Tile & Pottery
   Co. Ltd., earthenwares
   and tiles, (decorative
   pottery, 1897–1938,
   1948–57)
	P
	early incised mark

factory mark, VIII for
1908

c. 1914–38   'ROYAL LANCASTRIAN'

marks of notable designers:

Lewis F. Day   Walter Crane   C. E. Cundall   R. Joyce

Jessie Jones G. M. Forsyth Gladys Rodgers W. Mycock

COALPORT (Salop)
John Rose, *c.* 1796–
(transferred to Stoke-on-Trent
c. 1926)

rare early mark in red

1815–25 on many wares
decorated in Swansea
style

c. 1810–25, in underglaze
blue

underglaze blue mark
c. 1810–20

COALBROOKDALE

impressed

C. B. DALE

marks used from *c.* 1820

1830–50

JOHN ROSE & CO.
COALBROOKDALE
SHROPSHIRE

35

c. 1851–61, painted or gilt

c. 1861–75, 'c'
Coalport, 's',
Swansea, 'N', Nantgarw

painted or gilt

printed mark c. 1870–80
incorporating Patent
Office Registration
mark

c. 1875–81, printed or
painted
late marks c. 1881–
'England' added 1891
'Made in England'
c. 1920

COALPORT A.D. 1750

wares made for London
dealer A. B. & R. P.
Daniell c. 1860–1917

large size anchor mark
on Coalport copies of
Chelsea, also on
Continental wares
without 'c'

CODNOR PARK   W. BURTON
(Derbyshire)   CODNOR PARK
  Burton, William,   impressed
  c. 1821–32, stoneware

CROWBOROUGH (Sussex) & REDHILL (Surrey)
  Walford, J. F., 1948–
  studio-potter

DARTINGTON (S. Devon)
  Trey, Marianne de
  studio-potter, 1947–
  Shinners Bridge Pottery   incised or painted

  Haile, T. S., *c.* 1936–43,
  1945–8, studio-potter

                            impressed

DENBY (Derbyshire)   BOURNES
  Bourne & Son Ltd.,   WARRANTED
  Joseph, *c.* 1809–
  stoneware

                        J. BOURNE & SON
  Joseph Bourne, 1833–60   PATENTEES
  'Son' added 1850   DENBY POTTERY
                        NEAR DERBY
                        impressed

DENHOLME (W. Yorkshire)   N. Taylor
  Taylor, Nicholas   Denholme
  1893–1909   incised
  earthenware

Derby (Derbyshire)
  c. 1750–1848
  soft-paste porcelain
    early marks of Planché
    period *c.* 1750–56

Derby

incised

Derby Porcelain Works
1756–1848
  'William Duesbury &
  Co.' *c.* 1760

incised

  'N' seen on dishes, etc.
  c. 1770–80

incised

  'Chelsea-Derby' marks
  c. 1770–84

in gold

  c. 1770–82, in blue or
  purple

  incised model numbers
  on figures, *c.* 1775–
  early 19th century

  common Derby mark
  1782–, incised, purple,
  blue or black
  c. 1800–25 in red
  enamel

mark of Isaac
Farnsworth 'repairer'

mark of Joseph Hill
'repairer'

'size' mark

'Duesbury & Kean',
c. 1795
in blue, crimson or purple

blue-painted mark in
imitation of Meissen
c. 1785–1825

Robert Bloor Period

printed in red
c. 1820–40

printed in red
c. 1830–48

mark in imitation of
Sèvres, *c.* 1825–48
in blue enamel

Locker & Co., King Street factory
c. 1849–59

similar marks used also
by:
Stevenson Sharp & Co.
1859–61
'Courtney late Bloor'
1849–63

Stevenson & Hancock
1861–1935, this mark
also used after 1935
when King St. factory
was taken over by Royal Crown Derby
Porcelain Co. Ltd.

Derby Crown Porcelain Co. Ltd. Est. 1876
c. 1878–90, together
　with year mark as　　　　　　　　　　　　　Derby
　shown in table on next
　page　　　　　　　　　　　　　　　　　　impressed

printed

Royal Crown Derby Porcelain Co. Ltd.
1890–
　printed mark of *c.* 1890
　'England' from 1891
　'Made in England'
　added from *c.* 1920
　together with year
　mark
(Part of Royal Doulton Tableware Ltd. from 1973)

TABLE OF DERBY YEAR-MARKS,
1882–

1882	1883	1884	1885	1886	1887	1888

1889	1890	1891	1892	1893	1894	1895

1896	1897	1898	1899	1900	1901	1902

1903	1904	1905	1906	1907	1908	1909

1910	1911	1912	1913	1914	1915	1916

1917	1918	1919	1920	1921	1922	1923

1924	1925	1926	1927	1928	1929	1930

1931	1932	1933	1934	1935	1936	1937

1938	1939	1940	1941	1942	1943	1944
I	II	III	IV	V	VI	VII

1945	1946	1947	1948	1949	1950	1951
VIII	IX	X	XI	XII	XIII	etc.

Derby Pot Works
creamwares, *c.* 1750–80

T. RADFORD SC.
DERBY

Thomas Radford,
engraver of prints
found on some
Cockpit Hill wares

RADFORD fecit
DERBY POT WORKS

Potts, W. W.
St. George's Works, *c.*
1831–, earthenware
(also at Burslem)

marks indicating
patent printing
processes, 1831 & 1835

DONYATT (Somerset)
Rogers, James, 19th century
(with descendants)
sgraffiato slipwares

Jas Rogers
Maker Octr 10th
1848

impressed on jug
dated 1864

ROGERS & SONS
CROCK STRETT
POTTERY

EAST HENDRED (Oxfordshire)
Thompson, Pauline
studio-potter, 1950–

incised or painted

EAST HORSLEY (Surrey)
Moore, Denis & Michael
Buckland
Green Dene Pottery
1953–
(initials also used)

impressed or painted

42

FARNHAM (Surrey)
Hammond, Henry
studio-potter, 1934–40,
1946–

incised   impressed

Barron, Paul
studio-potter, 1948–

B

impressed

FELIXSTOWE (Suffolk)
Kemp, Dorothy, 1939–
studio-potter

incised or impressed

FERRYBRIDGE (Yorkshire)
Ferrybridge Pottery, 1792–
known as Knottingley Pottery, 1792–1804

1792–6, *c.* 1801–34	TOMLINSON & CO. impressed or printed
Wedgwood, Ralph, *c.* 1796–1801	WEDGWOOD & CO.
c. 1804–	FERRYBRIDGE impressed

Reed & Taylor, *c.* 1843–56	R. & T.	R.T. & CO.
Woolf & Sons, L., *c.* 1856–83	L.W.	L.W. & S.
Poulson, Bros., Ltd. 1884–97	P.B.	P.BROS
Sefton & Brown, *c.* 1897–1919	S.B.	
Brown & Sons, T., *c.* 1919–	T.B & S.	

43

FREMINGTON (Devon)
 Fishley, Edwin Beer
 1861–1906, earthenware

E. B. FISHLEY
FREMINGTON
N. DEVON
 incised

FULHAM (London)
 Dwight, John, 1671–
 salt-glazed stoneware

no certain
marks

De Morgan, William
 c. 1872–1907
 decorator of earthenwares made to order
 from other factories, and own wares
  impressed mark, 1882–
  '& Co.' added after 1888

marks used at Merton Abbey, 1882–88
made own tiles from *c*.
1879, and wares from 1882

  impressed or painted
  1882–

Sands End Pottery, 1888–97
(period of partnership with
Halsey Ricardo)

44

1898–1907, partnership with
Frank Iles, Charles & Fred
Passenger at Fulham

decoration continued
until 1911, four years
after De Morgan retired

all impressed

earthenwares were decorated
in De Morgan style at
Mrs. Ida Perrin's studio,
Bushey Heath, 1921–33
by Fred Passenger

Fulham Pottery & Cheavin Filter Co. Ltd.
vases & commercial pottery
1889–present

FULHAM POTTERY
LONDON
1948–   impressed

GATESHEAD (Tyne and Wear)
Durham China Co. Ltd.
general ceramics, 1947–57

printed or impressed

HENLEY-ON-THAMES
(Berkshire)
Hawkins, John & Son
china and glass dealers
closed about 1935

'FAMOUS HENLEY CHINA'
EST. 1867
HAWKINS
HENLEY-ON-THAMES

HEREFORD
  Godwin & Hewitt, tiles
  1889–1910, mark printed
  or impressed

HONITON (Devon)
  Honiton Art Potteries
  Ltd., earthenware, *c.*
  1881–, printed or
  impressed *c.* 1915

THE HONITON
LACE ART POTTERY
CO.

  Collard, C., 1918–1947
  printed or impressed

COLLARD HONITON
ENGLAND

  Hull, N. T. S., 1947–1955

N.T.S. HULL

  1947–

HONITON POTTERY
DEVON

  Hull, Norman
  Norman Hull Pottery
  1947–55

NORMAN HULL
POTTERY

HORNSEA (Humberside)
  Hornsea Pottery Co. Ltd.
  earthenware, *c.* 1951
    printed or impressed, 1962–

HULL (Humberside)
  Longbottom, Samuel
  earthenware, late 19th
  century, closed 1899

S.L.
impressed

IPSWICH (Suffolk)
  Balaam, W., 1870–81
  Rope Lane Pottery
  slipwares

W. BALAAM
ROPE LANE POTTERY
IPSWICH
impressed

ISLEWORTH (London)
  earthenware, *c.* 1760–
  1825, Shore, J.
  Shore & Co.
  Shore & Goulding

SHORE & CO.
S. & CO.
S. & G.
ISLEWORTH

    (*Note:* S. & G. seen on Wedgwood type wares
    are Schiller & Gerbing, Bodenbach, Bohemia.
    See Pocket-Book of German Ceramic Marks)

JACKFIELD (Salop)
  Craven Dunnill & Co.
  Ltd., tiles, 1872–1951

CRAVEN & CO.

JACKFIELD

KEW (Surrey)
  Duckworth, Ruth
  studio-potter, 1956–

painted or incised

KILMINGTON MANOR (Wiltshire)
  Pleydell-Bouverie, Katharine
  stoneware, 1925–
  studio-potter
  (also at other addresses)

incised or stamped

47

LAMBETH (London) 'Coade Lambeth'
  Coade & Sealy, 1769–
  1811, artificial stoneware

  Doulton & Watts
  stoneware and earthenware
  c. 1815–1858
      c. 1826–1838
      on early brown salt-
      glazed wares

      c. 1826–1858

  all marks impressed
  moulded or incised

  Doulton & Co.
  Lambeth, *c.* 1858–1956
  Burslem, *c.* 1882–
      c. 1869–77, decorated
  coloured wares, year often
  appears in centre after 1872

  '4D' mark on decorated
  salt-glaze

  Note: 'England' added
  after 1891   *c.* 1877–80   *c.* 1880–1902

  mark on mural tiles
  c. 1879–1900

on wares decorated with coloured clays
c. 1887–1900

underglaze decorated earthenware

c. 1872–73

c. 1873–1908

underglaze decorated earthenware, *c.* 1881–1910

'Carrara' ware, stoneware covered with translucent crystalline enamel
c. 1888–1898

'Silicon' ware, unglazed stoneware, *c.* 1882–1912

fine earthenware and china, made at Burslem
c. 1882–1902

standard impressed mark
c. 1902–22
c. 1927–36

Lambeth stoneware
c. 1922–

Burslem factory marks   DOULTON
c. 1882–1902

DOULTON
& SLATERS
PATENT

c. 1900–   ROYAL   ROYAL
DOULTON DOULTON
FLAMBE   KALON
c. 1960–   ENGLISH
TRANSLUCENT
CHINA

selection of initials used
by Doulton decorators:

Atkins, Elizabeth, *c.* 1876–82   *EA*

Banks, Eliza, *c.* 1876–84   *E/B*

Barlow, Arthur B., 1871–8

Barlow, Florence E., *c.* 1873–1909   *FEB*

Barlow, Hannah B., *c.* 1872–1906

Barnard, Harry, *c.* 1880–90   *B*

Butler, Frank A., *c.* 1872–1911   *FFB*

Butterton, Mary, *c.* 1874–94

Capes, Mary, *c.* 1876–83

Dewsberry, David, 1889–1919 D.Dewsberry

Dunn, William, E., *c.* 1883–95

Lee, Frances E., *c.* 1875–90   FEL

Marshall, Mark V., 1879–   M·V·M
    1912

Pope, Frank C., 1880–1923   F·C·P

Raby, Edward J., 1892–1911   E.Raby

Rowe, William, 1883–1939   WR

Simeon, Henry, 1894–1936   HS

Simmance, Eliza, *c.* 1873–1928   S

Tinworth, George, 1886–1913

A full-list of painters, modellers and designers are
shown in *Royal Doulton* 1815–1965 by Desmond
Eyles, London, 1965, together with full guides,
etc. to precise dating

Green, Stephen
Imperial Pottery
stoneware, c. 1820–58

impressed marks

STEPHEN GREEN
IMPERIAL
POTTERIES
LAMBETH

Stiff, James   J. STIFF
London Pottery, c. 1840–
1913 stonewares
   c. 1863

J. STIFF & SONS
impressed

LANGLEY MILL (Nottingham)
  Lovatt & Lovatt, 1895–
stoneware and earthenware
printed or impressed marks
             c. 1900–

now Langley
Pottery Ltd. (1967)   c. 1900–   c. 1931–62

LEEDS (W. Yorkshire)
  c. 1770–1881
creamware, earthenware and stoneware

Green Bros., 1770–   LEEDS *POTTERY
impressed

Humble, Green & Co., 1774–76
52

Humble, Hartley, Greens
& Co., 1776–1780

LEEDS POTTERY

Hartley, Greens & Co.
1781–1830

1800–1830

LEEDS.POTTERY

HARTLEY GREENS & Co.
LEEDS * POTTERY

all marks impressed

1780–1810
impressed or enamelled

Britton & Son, Richard
1872–8, earthenware
  initials found on variety
  of transfer-printed wares

LP

R.B. & S.
printed

Rainforth & Co. 1800–17
Petty's Pottery, 1817–46
earthenware & creamware

RAINFORTH & CO.
PETTYS & CO. LEEDS

printed or impressed

Burmantofts
art-pottery, 1882–1904
  marks impressed

BURMANTOFTS
FAIENCE

Leeds Fireclay Co. Ltd.
earthenware, *c.* 1904–14

L.
F.C.

decorative wares, made
up until 1914, after
which only commercial
& utility wares were
produced

LEFICO

GRANITOFTS

Yates, William, *c.* 1840–76
(retailer only)

YATES
LEEDS
printed or painted

LETCHWORTH
(Hertfordshire)
  Cowlishaw, W. H.
  1908–14, earthenwares

ICENI WARE
impressed

LIVERPOOL (Merseyside)
  Chaffers, Richard, 1743–65
  tin-glazed earthenware
  and soft-paste porcelain
    dated example referring
      to son:

Christian, Philip
c. 1765–1776

'CHRISTIAN'
impressed

Billinge, Thomas
engraver, *c.* 1760–80

Billinge Sculp
Liverpool

Sadler, John & Green,
Guy, printers only, their
work seen on tiles,
Wedgwood's creamware,
Longton Hall, etc.,
1756–1799

J. Sadler, Liverpool

Green, Liverpool

Abbey, Richard
engraver and printer
1773–80, potter from
1790

ABBEY
LIVERPOOL

R. Abbey, sculp.

Johnson, Joseph
engraver, second half
18th century

'I. JOHNSON,
LIVERPOOL'

Herculaneum Pottery
earthenware and procelain
c. 1793–1841
Worthington, Humble
& Holland, 1794–1806

HERCULANEUM

impressed or printed marks, *c.* 1796–1833

1822–41

HERCULANEUM POTTERY
impressed or printed
in blue

Case, Thomas & Mort,
John, 1833–1836

printed, usually in red

Mort & Simpson

'Liver' bird printed or
impressed, *c.* 1836–41

Gibson, John &
Solomon, earthenware,
early 19th century

JOHN GIBSON
LIVERPOOL
1813

LONDON

VARIOUS RETAILERS OF POTTERY & PORCELAIN

Allsup, John, 1832–58
    printed

JOHN ALLSUP
ST. PAUL'S CHURCH-
YARD, LONDON

Blades, John
c. 1800–30

BLADES LONDON

Bradley & Co., J.
decorators and retailers
c. 1813–20

J. BRADLEY & CO.

Brameld, J. W.
c. 1830–50
partner of
Rockingham Works

I. W. BRAMELD

at various
London addresses

56

Daniell, A. B. & R. P.
c. 1825–1917
    printed mark on wares
    of Coalport, etc. made
    to order for Daniell's

Dreydel & Co., Henry
late 19th century
    mark of wares made
    to order both in England
    and on Continent

Goode & Co. (Ltd.), Thomas
c. 1860–present
'Ltd' from 1918
now in South Audley St.

Green & Co., J.
1834–42 at St. Paul's
Churchyard, elsewhere
until *c.* 1874

Haines, Batchelor & Co.
1880–90

    H.B.
    printed

Hales, Hancock &
Goodwin, Ltd., 1922–60
(Hales, Hancock & Co.
Ltd., and Hales Bros.)

    H.H. & G. LTD.
    printed

57

Hart & Son 1826–69	H. & S. printed
Howell & James *c.* 1820–1922 (also retailers of materials for amateur decorators)	HOWELL & JAMES

Mortlock, J.
1746–*c.* 1930
  many marks used
  including name of such
  manufacturers as
  Mintons
	MORTLOCK
	
	MORTLOCKS
	OXFORD STREET

Pearce, Alfred B. 1866–1940	ALFRED B. PEARCE 39 LUDGATE HILL LONDON
Pellatt & Co., Apsley *c.* 1789– (also glass retailers)	APSLEY PELLATT & CO.
Pellatt & Green *c.* 1805–30	PELLATT & GREEN LONDON
Pellatt & Wood *c.* 1870–90	PELLATT & WOOD

Phillips, *c.* 1799–1929
  c. 1858–97
  c. 1897–1906
  c. 1908–29
	
	W. P. & G. PHILLIPS
	PHILLIPS & CO.
	PHILLIPS LTD.

Walker, William
c. 1795–1800

WALKER MINORIES

MINOR FACTORIES AND STUDIO-POTTERS IN LONDON

Benham, Tony, 1958
    mark written or incised
    with year, studio-potter
(now at Wateringbury, Kent),
Billington, Dora
studio-potter, 1912–

incised or painted

Briglin Pottery Ltd.
earthenware, 1948–

BRIGLIN
impressed

Dalton, William B.
stoneware and porcelain
studio-potter, 1900–
c. 1955
(In U.S.A. from 1941)

incised or painted

Eeles, David
studio-potter, 1955
Shepherd's Well Pottery
London, then in 1962
to Mosterton, Dorset

D.E.

Fine Arts Porcelain Ltd.
earthenwares, 1948–52

printed

Fry, Roger, Omega
Workshops *c.* 1913–19,
studio-potter

Groves, Lavender
studio-potter, 1952–

Leach, Jeremy   J.L.   J.L.
studio-potter, *c.* 1959   D.S.

Martin Bros. (Robert Wallace, Walter, Edwin
and Charles), studio-potters, stoneware,
1873–1914

    1873–5   R. W. Martin fecit

    1873–4

    1874–8

    1878–9

SOUTHALL	MARTIN
MARTIN	SOUTHALL
POTTERY	POTTERY

    1879–82

    1882–

all marks either incised or impressed together
with month and year

Mills, Donald
studio-potter, 1946–55

Murray, William Staite
studio-potter, 1919–62
in S. Rhodesia from 1940

W. S. MURRAY
(date)
LONDON

Northen & Co., W.
Union Potteries,
Lambeth, stoneware,
1847–92, '& Co.'
added 1887

W. NORTHEN
POTTER
VAUXHALL
LAMBETH

O'Malley, Peter
studio-potter, 1953–

Parnell, Gwendolen
studio-potter, 1916–36

CHELSEA CHEYNE
(date)
G.P.

Parr, Harry
studio-potter, *c.* 1919–
c. 1948

HY PARR
CHELSEA (date)

Powell, Alfred & Louise
decorators of Wedgwood
earthenwares, *c.* 1904–39

Powell, John
painter and retailer
c. 1810–30

Powell
91, Wimpole St.

Richards, Frances E.
studio-potter, 1922–31
  mark incised

Rie, Lucie
studio-potter, *c.* 1938–
  mark impressed

Samuel, Audrey
studio-potter, 1949–

A S

Smith & Co., Thomas
stonewares, 1879–93

T. SMITH & CO.
OLD KENT ROAD
LONDON

Stabler, Harold &
Phoebe, earthenware
designers and potters
b. 1872–*d.* 1945 (wife
d. 1955)

Phoebe Stabler
(date)

Stabler (date)

Vergette, Nicholas
studio-potter, 1946–58

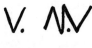

Walters, Helen
studio-potter, 1945–
(now Helen Swain,
mark 'HWS')

1945–53   1953–

62

White, William J.
Fulham Pottery
stoneware, *c.* 1750–1850

            W.W.
            (date)

            W. J. WHITE

      incised dated marks   (date)

LOWER DICKER (Sussex)
    U. Clark & Nephews,
    1843–1946, earthenware
    1933–
    Dicker Potteries Ltd. 1946–59

            U.C. & N.
            THE DICKER
            SUSSEX
            DICKER WARE

LOWESBY (Leicestershire)
    Lowesby Pottery
    Fowke, Sir Frederick
    c. 1835–40
    earthenwares

            LOWESBY

LOWESTOFT (Suffolk)
    soft-paste porcelain
    c. 1757– *c.* 1800
        decorators numbers,
        to approx. 17, painted
        on inner wall of foot-
        rim, *c.* 1760–75
    copies of Worcester

           1 3 5

           7 9 13

and Meissen marks
c. 1775–1790

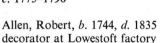

Allen, Robert, *b.* 1744, *d.* 1835
decorator at Lowestoft factory
and independent enameller
from *c.* 1800

painted

MADELEY (Salop)
Randall, Thomas M.
c. 1825–40, decorator of
English and Sèvres porcelain;
with factory at Madeley
for production of soft-paste
imitations of Sèvres

painted

MALVERN (Worcestershire)
Woods, Richard, *c.* 1850–
retailer only

R. WOODS
printed

MANCHESTER
Sutcliffe & Co., *c.* 1885–1901
decorative tiles

printed or impressed

MANSFIELD
(Nottinghamshire)
Billingsley, William
1799–1802
painter and gilder

BILLINGSLEY
MANFIELD
painted

MEXBOROUGH
(S. Yorkshire)
Emery, James
earthenware, 1837–61

J. EMERY
MEXBRO

incised

Rock Pottery
Reed, James, *c.* 1839–49

REED
impressed

Mexbro Pottery
Reed, John, *c.* 1849–73

Sowter & Co., *c.* 1795–
1804, Mexborough Old
Pottery
  marks impressed

SOWTER & CO.
MEXBRO

S. & CO.

Wilkinson & Wardle
Denaby Pottery, 1864–6
earthenware

Wardle & Co., John,
Denaby Pottery
earthenwares (including creamware)
1866–70
  printed mark

JOHN WARDLE & CO.

MIDDLESBROUGH
(Cleveland)
  Linthorpe Pottery, 1879–90
  earthenware (art pottery type)

LINTHORPE
impressed

    incised, impressed or
    painted signature of Dresser

Chr. Dresser

    Tooth, Henry, manager
    1879–1882

HT   HT

Middlesbrough Pottery Co.
1834–44
earthenware and
creamware

M.P. CO.

MIDDLESBRO'
POTTERY CO.

Middlesbrough   M.E. & CO.
Earthenware Co.
1844–52, earthenware
  initials used with various
  printed or impressed marks

                    MIDDLESBRO POTTERY
                    (with anchor)
Wilson & Co., Isaac   I.W. & CO.
Middlesbrough Pottery   MIDDLESBRO'
1852–87   impressed

MORTLAKE (London)   KISHERE
  Mortlake Pottery, *c.*
  1800–43, Kishere,   I.K.
  Joseph   impressed
  salt-glazed stoneware

NEW BARNET (Hertfordshire)   D.A.
  Arbeid, Dan, 1956–
  Abbey Art Centre   ARBEID
  studio-potter   painted or impressed
  (now at Saffron Walden, Essex)

NEWCASTLE UPON TYNE   DAVIES & CO.
(Tyne and Wear)   impressed
  Davies & Co., 1833–51
  Tyne Main Pottery
  earthenware

  Fell, Thomas, 1817–90   FELL
  St. Peter's Pottery   impressed
  earthenware and creamware
  1817–30

                    impressed

Fell & Co., *c.* 1830–90	F. & CO.
initials used with	T.F. & CO.
various marks:	T. FELL & CO.
Ford & Patterson	FORD & PATTERSON
Sheriff Hill Pottery	Sheriff Hill
c. 1820–*c.* 1830	Pottery
earthenware	impressed
Jackson & Patterson	J. & P.
1830–45	
Maling, Robert	MALING
Ouseburn Pottery	M
1817–59, earthenware	impressed
Maling, C. T.	MALING
Ford Pottery, 1859–90	C. T. MALING
earthenware, often	C.T.M.
with lustre decoration	

Maling & Sons, Ltd.
1890–1963
earthenwares, mark of
  c. 1875–1908

1890–   *c.* 1908   *c.* 1949–63

Patterson & Co.　　　　　PATTERSON & CO.
Sheriff Hill Pottery,　　　　printed or
1830–1904, earthenware　　　impressed

Sewell, 1804– *c.* 28　　　　　SEWELL
St. Anthony's Pottery, *c.* 1780–1878
earthenware (including creamwares)
1780–1820　　　　　　　　ST. ANTHONY'S
Sewell & Donkin　　　　SEWELL & DONKIN
1828–52
Sewell & Co., 1852–78　　　SEWELL & CO.
　　　　　　　　　　　all impressed or printed

Taylor & Co., *c.* 1820–5　　TAYLOR & CO.
Tyne Pottery　　　　　　　printed
earthenware

Wallace & Co., J.　　　　WALLACE & CO.
Newcastle or Forth Bank　　impressed
Pottery, 1838–93, earthenware

Warburton, John, &　　　J. WARBURTON
family, Carr's Hill　　　　N. ON TYNE
Pottery, earthenware, *c.* 1750–1817

NEWTON ABBOT (Devon)
　Phillips & Co., John　　ΦIΛEΩ II⅂I⅂ΟN
Aller Pottery, 1868–87　　printed or impressed

Aller Vale Art Potteries　　ALLER VALE
earthenware, 1887–1901　　impressed

Royal Aller Vale &
Watcombe Pottery Co.
(Torquay) *c.* 1901–62
  impressed or printed
  1901–

ROYAL ALLER VALE

ROYAL   DEVON
TORQUAY   MOTTO
POTTERY   WARE

Candy & Co. Ltd.
Great Western Potteries
earthenwares, 1882–

CANDY WARE
C
N A

NORTH SHIELDS
(Tyne and Wear)
  Carr, John
  earthenware, *c.* 1845–1900

J. CARR & CO.

NOTTINGHAM
  (Nottinghamshire)
  Lockett, William
  stoneware, *c.* 1740–80

'Wm. and Ann Lockett,
1755'

OXFORD (Oxfordshire)
  Blackman, Audrey
  studio-potter, 1949–
  'Astbury-type' figures

A. BLACKMAN

OXSHOTT (Surrey)
  Oxshott Pottery, 1919
  Wren, Henry, *c.* 1919–47   HW   hw

Wren, Denise, *c.* 1919–   DKW

Wren, Rosemary, *c.* 1945–
69

OXSHOTT

PINXTON (Derbyshire)
  Pinxton Works, *c.* 1796–1813
  John Coke, William Billingsley
  soft-paste porcelain
  (Billingsley, *c.* 1796–93)
  (Cutts, *c.* 1803–1813)

in red   **in purple**
from arms of Coke

  marks found on late
  pieces

PLYMOUTH (Devon)
  Plymouth Porcelain Works
  Cookworthy, William
  hard-paste porcelain, 1768–70
  (transferred to Bristol in 1770)
  workman's mark also seen
    on Bow, Worcester, Bristol
    and Wedgwood

underglaze-blue,
blue enamel,
red or gold

  Plymouth Pottery Co. Ltd.
  earthenware, 1856–63

P.P. COY.L
STONE CHINA

POOLE (Dorset)
  Carter & Co.
  earthenware, 1873–1921

CARTER & CO.
CARTER POOLE

  Carter, Stabler & Adams
  1921–
    'Ltd.' added 1925
    1956–
  1963– Poole Pottery Ltd.

POOLE
ENGLAND

printed

PRAZE (Cornwall)
  Crowan Pottery, 1946–62
  Davis, Harry & May
  studio-potters

impressed

PRESTBURY (Cheshire)
  Nowell, C. D., *c.* 1946–59
  studio-potter
  (at Disley *c.* 1946–51)

C D Nowell

PRESTBURY

PRESTWOOD (Buckinghamshire)
  Newland, William
  studio-potter, 1948–

WN

(date)

  Casson, Michael & Sheila
  studio-potters, 1953–
    Sheila Casson, 1951–59

CM   M

w
s

RAINHAM (Kent)
  Upchurch Pottery, 1913–61
  Baker, W. & J.
    'Seeby', name of agent
    1945–61

UPCHURCH

UPCHURCH
SEEBY

  Rainham Pottery Ltd.
  earthenware, 1948–
  Wilson, Alfred, now
  E. J. Baker

Rainham
impressed or painted

RAMSBURY (Wiltshire)
  Holdsworth Potteries
  Holdsworth, Peter, 1945–

READING (Berkshire)
Collier Ltd., S. & E.
terra-cotta, *c.* 1848–1957

RICHMOND (Surrey)
Sykes, Steven, 1948–55
studio-potter

Steven Sykes
(signature)

ROCKINGHAM (Yorkshire)
Rockingham Works
(nr. Swinton) earthenware
c. 1750–1842 (porcelain
also made from about 1826)
c. 1778–87

BINGLEY
impressed

Brameld & Co., 1806–42

BRAMELD
impressed

    c. 1826–30

ROCKINGHAM
WORKS,
BRAMELD

ROCKINHGAM
BRAMELD

    c. 1830–42

ROYAL
ROCKINGHAM
WORKS
BRAMELD

    'griffin-mark', *c.* 1826–30
from crest of Earl Fitzwilliam,
Marquis of Rockingham

from *c.* 1830–42
    'Royal' added to title
of factory
mark in red *c.* 1826–30, puce 1830–42
'Manufacturer to the King' added to mark
in 1830–37 (William IV)

Baguley, Alfred & Isaac
Rockingham Works
decorator only of
porcelain in Rockingham
style, *c.* 1842–65 (Mexborough)
   c. 1865–91

'Griffin mark'
with
'Baguley'

printed

ROLVENDEN (Kent)
Watson, Dorothy
Bridge Pottery 1921–

impressed or printed

ROTHERHAM (S. Yorkshire)
Holmes Pottery, 1870–87
Jackson & Co., J.
earthenware
Shaw & Sons, Ltd., G.
1887–1948

J.J. & CO.

J. & CO.

G.S. & S.
printed

Northfield Pottery
earthenware
Hawley, W. & G., 1863–8,
Hawley Bros Ltd.,
1868–1903, 'Ltd'. added 1897

W. & G. HAWLEY

H.B.
HAWLEY BROS.

Northfield Hawley Pottery Co. Ltd.
earthenware, 1903–19

  impressed or printed
  mark introduced about
  1898 by Hawley Bros.

Walker & Son   WALKER
earthenware, *c*. 1772–

RUSTINGTON (Sussex)
Champion, G. H. & E. E.
studio-potters, 1947–

RYE (Sussex)   SUSSEX WARE
   1869– mark of *c*. 1900
   pottery (including tin-glaze)
   c. 1869–1920
   (Sussex Rustic Ware)
   's.A.W.' Sussex Art Ware
   c. 1920–39
   J. C. Cole & W. V.   RYE
   Cole, 1947–
      various marks including
      name 'RYE'
   Walter V. Cole, 1957–

Cadborough Pottery,   OLD SUSSEX WARE
   1807–71, earthenware   RYE

   Mitchell, William, *c*.   MITCHELL
   1840–, W. Mitchell &   M
   Sons, 1859–69,
   Mitchell, F. & H., 1869–71

   Iden Pottery, 1961–
   Townsend, D. & Wood, J. H.
   studio-potters
   (moved from Iden to Rye
   in 1963)

74

Everett, Raymond, 1963–
studio-potter

ST. IVES (Cornwall)
  Leach, Bernard, 1921–
    Leach Pottery marks
  studio-pottery
    personal marks of B. Leach

Hamada, Shoji
1920–23, 1929–*c*. 30

Leach, Janet, 1956–

Leach, John, *c*. 1950–8
(at Langport, Somerset since 1964)
Marshall, William, 1954–

incised

impressed

Mc. Kenzie, Warren, 1950–2

(at Dartington from 1963–)
  mark used at Dartington

Quick, Kenneth, 1945–63
(at St. Ives 1945–*c*. 55 and
1960–63)
  mark used at Tregenna Hill Pottery
  c. 1955–60

75

ST. MARY CHURCH (Devon) WATCOMBE
  Watcombe Pottery Co.   TORQUAY
  1867–1901

    printed mark, 1875–1901

    Royal Aller Vale &
    Watcombe Pottery Co.
    c. 1901–62

                    WATCOMBE
                    POTTERY

                    ROYAL
                    TORQUAY
                    POTTERY

SALISBURY (Wiltshire)   PAYNE SARUM
  Payne, retailer only   printed
  c. 1834–41

SMETHWICK   TAYLOR
(nr. Birmingham)   impressed
  Ruskin Pottery, 1898–1935
  earthenware
  Taylor, W. Howson, *c.* 1898–

    painted or incised

    impressed mark, *c.* 1904–15
    with added date

STANMORE (London)   E.C./(date)
  Collyer, Ernest & Pamela
  studio-potters, 1950–

  Collyer-Nash   P.N. (Pamela Nash)

STEDHAM (Sussex)   Ray Marshall
  Marshall, Ray   (date)
  studio-potter, 1945–
  impressed mark   signature

STOCKTON-ON-TEES (Cleveland)
Ainsworth, W. H. & J. H.
1865–1901, earthenware

impressed

Harwood, J.
Clarence Pottery, 19th
century earthenware
  impressed mark, *c.* 1849–77

HARWOOD
STOCKTON

Skinner & Co., George
Stafford Pottery
earthenware, *c.* 1855–70

G.S. & CO.
printed

Skinner & Walker
1870–80

S. & W.
QUEEN'S WARE
STOCKTON

Smith & Co.,   W.S. & CO.   W.S. & CO.
William, *c.* 1825–55   STAFFORD
Stafford Pottery   W.S. & CO'S   POTTERY
             WEDGWOOD

Smith, George F.
North Shore Pottery
c. 1855–60, earthenware

G.F.S.

Smith (Junr), William
c. 1845–84

W. S. JUNR. & CO.
all printed or impressed

STOURBRIDGE (West Midlands)
Sunfield Pottery, 1937–
earthenware and stoneware

77

SUNDERLAND   ATKINSON & CO.
(Tyne and Wear)   impressed or
  Southwick Pottery,   printed
  1788–99, Atkinson & Co., earthenware

  Deptford Pottery,   COPYRIGHT BALL
  1857–1918   BROS.
  Ball, William,   SUNDERLAND
  earthenware, Ball Bros., 1884–

  Wear Pottery   J. BRUNTON
  Brunton, John,   printed
  1796–1803, earthenware

  South Hylton &   DAWSON   I. DAWSON
  Ford Potteries
  Dawson, John, *c.* 1799–1864
  c. 1799–1848, earthenware
  Thomas Dawson & Co.,   DAWSON & CO.
  c. 1837–48, earthenware
    printed marks   FORD POTTERY   J. DAWSON
                        SOUTH HYLTON

  Garrison or   J. PHILLIPS
  Sunderland Pottery   SUNDERLAND
  earthenware, *c.* 1807–65   POTTERY
    c. 1807–12

    c. 1813–19   PHILLIPS & CO.   DIXON & CO.
                             DIXON, AUSTIN
    c. 1820–26   & CO.
                             DIXON, AUSTIN
    c. 1827–40   PHILLIPS & CO.

    c. 1840–65   DIXON, PHILLIPS
                              & CO.

Wear Pottery, 1803–74
Moore & Co., Samuel
earthenware

MOORE & CO.
SUNDERLAND

North Hylton
Pottery, 1762–67,
earthenware, Maling, William, 1762–, continued
by family until 1815

MALING
impressed

Phillips & Co.,
John, 1815–67
(Phillips &
Maling, 1780–1815)

JOHN PHILLIPS
HYLTON POT
WORKS

Southwick Pottery, *c.* 1800–97
    c. 1800–29   A. SCOTT & CO.
                           SCOTT, SOUTHWICK
      c. 1829–44   A. SCOTT & SONS
                               S. & SONS
      c. 1844–54   S.B. & CO.
                          SCOTT BROTHERS
      c. 1854–97   A. SCOTT & SON
                               S. & S.

Union Pottery,
c. 1802

UNION POTTERY
printed

SWADLINCOTE (S. Derbyshire)
Ault, William, 1887–1923
earthenware
    The wares of this
    pottery sometimes
    bear the signature
    of the designer
    Christopher Dresser
    and date from
    1891–6

printed or
impressed

printed

Ault & Tunnicliffe Ltd.
1923–37
(*see* Ashby Potter's Guild)

Ault Potteries Ltd., 1937–
(now Pearson & Co., Group)
  marks impressed or printed

SWINTON (Yorkshire)
  Don Pottery, earthenware
  1790–1893
    1800–34

DON POTTERY

GREEN
DON POTTERY

    1820–34, impressed or
    printed

Barker, Samuel, 1834–93

      '& Son' or '& Sons'
      added 1851–93

BARKER
DON POTTERY

Bingley & Co., Thomas
earthenware, 1778–87

BINGLEY
impressed

Twigg, Joseph & brothers
Kilnhurst Pottery & Newhill Pottery, *c.* 1822–81
earthenware
    impressed or
    printed, *c.* 1822–

J.T.

    impressed, *c.*
    1822–66

TWIGG
NEWHILL

    impressed, *c.*
    1839–81

TWIGG
K.P.

80

TONBRIDGE (Kent)
  Slack & Brownlow
  earthenware, *c.* 1928–34

TONBRIDGE WARE
printed or impressed

TORQUAY (Devon)
  Torquay Terra-Cotta Co. Ltd.
  Dr. Gillow, 1875–1909
  earthenware figures, busts, etc.

impressed or printed

TRING (Hertfordshire)
  Pendley Pottery, 1949–
  Fieldhouse, Murray
  studio-potter (now at
  Northfields Studio)

incised or printed

TRURO (Cornwall)
  Chapel Hill Pottery,
  1872–, Lake & Son Ltd.,
  W. H., earthenware

LAKE'S CORNISH
POTTERY TRURO
printed or impressed

WAREHAM (Dorset)
  Sibley Pottery Ltd., 1922–
  62, earthenware and
  stoneware

SIBLEY POTTERY LTD
DORSET
ENGLAND
impressed or printed

WATTISFIELD (Suffolk)
  Watson Potteries Ltd., Henry
  earthenware and stoneware
  c. 1800–; mark of about
    1948, early wares unmarked

WELWYN GARDEN CITY (Hertfordshire)
  Coper, Hans, 1947–
  studio-potter

81

WENFORD BRIDGE (nr. Bodmin, Cornwall)
Wenford Bridge Pottery
c. 1939–42; 1949–
impressed mark
(*see also* WINCHCOMBE)

WESTON-SUPER-MARE (Avon)
Matthews, John
terra-cotta, 1870–88
impressed mark with
Royal Arms

JOHN MATTHEWS
LATE PHILLIPS
ROYAL POTTERY
WESTON-SUPER-MARE

WHITTINGTON (Derbyshire)
Walton Pottery Co. Ltd.
1946–56
Gordon, William
salt-glazed stoneware

WINCANTON Somerset)
Ireson, Nathaniel
c. 1730–50
tin-glazed earthenware

IRESON
WINCANTON

WINCHCOMBE (Gloucestershire)
c. 1926–39
Cardew, Michael A.
also at Wenford Bridge
c. 1939–42
studio-potter

mark impressed

Finch, Raymond, 1939–
studio-potter, impressed
mark used from *c.* 1926

WITHERNSEA (Humberside)
Eastgate Potteries, Ltd.
earthenware, 1955–

EASTGATE
ENGLAND
(on a gate)

WOODVILLE (Derbyshire)
Ashby Potters' Guild
earthenware, 1909–22

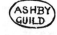

impressed

Mansfield Bros., Ltd.
Art Pottery Works, *c.* 1890–
1957

M.B.
impressed

WORCESTER (Worcestershire)
Worcester Porcelain Factory
1751 (Lund & Miller's Bristol factory
est. 1748, taken over in 1752)
soft-paste porcelain (soapstone)

workmen's marks
in underglaze blue

'open' crescent on painted
wares, 1755–83

83

crescent-mark with
crossed-hatched lines
on printed wares

in underglaze blue

any crescents in gilt or enamel colour
probably indicate outside decorator or
reproduction
on painted and printed
wares

painted in blue

marks on wares decorated
with 'Japan patterns'
c. 1760–75

in blue

'fretted square' mark
usually on heavily decorated
wares with scale-blue ground
c. 1755–75 (frequently seen
on reproductions)

in blue

Worcester imitation of Meissen
crossed-swords mark
c. 1760–70

in blue

printed numerals disguised as Chinese
characters, numbers 1–9, until recent
excavations at Worcester factory site these were
thought to be marks of Caughley (Salop)

'Flight' period, 1783–92
  'small crescent', 1783–92

  mark in blue, 1783–92

  mark in blue, 1788–92

'Flight & Barr' period
1792–1807

F. & B.

'Barr', *c.* 1792–1807

incised

'Barr Flight & Barr' period
1807–13

BFB
impressed

Barr, Flight & Barr	BARR, FLIGHT
Worcester	& BARR
Flight & Barr	ROYAL PORCELAIN
Coventry Street,	WORKS
London	WORCESTER
Manufacturers to their	LONDON HOUSE
Majesties and	NO. 1
Royal Family	COVENTRY STREET

'Flight, Barr & Barr' period
1813–40

impressed

(factory taken over by Chamberlains, 1840–52)

Kerr & Binns, 1852–62

Kerr & Binns, '54' = 1854
    mark on outstanding
    examples, including decorator's
    initials (bottom left)

standard mark, printed or
impressed, *c.* 1852–62
Note: crown added
in 1862

'Worcester Royal Porcelain Company Ltd.'
(Royal Worcester) 1862–present

standard mark, 1862–present
early version, with 'C'
in centre replacing crescent
in Kerr & Binn's version
numbers below = last 2 years
of date

From 1867 a letter indicating the year of
manufacture was printed under the factory mark
according to the following table:

A 1867	G 1872	M 1877	T 1882	Y 1887
B '1868	H 1873	N 1878	U 1883	Z 1888
C 1869	I 1874	P 1879	V 1884	O 1889
D 1870	K 1875	R 1880	W 1885	
E 1871	L 1876	S 1881	X 1886	

'a' in Old English script in 1890; date letter omitted in 1891.

'Royal Worcester England' written around mark from 1891, after which, dots, stars and other letters and forms were added to the mark each year as listed below until 1963 when the year in full is added.

1892, dot to left of crown, 1893 dot either side of crown; dots were then added to either side of crown until 1915, thus:

1894 3 dots	1900	9 dots	1906 15 dots	1912 21 dots
1895 4 dots	1901	10 dots	1907 16 dots	1913 22 dots
1896 5 dots	1902	11 dots	1908 17 dots	1914 23 dots
1897 6 dots	1903	12 dots	1909 18 dots	1915 24 dots
1898 7 dots	1904	13 dots	1910 19 dots	
1899 8 dots	1905	14 dots	1911 20 dots	

In 1916 the dots alongside the crown were replaced by a star under the mark, dots were then added to either side of this star until 1927:

1916 1 star	1922 star & 6 dots
1917 star & 1 dot	1923 star & 7 dots
1918 star & 2 dots	1924 star & 8 dots
1919 star & 3 dots	1925 star & 9 dots
1920 star & 4 dots	1926 star & 10 dots
1921 star & 5 dots	1927 star & 11 dots

then as follows:

1928 ▭   1929 ◇   1930 ÷

1931 ∞   1932 ∞∞   1933 ∞∞ ·

further dots were then added to three interlaced circles as follows:

1934 circles & 2 dots	1938 circles & 6 dots
1935 circles & 3 dots	1939 circles & 7 dots
1936 circles & 4 dots	1940 circles & 8 dots
1937 circles & 5 dots	1941 circles & 9 dots

from 1941 to 1948 inclusive there were no changes in the year-mark

1949 V	1953 W and 3 dots
1950 W	1954 W and 4 dots
1951 W and 1 dot	1955 W and 5 dots
1952 W and 2 dots	

1956 R in place of W	1960 R and 10 dots
with 6 dots	1961 R and 11 dots
1957 R and 7 dots	1962 R and 12 dots
1958 R and 8 dots	1963 R and 13 dots
1959 R and 9 dots	

From 1963 all new patterns have the year in full.

(*By courtesy of the Worcester Royal Porcelain Co. Ltd.*)

Hancock, Robert, *b.* 1730, *d.* 1817
engraver of transfer-prints
c. 1756–65

R̶1̶. Worcester

(Hancock associated with   initials of Hancock
Turner of Caughley in   and rebus of Richard
1776)   Holdship on prints

Chamberlain, *c.* 1786–1852
decorators from *c.* 1786–*c.* 1790, then
manufacturers of soft-paste porcelain
    c. 1790–1810

Chamberlains
Worcs No 276
in red

written or printed   *Chamberlain's*
c. 1811–40   *Worcester,*
(under crown)   *& 155*
New Bond Street
London,
Royal Porcelain
Manufactory

c. 1814–16   *Chamberlain's*
Worcester,
& 63 Piccadilly,
London

written or printed

incised, *c.* 1815–25	CHAMBERLAINS ROYAL PORCELAIN WORCESTER
printed mark under crown, *c.* 1840–5 ('& Co.' from this date)	CHAMBERLAIN & CO. WORCESTER 155 New Bond St. & No. 1 COVENTRY ST. LONDON
written or printed *c.* 1846–50	CHAMBERLAIN & CO. WORCESTER
impressed or printed *c.* 1847–50	CHAMBERLAINS
printed *c.* 1850–52	

(then Kerr & Binns, p. 86)

Doe and Rogers, *c.* 1820–40 porcelain decorators	Doe & Rogers Worcester
Grainger, Wood & Co. *c.* 1801–12, porcelain rare mark	Grainger Wood & Co. Worcester, Warranted
Grainger, Lee & Co. *c.* 1812–*c.* 39 porcelain	Grainger, Lee & Co. Worcester painted

c. 1820–30 painted	New China Works Worcester
c. 1812–30 painted	Royal China Works Worcester

Grainger, George *c.* 1839–1902 porcelain	GEO. GRAINGER CHINA WORKS WORCESTER
painted or printed mark *c.* 1839–60	
'& Co.' added *c.* 1850	G. GRAINGER & CO. WORCESTER

'S.P.' for 'Semi-
Porcelain', *c.*
1850–

     G.G. & CO.   S.P.
        S.P.   G.G.W.

initials included in
printed marks, 1850–60
1850–89

    impressed or printed
        G.W.

        G. & CO. W.

printed mark on copies
of 'Dr. Wall' period wares
c. 1860–80

   GRAINGER & CO.
     WORCESTER

printed or impressed
c. 1870–89

c. 1889–1902 ('England'
added in 1891)

letters added under mark to indicate year of
manufacture from 1891–1902:

A 1891	D 1894	G 1897	J 1900
B 1892	E 1895	H 1898	K 1901
C 1893	F 1896	I 1899	L 1902

George Grainger & Co. was taken over by
Worcester Royal Porcelain Co. Ltd. in 1889 and
closed down in 1902.

Hadley & Sons, James
porcelain and earthenware
1896–1905

Hadley

signature on work   incised or impressed
modelled by Hadley for
Worcester Royal Porcelain Co.
c. 1875–94

printed or impressed
1896–97
1897–1902,   FINE ART
impressed   HADLEY'S
                             TERRA-COTTA

printed mark 1897–1902
(centre ribbon omitted
from 1900)

printed mark, 1902–5

Locke & Co., porcelain   LOCKE & CO.
1895–1904   WORCESTER

'globe-mark', *c.* 1895–1904
'Ltd,' added in *c.* 1900

Sparks, George, *c.*
1836–54, decorator of
Worcester and Coalport porcelain

Sparks Worcester
written mark

WROTHAM (Kent)
  Greene, John
  slipware potter, *c.* 1670

I.G.

Hubble, Nicholas
slipware potter, second
half of 17th century

N.H.

Ifield, Thomas, Henry
& John
slipware potters whose
  initials are found on wares
  dating from *c.* 1620–75

T.I.
H.I.   I.I.

Livermore, John
(*d.* 1658) slipware potter,
wares dated from 1612–49

I.L.

Richardson, George
slipware potter, wares
dated from 1642–77

G.R.

all above slip-trailed

Wells, Reginald,
(1877–1951)
studio-potter

WELLS
incised

c. 1909		COLDRUM
		WROTHAM
c. 1910–24 (at		COLDRUM
Chelsea)		CHELSEA
c. 1910		R. F. WELLS
c. 1918–51		SOON
(at Storrington,		impressed or incised
Sussex, *c.* 1925–51)		

YARMOUTH (Norfolk)
Absolon, William, 1784–1815
independent enameller of
the wares of various
earthenwares and glass

painted in brown

STAFFORDSHIRE
Since the early seventeenth century the area in,
and around, Stoke in Staffordshire has been the
centre of the English ceramic industry.
Manufacture was first confined to earthenwares,
but later included salt-glazed stonewares,
jasperwares, bone-china and the mass of various
hybrid pottery and porcelain bodies introduced
about 1800 and later. The smaller pottery towns
are today grouped together to form
Stoke-on-Trent.
   In this section of the book, the various

Staffordshire potters are listed alphabetically under the names of the towns in which they potted.

Many of the more recent factories have often changed their mark many times and the following general aids to dating are often sufficient enough as a guide.

Few serious collectors seek pieces which include 'ENGLAND' in the mark, for this implies the piece was made in, or after, 1891 in order to comply with the American McKinley Tariff, which called for the country of origin to be marked on imported wares. The term 'MADE IN ENGLAND' suggests a date of about 1920.

The mass of blue-printed earthenwares are difficult to attribute if unmarked. Many have just a Royal Arms as a mark; this is a sure indication of a 19th-century date, whereas often similar marks, or 'back-stamps', include the name of the design and the initials of the potter. These initials may well be included in the index at end of the book. Versions of the Royal Arms used after 1837 lack the small inescutcheon on the quartered shield which is present on arms previous to this date.

In addition to factory marks, many wares will be found to bear the well-known 'diamond' or 'lozenge'-mark (see Appendix A, page 284). This mark was applied by either printing, impressing, or applying as a relief medallion and indicates that the design of the form or decoration had been registered with the London Patent Office and was protected against 'piracy' for a period of three years. If the numbers and letters in the four corners of this 'diamond-mark' can be accurately read, the reader should consult the key diagrams and tables on pages 284–7 to check the day, month and year the design was initially registered between 1842 and 1883. After this year wares bear only a registered number (e.g. Rd. 12345), which can be dated to the year, up until 1909.

Appendix B in this book is an abbreviated copy of the Class IV (pottery, porcelain, etc.) Index, giving the name and whereabouts of the firms registering ceramic designs between 1842 and 1883. This list is reproduced with the kind permission of the Public Record Office.

BILSTON (Staffs., now West Midlands)
Myatt Pottery Co., *c.* 1850–94
earthenware, mark of 1880   MYATT

BURSLEM (Staffs, now West Midlands.)
Albert Potteries Ltd.
earthenware, 1946–54   printed or impressed

Allman, Broughton & Co.,   A.B. & CO.
earthenware, 1861–8   printed or impressed

Baggaley, Jacob   J.B.
earthenware, 1880–6   impressed

Bagshaw & Meir   B. & M.
earthenware, 1802–8   printed or impressed

Ball, Izaac   I.B.
slipware, *c.* 1700

Bancroft & Bennett
earthenware, 1846–50

Barker & Son   B. & S.
earthenware, *c.* 1850–60   printed
BARKER & SON
printed or impressed

Barker, Sutton & Till   B.S. & T.
earthenware, 1834–43

Bates, Elliott & Co.   B.E. & CO.
general ceramics, 1870–5

Bates, Gildea & Walker, general ceramics, 1878–81	B.G. & W. printed
Bates, Walker & Co. general ceramics, 1875–78	B.W. & CO. printed
Bathwell & Goodfellow earthenware, 1818–23 (also Tunstall 1820–2)	BATHWELL & GOODFELLOW impressed
Beech, James earthenware, 1877–89 Swan Bank Works (also at Tunstall)	J.B. printed
Blackhurst & Bourne earthenware, 1880–92	B. & B. printed
Blackhurst & Tunnicliffe earthenware, *c.* 1879	B. & T. printed
Bodley & Co. earthenware, 1865	
Bodley & Co., E. F. earthenware, *c.* 1862–81	E.F.B. & CO. SCOTIA POTTERY
Bodley & Son bone-china, 1874–5	BODLEY B. & SON printed

Bodley, E. J. D.
general ceramics, 1875–92

E.J.D.B.
printed,
impressed or as
monogram

Bodley & Harrold
Scotia Pottery
1863–5, earthenware

B. & H.
Bodley & Harrold
printed

Boote, Ltd., T. & R.
Waterloo Pottery
general ceramics and
tiles, 1842–*c.* 1966

T. & R.B.   T.B. & S.

T. & R. BOOTE
printed or impressed

printed mark
1890–1906
'England' added
from 1891

Booth & Co., Thomas
(also at Tunstall)
earthenware, 1868–72

T.B. & CO.
printed

Bridgwood & Clarke
(also at Tunstall)
earthenware, 1857–64

BRIDGWOOD &
CLARKE
impressed
B. & C.   B. & C.
BURSLEM
printed

Brown & Steventon, Ltd.
earthenware, 1900–23

B. & S.
printed
'sun-face' mark
from 1920–

Buckley, Heath & Co.
earthenware, 1885–90

printed or impressed

Buckley, Wood & Co.
earthenware, 1875–85

B.W. & CO.
printed or impressed

Burgess, Henry
earthenware, 1864–92

H.B.
impressed or printed
under Royal Arms

Burgess & Leigh
earthenware, *c.* 1862–

B. & L.
impressed or printed

'Ltd.' added to marks
from *c.* 1919, large
variety of printed
marks from 1880,
'England' added from
1891

printed

monogram mark
1862–

impressed or printed

Burslem Pottery Co. Ltd.
earthenware, 1894–1933

printed

ENGLAND

Burslem School of Art
earthenware, figures, etc.
in 'Astbury' style
1935–41

impressed

Clarke & Co., Edward
earthenware, *c.* 1880–87
(also at Tunstall, *c.* 1865–
77, and Longport, *c.*
1878–80)

EDWARD CLARKE

EDWARD CLARKE &
CO.
printed

Clowes, William
general ceramics
c. 1783–96

W. CLOWES
impressed

Collinson & Co.,
Charles, earthenware,
1851–73

C. COLLINSON & CO.
printed

Cooper & Co., J.
earthenware, 1922–5
printed or impressed
in circle
Cooper Pottery, Susie
('Ltd.' from *c.* 1961)
general ceramics
　c. 1930–

J. COOPER & CO.
ENGLAND
DUCAL WORKS
Susie Cooper
CROWN WORKS
BURSLEM
ENGLAND

printed mark, 1932–

A SUSIE COOPER
PRODUCTION
CROWN WORKS
BURSLEM
ENGLAND

Cooper China Ltd., Susie
(also at Longton, *c.* 1950–9)
china, *c.* 1959–
Member of the
Wedgwood Group

Susie Cooper
BONE CHINA
ENGLAND

Cork & Edge
earthenware,
1846–60

C. & E.
printed with a
variety of designs

Cork, Edge & Malkin
earthenware, 1860–71

C.E. & M.
printed with varying
'backstamps' often
including pattern-name

Dale, John   J. DALE   I. DALE
'Staffordshire   BURSLEM   BURSLEM
figures', early 19th century

Daniel & Cork   DANIEL & CORK
earthenware, 1867–9   printed

Davison & Son, Ltd.
earthenware,
c. 1898–1952

DAVISON
& SON LTD
BURSLEM
ENGLAND

mark of 1948–   printed

Dean, S. W.
earthenware, 1904–10

  printed mark

Deans (1910) Ltd.
earthenware, 1910–19
  printed mark

DEANS (1910) LTD.
BURSLEM
ENGLAND

Doulton & Co.
earthenware and
porcelain, *c.* 1882
(Doulton Fine China Ltd.
from 1955 and Royal
Doulton Tableware Ltd., 1973–)
  impressed name of
  new material from
  1960

see under
LAMBETH
for major
marks

ENGLISH
TRANSLUCENT
CHINA

Duke & Nephews, Sir James
various hybrid porcelains
c. 1860–3

  impressed hand

Dunn, Bennett & Co.
earthenware, 1875–
('Ltd.' added from 1907–)
(now Royal Doulton Group)
  marks 1875–1907

D.B. & CO.
printed

printed mark, 1937–   DUNN BENNETT & CO. LTD.
                      BURSLEM
                      ENGLAND

added to mark on
'Ironstone' from 1955–   'Vitreous Ironstone'

Edge, Malkin & Co.   E.M. & CO.
earthenware, 1871–1903

                     E.M. & CO.
'L T D.' added from 1899   B
                     printed

Edwards & Son, James   J.E. & S.
various pottery, 1851–82

                       EDWARDS
'Dale Hall', Burslem   D.H.
                       printed or impressed
Edwards, James & Thomas   J. & T.E.
earthenware, 1839–41

    printed or impressed   J. & T. EDWARDS
                           B

Ellgreave Pottery Co. Ltd.   'Lottie Rhead Ware'
earthenware, 1921–
(Wood & Sons Ltd.)
    and other fully   'Heatmaster'
    named marks

Elton & Co. Ltd., J. F.   J.F.E. CO. LTD.
earthenware, 1901–1910   BURSLEM
    (also in monogram)   printed or impressed

Emery, Francis J.
earthenware, *c.* 1878–93

F. J. EMERY
printed

Evans & Booth
earthenware, 1856–69

E. & B.
printed

Ford & Co., Samuel
earthenware, 1898–1939
(*see* Smith & Ford)

'F. & CO.' alternative to
'S. & F.'

printed

c. 1936–9

'Samford Ware'

Ford & Riley
earthenware, 1882–93

F. & R.
B

Ford & Sons ('Ltd.'
added 1908),
earthenware, *c.* 1893–1938

F. & S.
B

also 'CROWN
FORD', 'NEWCRAFT'

F. & SONS, LTD.
printed

Ford & Sons (Crownford)
earthenware, 1938–

printed, 1961–

Gibson & Sons, Ltd.
earthenware, 1885–

G. & S. LTD.
B

Gibson & Sons, Ltd.
'Harvey Pottery'
  printed, *c.* 1904–9

'Royal Harvey', *c.* 1950–5
  large variety of fully named marks, 1909–

Gildea & Walker, 1881–5
earthenware

G. & W.

c. 1881–5:
$\dfrac{4}{82}$ = APRIL, 1882

TRADE MARK.

Gildea, James
earthenware, 1885–8

  printed mark includes
  a pattern-name

Godwin, B. C.
earthenware, *c.* 1851–

B.C.G.
printed

Godwin, Thomas &
Benjamin, general
ceramics, *c.* 1809–34

T. & B.G.
T.B.G.
printed

Godwin, Thomas
earthenware, 1834–54

THOS GODWIN
BURSLEM
STONE CHINA

Godwin, Rowley & Co. earthenware, 1828–31	G.R. & CO. printed
Hall & Sons, John earthenware, 1814–32 *c.* 1822–32	I. HALL HALL I. HALL & SONS impressed or printed
Hammersley & Son, Ralph, earthenware, 1860–1905 '& Son' added 1884–	R.H. R.H. & S. printed
Hancock, Whittingham & Co., earthenware, 1863–72	H.W. & CO. printed
Harding, Joseph earthenware, 1850–1	J. HARDING printed
Harrison & Phillips earthenware, 1914–15	H. & P. BURSLEM printed
Heath & Son earthenware, *c.* 1800	HEATH & SON impressed
Heath, John general ceramics, 1809–23	HEATH impressed
Heath, Thomas earthenware, 1812–35	T. HEATH impressed or printed

Heath & Blackhurst & Co.,
earthenware, 1859–77

H. & B.
H.B. & CO.

Heath & Greatbatch
earthenware, 1891–3

H. & G.
B
printed or impressed

Hill Pottery Co. Ltd.
general ceramics, *c.* 1861–7

J.S.H.
printed
(also as monogram)

Hobson, Charles
earthenware, 1865–80
's' added 1873–5

C.H.
C.H. & S.
impressed or printed

Hobson, G. & J.
earthenware, 1883–1901

HOBSON'S
printed

Hobson, George
earthenware, 1901–23
printed or impressed

Holdcroft & Co., Peter
earthenware, 1846–52

P.H. & CO.
printed

Holdcroft, Hill & Mellor,
earthenware,
1860–70

H.H. & M.
printed

Hollinshead & Griffiths
earthenware, 1890–1909

CHELSEA ART POTTERY
H. & G.
BURSLEM

mark includes lion and crown

Holmes, Plant & Maydew earthenware, 1876–85	H.P. & M. printed
Hope & Carter earthenware, 1862–80	H. & C. printed
Hughes, Thomas earthenware, 1860–94	THOMAS HUGHES IRONSTONE CHINA impressed
Hughes & Son Ltd., Thomas, general ceramics, 1895–1957	THOS. HUGHES & SON ENGLAND
Hulme & Sons, Henry earthenware, 1906–32 (mark previously used by Wood & Hulme)	W. & H. B

Hulme, William   printed
earthenware, 1891–1941   1891–1936

printed or impressed,   ALPHA WARE
1936–41   H
                                      ENGLAND

Jackson, Job & John   J. & J. JACKSON
earthenware, 1831–5   JACKSON'S
                                    WARRANTED
                              impressed or printed

Johnson, Ltd., Samuel
earthenware, 1887–1931
   'Ltd.' 1912–
   'BRITANNIA POTTERY',
   1916–31

S.J.

S.J.B.

S.J. LTD.
printed

Jones, George
earthenware, *c.* 1854

GEORGE JONES

Keeling & Co. Ltd.
earthenware, 1886–1936

   'England' usually added
   from 1891
   'Losol Ware', *c.* 1912–

K. & CO.

K. & CO. B.

all
printed

Kennedy, William Sadler
earthenware, 1843–54

W. S. KENNEDY
impressed or printed

Kennedy & Macintyre
earthenware, 1854–60

W. S. KENNEDY
& J. MACINTYRE
impressed or printed

Kensington Pottery Ltd.
c. 1937–
(also at Hanley 1922–37)
now Price & Kensington Potteries Ltd.

Kent (Porcelains) Ltd., William
earthenware 1944–62

King & Barrett, Ltd.   K. & B.
general pottery, 1898–40   impressed or printed

Lakin & Poole   LAKIN & POOLE
pottery and figures, *c.* 1791–5

L. & P.
BURSLEM
impressed

Leighton Pottery Ltd.   'ROYAL LEIGHTON WARE'
earthenware, 1940–54

Machin & Potts   MACHIN & POTTS
general ceramics
1833–7   MACHIN & POTTS
colour-print patent 1835   PATENT

Machin & Thomas   M. & T.
earthenware, *c.* 1831–2   printed

Macintyre & Co. Ltd.,   MACINTYRE
James, earthenware, *c.*   J. MACINTYRE
1860–1928, '& Co.' from   J.M. & CO.
  1867– (continued with   printed or impressed
  industrial wares only)

Maddock & Seddon   M. & S.
earthenware, *c.* 1839–42

Maddock, John   M
earthenware, 1842–55   printed
  (not to be confused with
  'M' for Minton)

Maddock & Sons (Ltd.) general pottery, 1855– specialist hotel-ware 'Ltd.' added 1896–	various fully named marks, and 'ROYAL VITREOUS' 'ROYAL IVORY' 'IVORY WARE' 'EMBASSY'

Malkin, Frederick
earthenware, 1891–1905

　printed, *c.* 1900–5

Malkin, Samuel
slip-wares, early 18th century

S.M.
moulded in
relief

Mayer, Thomas, John
& Joseph, general
ceramics, 1843–55

T. J. & J. MAYER
printed

Mellor, Taylor & Co.　'ROYAL IRONSTONE CHINA'
earthenware, *c.* 1880–1904

　printed or impressed　　'SEMI PORCELAIN'
　with name of firm

Mellor, Venables & Co.　MELLOR, VENABLES
general ceramics, 1834–51　　& CO.

M.V. & CO.
printed or impressed

Midwinter Ltd., W. R.
earthenwares, 1910–
　　added numbers indicate
　　month and year
(*now Wedgwood Group*)

various fully-named
marks with:
'PORCELON'
'STYLECRAFT'

Moorcroft Ltd., W.
earthenware, 1913–

MOORCROFT
BURSLEM

　　signature of William
　　Moorcroft (*d.* 1945)

　　mark of Walter Moorcroft
　　(son)

Morgan, Wood & Co.
earthenware, 1860–70

M.W. & CO.
printed
(at times with bee)

Mountford, A. J.
earthenware, 1897–1901

BURSLEM
printed

New Wharf Pottery Co.
earthenware, 1878–94

N.W.P.C.O.
B
printed

Newport Pottery Co. Ltd.
earthenware, 1920–
(*now Wedgwood group*)

various fully named
marks

　　c. 1938–66

'Clarice Cliff'

113

Parrott & Co. Ltd.
earthenware, 1921
(manufacture ceased *c.* 1962)

Phillips & Son, Thomas
earthenware, *c.* 1845–6

T. PHILLIPS & SON
BURSLEM
printed or impressed

Pinder, Thomas
earthenware, 1849–51

PINDER BURSLEM
printed or impressed

Pinder, Bourne & Hope
earthenware, 1851–62

P.B. & H.
printed

Pinder, Bourne & Co.
earthenware, 1862–82
(taken over by Doultons
in 1878, but name unchanged
until 1882)

P.B. & CO.

Plant Bros. Crown Pottery
porcelain, 1889–1906
(at Longton from 1898)

Plant, Enoch
earthenware, 1898–1905
    (such crowns are a
    common form of mark)

printed or impressed

Poole, J. E.
earthenware, *c.* 1796–
early 19th century

POOLE
impressed

Price Bros.
earthenware, 1896–1903

Price Bros. (Burslem) Ltd.   printed
earthenware, 1903–61   'star-mark', as above
                                                    until 1910

   trade-names:
   'PALM ATHLO'
   'ATHLO WARE'
   'MATTONA WARE'

Price & Kensington   PRICE
Potteries Ltd.   KENSINGTON
earthenware, 1962–   printed within wreath

Radford Handcraft   G. RADFORD
Pottery, earthenware,   BURSLEM
1933–48   printed signature

Riley, John & Richard   J. & R. RILEY
general ceramics, 1802–28

   marks painted,   RILEY'S
   printed or impressed   SEMI-CHINA

Robinson, Joseph   J.R.
earthenware, 1876–98   B
                                         printed or impressed

Roddy & Co., E.   STAFFORDSHIRE
earthenware, 1925–8   RODDY
                                                  WARE

115

Sadler & Sons, Ltd., James, earthenware, 1899– impressed or printed from 1937–	ENGLAND J.S.S.B. impressed SADLER BURSLEM ENGLAND
Simpson, Ralph slip-wares, 1651–*c.* 1724 name slip-trailed on front of large chargers	RALPH SIMPSON slip-trailed
Simpson, John slip wares, first half of 18th century	JOHN SIMPSON I.S. slip-trailed
Smith & Co., Ambrose earthenware, *c.* 1784–6	A.S. & CO. impressed or printed
Smith & Ford earthenware, 1895–8 printed (*see also* Samuel Ford)	
Stanyer, A. earthenware, *c.* 1916–41	A.S. A.S. B ENG. ENG. B impressed
Steel, Daniel, 1790–1824 earthenwares and 'Wedgwood-type' stonewares	STEEL impressed

Stubbs, Joseph earthenwares, *c.* 1822–35	JOSEPH STUBBS LONGPORT impressed or printed

Stubbs & Kent
earthenware, *c.* 1828–30
  mark impressed or
  printed

Sudlow & Sons, Ltd., R.
earthenware, 1893–
(Part of Howard Pottery
Co. Shelton from 1965)

full-name marks
impressed or printed
from *c.* 1920–

Till & Sons, Thomas
earthenware, *c.* 1850–1928

1861–

'Globe-mark' from 1880
'Tillson' ware, *c.* 1922–8

Tundley, Rhodes &
Proctor, earthenware,
1873–83, then:

T.R. & P.
printed

Rhodes & Proctor,
1883–5, earthenware

R. & P.
printed

Venables & Baines
earthenware, *c.* 1851–3

VENABLES &
BAINES

Venables & Co.
earthenware, *c.* 1853–5

J. VENABLES
& CO.
printed or impressed

Vernon & Son, James
earthenware, 1860–80
1875–

J.V.

J.V. & Son

J.V. & S.   J.V. junr.

Wade & Son, Ltd.,
George, earthenware
1922–,
1936–

1947–

WADE
Figures

Wade & Co.
earthenware, 1887–1927

WADES

W. & CO.
B

Wade, Heath & Co., Ltd.,
earthenware,
1927–

WADES
(with lion)

c. 1934–

WADEHEATH
ORCADIA
WARE

c. 1934–

WADEHEATH
(with lion)

Trade-names: 'Flaxman Ware', 'ROYAL
VICTORIA'

Walley, John
earthenware, 1850–67

J. WALLEY
J. WALLEY'S
WARE
printed or impressed

Walton, John
earthenware groups and
figures, *c.* 1818–35

impressed on raised
scroll

Wedgwood & Sons, Ltd.
Josiah, general ceramics, 1759–
very rare incised initials or   'J.W.'
signature, *c.* 1760
rare, *c.* 1759–69   wedgwood WEDGWOOD
c. 1759   WEDGWOOD

Wedgwood & Bentley   WEDGWOOD
partnership, 1769–80   & BENTLEY
concerned only with
the manufacture of   WEDGWOOD
ornamental neo-classical   & BENTLEY
wares   ETRURIA

impressed on cameos, etc.   W. & B.
impressed or raised mark

c. 1780–98   Wedgwood

rare impressed mark   WEDGWOOD & SONS
c. 1790
printed on bone-china   WEDGWOOD
c. 1812–22   red, blue or gold

rare printed mark on stone china, *c.* 1827–61	WEDGWOOD'S STONE CHINA
impressed mark *c.* 1840–5	WEDGWOOD ETRURIA
impressed on 'pearlware' *c.* 1840–68	PEARL
as above, post–1868	P

From 1860 the Wedgwood factory in addition to their usual name-mark, adopted a system of date-marking consisting of three letters side by side: the first indicates the month, the second a potter's mark and the third the year of manufacture. As from 1907 the first letter, which had hitherto denoted the month of manufacture, was replaced by a number indicating the cycle of year marks in use; previously there was no indication whether the piece was made in the first second, or third cycle.

This system was further changed in 1930 when the cycle number was replaced by the chronological number of the month, e.g.: January = 1, February = 2, etc., and the initial which had previously indicated the year was now replaced by the last two years of the actual date of manufacture.

Examples:

Month	Potter	Year	
Y	O	R	May, 1863
L	O	E	July, 1902
Cycle	Potter	Year	
3	O	N	1911
4	O	A	1924

Month	Potter	Year	
3	O	32	March, 1932
11	O	48	November, 1948

Monthly marks indicated by the first letter from
1860–1864:

January	J	April	A	July	V	October	O
February	F	May	Y	August	W	November	N
March	M	June	T	September	S	December	D

1865–1907:

January	J	April	A	July	L	October	O
February	F	May	M	August	W	November	N
March	R	June	T	September	S	December	D

First cycle of year marks:

O	1860	R	1863	U	1866	X	1869
P	1861	S	1864	V	1867	Y	1870
Q	1862	T	1865	W	1868	Z	1871

Second cycle of year marks:

A	1872	H	1879	O	1886	V	1893
B	1873	I	1880	P	1887	W	1894
C	1874	J	1881	Q	1888	X	1895
D	1875	K	1882	R	1889	Y	1896
E	1876	L	1883	S	1890	Z	1897
F	1877	M	1884	T	1891		
G	1878	N	1885	U	1892		

Note: 'ENGLAND' added to mark from 1891

Third cycle of year marks:

A	1898	H	1905	O	1912	V	1919
B	1899	I	1906	P	1913	W	1920
C	1900	J	1907	Q	1914	X	1921
D	1901	K	1908	R	1915	Y	1922
E	1902	L	1909	S	1916	Z	1923
F	1903	M	1910	T	1917		
G	1904	N	1911	U	1918		

Fourth cycle of year marks:

A	1924	C	1926	E	1928
B	1925	D	1927	F	1929

the last two years of the date then appear in full.

'Portland Vase' mark printed on bone-china from *c.* 1878 occasionally seen impressed on earthenware, *c.* 1891–1900 *Note:* 'ENGLAND' added after 1891 'MADE IN ENGLAND' from about 1910 'Bone China' added *c.* 1920

WEDGWOOD
BONE CHINA

MADE IN ENGLAND

printed on creamwares from *c.* 1940

OF ETRURIA
WEDGWOOD
MADE IN
ENGLAND
BARLASTON

Lessore, Emile, decorator *c.* 1858–76

E Lessore

Thomson, E. G.,
decorator, *c.* 1870

E. G. Thomson

Barnard, Harry, decorator
c. 1900

marks on red stonewares,
probably Wedgwood
second-half of
18th century

impressed

Whittingham, Ford & Co.,
1868–73,
earthenware

w.f. & co.
printed

Whittingham, Ford & Riley,
earthenware, 1876–82

w.f. & r.
printed

Wilkinson, Arthur J.,
1885–*c.* 1970, earthenwares
'ROYAL SEMI-PORCELAIN', *c.* 1891–
'ROYAL IRONSTONE CHINA', *c.* 1896–
'IRONSTONE CHINA', *c.* 1910
'Clarice Cliff', *c.* 1930
'Honeyglaze', *c.* 1947
(merged with W. R. Midwinter Ltd., 1964)

many fully-named
marks including:

Withinshaw, W. E.,
1873–8, general ceramics

w.e.w.
W. E. WITHINSHAW
printed or impressed

Wood, Enoch
c. 1784–*c.* 1790 general
ceramics

WOOD   E. WOOD
        W (***)
E.W.   W.

Enoch Wood's marks can be seen impressed, moulded or incised	ENOCH WOOD SCULPSIT
	E. WOOD SCULPSIT
	ENOCH WOOD
Wood & Caldwell 1790–1818, earthenware especially figures, etc.	WOOD & CALDWELL impressed
Wood & Sons, Enoch 1818–1846, earthenware blue-printed wares made for U.S.A. include the American eagle in mark	ENOCH WOOD & SONS BURSLEM STAFFORDSHIRE
	E.W. & S.
E. WOOD & SONS E. & E. WOOD BURSLEM	E. & E. WOOD E. & E.W. all printed

Wood, H. J.
1884–, earthenware
   many various fully-named marks including:
   'Bursley-Ware' *c.* 1930–
   'E. Radford' *c.* 1935–
   'CHINESE ROSE' *c.* 1960–, etc.

Wood, Isaiah 1710–15, earthenware	ISA WOOD 1712 incised

Wood, John Wedge 1841–4 (also at Tunstall 1845–60)	w.w. impressed J. WEDGWOOD printed

Wood, Ralph (Snr.)
(1715–72), son of same
name (1748–95)
grandson (1781–1801)
  impressed or incised marks
  c. 1770–1801
	R. WOOD Ra. WOOD
	Ra. WOOD
	BURSLEM
	Ralph Wood

rebus of trees (rare)
c. 1770–90

Wood & Son 1865–, earthenware, etc. '& Sons', from 1907 'Ltd.' added *c.* 1910	various fully-named marks from *c.* 1890–

Wood & Co., Thomas 1885–96, earthenwares	T.W. & CO. printed or impressed

Wood & Sons, Thomas *c.* 1896–7, earthenware	T.W. & S. printed

Wood & Co., W. 1873–1932, earthenware	W.W. & CO. printed or impressed

mark of initials printed in 'Staffordshire
knot', 1880–1915, with crown, 1915–32

Wood & Baggaley 1870–80, earthenware	W. & B. printed
Wood & Barker, Ltd. 1897–1903, earthenware	W. & B. Ltd. printed
Wood & Bowers 1839, earthenware	W. & B. (can be confused with Wood & Baggaley)
Wood & Clarke *c.* 1871–2, earthenware	W. & C. printed with 'lion rampant'
Wood & Hulme 1882–1905, earthenware	W. & H. B printed or impressed
Wooldridge & Walley 1898–1901, earthenware	W. & W. B printed

COBRIDGE (Staffordshire)

	J. & G.A.
Alcock, John & George 1839–46, earthenware and 'INDIAN IRONSTONE'	J. & G. ALCOCK COBRIDGE impressed or printed
Alcock, Junior, John & Samuel, *c.* 1848–50 earthenware	J. & S. ALCOCK JR. printed or impressed

---

Alcock, John
1853–61, earthenware

JOHN ALCOCK
COBRIDGE
printed

Alcock & Co., Henry
1861–1910, earthenware
fully-named mark from
1880, 'Ltd.' from 1900

H.A. & CO.
printed

Alcock Pottery, The Henry
1910–35, earthenware

fully named
'coat of arms' mark
printed

Alcock & Co., Samuel
c. 1828–53, general ceramics
(Also at Burslem
c. 1830–59)
printed, painted or
impressed, sometimes
with Royal Arms or
bee-hive

SAMUEL ALCOCK & CO.
COBRIDGE
printed or impressed
S.A. & CO.
S. ALCOCK & CO.

Bates & Bennett
1868–95, earthenware

B. & B.
printed or impressed

Birks Brothers & Seddon
1877–86, earthenware

IMPERIAL IRONSTONE
CHINA
BIRKS BROS. & SEDDON
printed below Royal Arms

Blackhurst & Co. Ltd., John
1951–9, earthenware

J. BLACKHURST
ENGLAND

Brownfield, William
1850–91, earthenware (also
porcelain after 1871) much
'parian ware'

W.B.

printed, impressed
or moulded

impressed, often with
crown, from 1860–
'S' or '& Son', added 1871
'& Sons', added 1876
printed 'double-globe' mark, 1871–91

BROWNFIELD

Brownfields Guild Pottery
Society Ltd., 1891–1900,
general ceramics
(Brownfield's Pottery Ltd.,
c. 1898–1900)

B.G.P. CO.
impressed

printed monogram

printed within circular
strap device

BROWNFIELDS

Cartledge, John
c. 1800, earthenware
figures

JOHN CARTLEDGE
rare incised mark

Clews, James & Ralph
1818–34, pottery and porcelain

CLEWS WARRANTED
STAFFORDSHIRE
impressed under
crown

impressed mark on
blue-printed wares

C.C. & CO.

Cockson & Chetwynd
1867–75, earthenware

COCKSON &
CHETWYND
printed

Cockson & Seddon
1875–7, earthenware

IMPERIAL IRONSTONE
CHINA
COCKSON & SEDDON
printed under Royal
Arms

Crystal Porcelain Pottery
Co. Ltd., 1882–6,
pottery and porcelain
  (dove sometimes
  included in mark)

C.P.P. CO.
printed or impressed

Daniel, John
c. 1770–*c.* 86, earthenware

JOHN DANIEL
incised

Dillon, Francis
1834–43, earthenware

DILLON
impressed

F.D.
printed with various
back-stamps

Furnival & Co., Jacob
c. 1845–70, earthenware

J.F. & CO.
printed

Furnival & Sons, Thomas
1871–90, earthenware
   various 'T. F. & Sons'
   monograms

Furnivals (Ltd.)
1890–1968, earthenware
   'Ltd.' added *c.* 1895

FURNIVALS
ENGLAND

c. 1905–13
(Taken over by Barratt's
of Staffordshire in 1967,
closed 1968)

1913 date included in
marks from that year

FURNIVALS
(1913)
ENGLAND

Globe Pottery Co. Ltd.
1914–, earthenware (now
Royal Doulton Group)

fully-named
printed 'globe' marks

Godwin, Benjamin E.
1834–41, earthenware

B.G.
printed with back-
stamp

Godwin, John & Robert
1834–66, earthenware

J. & R.G.
printed

Harding & Cockson 1834–60, earthenware	COBRIDGE H. & C. printed
Hughes & Co., Elijah 1853–67, earthenware	E. HUGHES & CO. impressed
Hulme, William 1948–54, earthenware printed mark	
Jones, Elijah 1831–9, earthenware	fully named impressed mark or E.J. printed
Jones & Walley 1841–3, earthenware	fully named impressed or moulded mark or printed J. & W.
Meakin, Henry 1873–6, earthenware	IRONSTONE CHINA H. MEAKIN printed with Royal Arms

North Staffordshire Pottery Co. Ltd.
1940–52, earthenware

trade-mark registered
in 1944

Portland Pottery Ltd.
1946–53, earthenware
  ('P.P.C.' monogram,
  Portland Pottery, Cobridge)

Regal Pottery Co. Ltd.
1925–31, earthenware

Richardson, Albert G.
c. 1920–21

REGAL WARE
A.G.R.
printed

Richardsons (Cobridge) Ltd.,
1921–25

REGAL WARE
R(C) LTD.
printed

Robinson, Wood &
Brownfield, 1838–41,
earthenware, printed

R.W. & B.

Sant & Vodrey
1887–93, earthenware

S. & V.
COBRIDGE
printed or impressed

Shaw, Ralph
c. 1740–, earthenware

Made by Ralph Shaw
October 31, Cobridge
gate

Simpsons (Potters) Ltd.
1944–, earthenware
  including various trade-names:
    'Ambassador Ware', 'Solian Ware', 'Loh
    Yueh Mei Kuei', 'Vogue', 'Chinastyle',
    'Marlborough Old English Ironstone',
    'Chanticleer'

fully-named marks

Stevenson, Andrew *c.* 1816–30, earthenware	STEVENSON A. STEVENSON

impressed 'ship'
mark could also refer to
following potter

Stevenson, Ralph *c.* 1810–32, earthenware	R. STEVENSON

marks impressed   R.S.

Stevenson & Son, Ralph *c.* 1832–35, earthenware marks printed	R.S. & S. R. STEVENSON & SON

Stevenson, Alcock & Williams, earthenware *c.* 1825, marks printed	STEVENSON ALCOCK & WILLIAMS

Stevenson & Williams *c.* 1825, earthenware	R.S.W.

marks printed   STEVENSON & WILLIAMS

Viking Pottery Co.
1950–63, general ceramics

Walley, Edward 1845–56, general ceramics marks impressed or printed	E. WALLEY W.

Warburton, John *c.* 1802–25, earthenwares and stonewares	WARBURTON impressed
Warburton, Peter *c.* 1802–12, general ceramics *c.* 1810–12	WARBURTON'S PATENT printed or written under crown
Warburton, Peter & Francis 1795–1802, earthenware marks impressed	P. & F.W. P. & F. WARBURTON
Wood, Son & Co. 1869–79, earthenware	WOOD, SON & CO. printed under Royal Arms
Wood & Brownfield *c.* 1838–50, earthenware	W. & B. impressed or printed
Wood & Hawthorne 1882–7, earthenware	WOOD & HAWTHORNE printed under Royal Arms

FENTON (Staffordshire)

Bailey Potteries, Ltd. 1935–40, earthenware	BEWLEY POTTERY MADE IN ENGLAND printed
Baker & Co., W. 1839–1932, earthenware	W. BAKER & CO. printed or impressed

printed or impressed　　BAKER & CO.
'Ltd.' added 1893

Barkers & Kent　　　　　B. & K.
1889–1941, earthenware　　B. & K.L.
'Ltd.' added 1898　　printed or impressed

Beardmore & Co., Frank　　F.B. & CO.
1903–14, earthenware　　F
　impressed on printed mark

　printed mark

Bourne, Charles　　　　　C.B.
1817–30, porcelain　　(pattern no.)

Bowker, Arthur　　　　STAFFORDSHIRE
1948–58, porcelain　　FINE BONE CHINA
　　　　　　　　　　　　OF
mark printed under crown　ARTHUR BOWKER

Brain & Co. Ltd.　　　　HARJIAN
1903–67　　　　　　　ENGLAND
porcelain

　1905–　　　　　　　　E.B. & CO.
（now Coalport　　　　　　　F
a division of　　impressed or
the Wedgwood　　　　printed within
Group at　　　　　　Staffordshire
Foley Works)　　　　　knot

(Coalport China Ltd., taken over by
E. Brain & Co. Ltd. in 1958)

British Art Pottery Co. (Fenton) Ltd.
1920–6, porcelain

   mark printed or impressed

Broadhurst & Sons, James
c. 1862–, earthenware
   printed in mark, 1862–70   J.B.

   printed in mark, 1870–1922   J.B. & S.
   'Ltd.' added 1922

Challinor & Co., E.   E. CHALLINOR & CO.
1853–62, earthenware   printed

Challinor, E. & C.   E. & C.C.
1862–91, earthenware

             E. & C. CHALLINOR
                 FENTON
                 printed

Challinor, C. & Co.   C. CHALLINOR & CO.
1892–6, earthenware   ENGLAND

Clulow & Co.   CLULOW & CO.
c. 1802, earthenware   FENTON

Crown Staffordshire Porcelain Co. Ltd.
1889–, porcelain
(renamed Crown Staffordshire China Co. Ltd. in
1948)

printed 1889–1912
(Wedgwood China Div.
from 1973)
  printed marks of from
  1906, this firm makes
  bone-china reproductions
  of Chelsea 'raised-
  anchor' birds

'STAFFORDSHIRE'
with a crown within
wreath

Edge, Barker & Co.
1835–6, earthenware

E.B. & CO.
printed

Edge, Barker & Barker
1836–40, earthenware

E.B. & B.
printed

Edwards, John
1847–1900, general ceramics
  '& Co.' added *c.* 1873–9
  named marks including
  'PORCELAINE DE TERRE' or
  'WARRANTED IRONSTONE CHINA'
  from *c.* 1880–1900

J.E.

J.E. & CO.
PORCELAINE
IRONSTONE

Elkin, Knight & Co.
1822–6, earthenware
  marks impressed or
  printed

E.K. & CO.

ELKIN KNIGHT
& CO.

Elkin, Knight & Bridgwood
c. 1827–40, earthenware
and porcelain

E.K.B.
printed

Forester & Sons, Thomas   T.F. & S.
1883–1959, earthenware

   'Ltd.' added, 1891–
   'Phoenix China', 1912–

Forester & Hulme   F. & H.
1887–93, earthenware   printed under bee

Hulme & Christie   H. & C.
1893–1902, earthenware   F
   mark printed with a dove

Garner, Robert   R.G.
late 18th century, earthenware   moulded

Gimson & Co., Wallis   WALLIS GIMSON &
1884–90, earthenware   CO.
   printed under beehive

Ginder & Co., Samuel   S. Ginder & Co.
1811–43, earthenware   printed

Greatbatch, William   GREATBATCH
c. 1760– *c,* 1780, modeller   printed
potter and engraver of
transfer-prints

Green, Thomas   T. GREEN
1847–59, general   FENTON POTTERIES
ceramics   printed

Green, Thomas

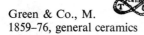

Green & Co., M.   M. GREEN & CO.
1859–76, general ceramics   printed

Green, T. A. & S.   T.A. & S.G.
1876–89, china   initials printed in
    'Staffordshire knot'
From 1889 this firm became known as
'Crown Staffordshire Porcelain Co.'

Greenwood, S.   S. GREENWOOD
late 18th century   rare impressed mark
black basaltes

Hines Bros.   H.B.
1886–1907, earthenware   impressed

    HINES BROS.
    printed

Hoods, Ltd.   H. LTD.
c. 1919–, earthenware   printed
(firm now closed)

Hughes & Co., E.   H
1889–1953, porcelain
  impressed mark, 1889–98

  impressed or printed   H.F.
  1898–1905

printed mark
c. 1908–12

various 'globe' marks
from 1912–41
1940 firm retitled Hughes (Fenton) Ltd.

Hulme & Christie   H. & C.
1893–1902, earthenware   F
(Christie & Beardmore   printed with dove
1902–3)

Jones, A. G., Harley-   H.J.
1907–34, earthenware
and porcelain
   initials printed with   A.G.H.J.
   various trade-names:
   'FENTONIA WARE', 'PARAMOUNT',
   'WILTON WARE'

Kirkby & Co., William   W.K. & CO.
1879–85, general ceramics
   'K. & Co.', also used in   K. & CO.
   monogram form   printed or impressed

Knight, Elkin & Co.   K.E. & CO.
1826–46, earthenware

                  KNIGHT ELKIN
   printed initials with   & CO.
   variously designed
   backstamps   K. & E.

Knight, John King   J. K. KNIGHT
1846–53, earthenware   printed

Knight, Elkin & Bridgwood *c.* 1829–40, earthenware marks printed	K.E. & B. K.E.B.
Knight, Elkin & Knight 1841–4, earthenware	K.E. & K. printed
Malkin, Ralph 1863–81, earthenware	R.M. printed
Malkin & Sons, Ralph 1882–92, earthenware	R.M. & S. printed
Moore & Co. 1872–92, earthenware	M. & CO. impressed or printed
Moore, Leason & Co. 1892–6, earthenware	M.L. & CO. printed in shield under crown or initials alone impressed or printed
Morley, Fox & Co. Ltd. 1906–44, earthenware	M.F. & CO. printed

c. 1906–

'HOMELEIGHWARE', 1929–

Morley & Co. Ltd., William
1944–57, earthenware

Pratt & Co. (Ltd.), F. & R.   F. & R.P.
c. 1818–, earthenware

                               PRATT

'Co.' added 1840   F. & R.P. CO.

c. 1847–60   F. & R. PRATT & CO.
                                  FENTON
this firm is known   MANUFACTURER'S
to have made a great   TO H.R.H. PRINCE ALBERT
number of the popular
printed pot-lids and
similarly printed jugs,
etc. *c.* 1850
the firm was taken over in *c.* 1925
by Cauldon Potteries Ltd., who continue
original name together with their own

Pratt & Co., John   J.P. & CO. (L.)
1872–8, earthenware   printed

Pratt, Hassall & Gerrard   P.H.G
1822–34, general ceramics   P.H. & G.
                                  printed

Pratt & Simpson   P. & S.
1878–83, earthenware   printed

Radford (Ltd.), Samuel
1879–1957, porcelain
  'R.S.' monogram from
  about 1880, 'England'
  added 1891

various 'S.R.' monograms
used during this century

Rainbow Pottery Co.
1931–41, earthenware

RAINBOW POTTERY
FENTON
MADE IN ENGLAND
printed or impressed

Reeves, James
1870–1948, earthenware
printed or impressed

J.R.

J.R.
F

J. REEVES

Rubian Art Pottery Ltd.
1906–33, earthenware
   impressed or printed
   c. 1926–33

L.S. & G.

RUBAY ART WARE

Sterling Pottery Ltd.
1947–53, earthenware

other marks include:
'RIDGWAY'

printed

Stubbs Bros.
1899–1904, bone-china
   printed

Victoria Porcelain (Fenton) Ltd.
1949–57, earthenware
   printed

143

Victoria & Trentham Potteries Ltd.
1957–60, general ceramics
  lion mark as above but includes new name

Wathen & Lichfield   W. & L.
1862–4, earthenware   FENTON

Wathen, James, B.   J.B.W.
1864–9, earthenware   J.B.W.
                                     F
                                   printed

Wileman, James & Charles   J. & C.W.
1864–9, general ceramics   J.F. & C.W.
                                   C.J.W.
  'J. Wileman & Co.'   J.W. & CO.

Wileman, James F.   J.F.W.
1869–92   J. F. WILEMAN

Wileman & Co.
1892–1925
  'SHELLEY' mark used
  from *c.* 1911

Wilson & Sons, J.
1898–1926, bone-china

printed

FOLEY (Staffordshire)
 Hawley & Co.   HAWLEY
 1842–87, earthenware   HAWLEY & CO.
                                                 impressed

 Mayer, John   J.M.
 1833–41, earthenware   F
                                                 printed

HANLEY (Staffordshire)
 Adams & Co., John   J. ADAMS & CO.
 1864–73, earthenwares and   ADAMS & CO.
 stonewares, etc.   impressed

 Adams & Bromley   A. & B.   A. & B.
 1873–86, earthenware   SHELTON
 stonewares, etc.   ADAMS & BROMLEY
                                     printed or impressed

 Alcock, Lindley & Bloore (Ltd.)
 1919, earthenware
 (now Allied English Potteries)
   printed or impressed

 Art Pottery Co.   ART POTTERY CO.
 1900–11, earthenware   ENGLAND
   printed mark   (with crown)

 Ashworth & Bros. (Ltd.)
 1862–1970, earthenware   ASHWORTH
   1862–80   impressed
 (now Mason's Ironstone
 China Co. Ltd.)   A. BROS.
 Wedgwood Group from 1973
                          145

Ashworth & Bros.
  printed *c.* 1862–90
  with designs including
  pattern names
  From 1862 Ashworths used mark similar
  to that of Mason's 'Patent Ironstone'
(Mason's Ironstone China
Ltd. from 1968)
  'England' added 1891

G.L.A. & BROS.

  printed mark from
  about 1880

  'LUSTROSA' trade-name
  1932–

  printed on ironstone
  c. 1957–

Baddeley, Thomas   T. BADDELEY
1800–34, engraver of   HANLEY
plates for transfer-prints   printed

Baddeley, William   EASTWOOD
1802–22, 'Wedgwood-   impressed
type' ware

Bakewell Bros. Ltd.   BAKEWELL BROS.
1927-43, earthenware   LTD.
                             printed

Bates, Brown-Westhead   B.B.W. & M.
& Moore   printed or impressed
1859–61, general ceramics

Baxter, John Denton   I.D.B.
1823–7, earthenware   J.D.B.
                           printed
Bednall & Heath   B. & H.
1879–99, earthenware   printed

Bennett & Co., J.   J.B. & CO.
1896–1900, earthenware   printed or impressed

Bennett (Hanley) Ltd., William   W.B.
1882–1937   H
earthenwares   printed or impressed

Bevington, James & Thomas   J. & T.B.
1865–78, porcelains   impressed

Bevington & Co., John   J.B. & CO.
1869–71, earthenware   H
printed in backstamp

Bevington, John
1872–92, porcelains

This mark was   underglaze-blue
obviously adopted to
imitate that of Meissen on pieces made in
'Dresden' style

Bevington, Thomas
1877–91, general ceramics

printed

Birch & Whitehead
c. 1796, 'Wedgwood type'
wares

B. & W.
impressed

Bishop & Stonier
1891–1939, general
ceramics

B. & S.
printed or impressed

printed marks
1891–
'England' added
on fully named
marks from *c.* 1899–

1936–9

BISHOP
ENGLAND

Blue John Pottery Ltd.
1939, earthenware

various 'Blue John'
printed marks

Booth, G. R.	PUBLISHED BY
1829–44, earthenware	G. R. BOOTH & CO.
'& Co.' added *c.* 1839	HANLEY
impressed mark	STAFFORDSHIRE

Booth & Colcloughs Ltd.	various marks
1948–54, general ceramics	including
(see Ridgway Potteries Ltd.)	name
also trade-names:	
'Blue Mist', 'Malvern Chinaware'	
and 'Royal Swan'	

Bourne, Samuel	S. BOURNE
early 18th century	impressed
pottery figures	

Bournemouth Pottery Co.	BOURNEMOUTH
(Bournemouth, 1945–52)	POTTERY
Hanley 1952–, earthenware	ENGLAND

Boyle, Zachariah	BOYLE	
1823–50, general		
ceramics		
'& S.' added from	Z.B.	Z.B. & S.
1828		

Brown-Westhead, Moore & Co.	B.W.M.
1862–1904	
general ceramics	B.W.M. & CO.
	printed or impressed

impressed

printed or impressed
1891–

later marks include
initials & 'CAULDON'

T. C. BROWN
WESTHEAD-MOORE
& CO.

Bullers Ltd.
c. 1937–55, earthenware

BULLERS MADE
IN ENGLAND
painted

Bullock & Co., A.
1895–1915, earthenware

A.B. & CO. H.
A.B. & CO.
printed or impressed

Burgess, Thomas
1903–17, earthenware
  (mark of Harrop & Burgess
  was continued)

H & B

printed or impressed

Burton, Samuel & John
1832–45, earthenware

S. & J.B.
impressed on
applied tablet

Cauldon Ltd.
1905–20, general ceramics

CAULDON
ENGLAND
printed under crown

marks previously used by Ridgway
and Brown—Westhead, Moore & Co., used
with addition of 'CAULDON'

Cauldon Potteries, Ltd.
1920–62, general ceramics

ROYAL CAULDON
ENGLAND
EST. 1774

   similar printed marks used from 1930–62,
   when factory was taken over by
Pountney & Co. Ltd. of Bristol (now
Cauldon Bristol Potteries Ltd., Redruth, Cornwall)

Ceramic Art Co. Ltd.
1892–1903, decorators

THE CERAMIC ART
CO. LTD. HANLEY
STAFFORDSHIRE
ENGLAND
printed

Clementson, Joseph
c. 1839–64, earthenware

J.C.
J. CLEMENTSON
printed

Clementson Bros.
1865–1916, earthenware
and stoneware
   printed 1867–80
   various fully named printed marks with
   phoenix from 1870–
   'Ltd.' added 1910

CLEMENTSON BROS.
with Royal Arms

   printed, 1913–16

CLEMENTSON BROS.
ENGLAND
under crown

Clementson, Young & Jameson
1844, earthenware

C.Y. & J.

Clementson & Young
1845–7, earthenware

CLEMENTSON &
YOUNG
impressed or printed

Coalbrook Potteries 1937–, decorative wares printed–	COALBROOK MADE IN ENGLAND
Coopers Art Pottery Co. *c.* 1912–58, earthenware	ART POTTERY CO. ENGLAND with crown

Cotton, Ltd., Elijah
1880–, earthenware
  Trade-names: 'NELSON WARE', *c.* 1913–;
  'LORD NELSON WARE', 1956–
	various fully-
	named marks

Creyke & Sons, G. M.
1920–48, earthenware
  initials also used in
  monogram form
  Trade-name 'BROADWAY'
  c. 1935–
	G.M.C.
	printed or impressed

Davenport, Banks & Co.
1860–73, earthenware
 	
  impressed or printed
  marks
	D.B. & CO.
	
	DAVENPORT
	BANKS & CO.
	ETRURIA

Davenport, Beck & Co. 1873–80, earthenware	D.B. & CO.
Davis, J. Heath 1881–91, earthenware	J. H. DAVIS HANLEY

Diamond Pottery Co. Ltd.	D.P. CO.
1908–35, earthenware	D.P. CO. LTD.
	printed

Dimmock (Junr.) & Co., Thomas	D.
1828–59, earthenware	

impressed or printed
'double D' monogram

Dimmock & Co., J.	J.D. & CO.
1862–1904, earthenware	

firm taken over by
W. D. Cliff in *c.* 1878–
'Cliff' used in varying
forms *c.* 1878–1904

CLIFF
ENGLAND

written on ribbon	ALBION WORKS
under 'lion rampant'	printed

Dudson, James	DUDSON
1838–88, earthenware	impressed
(this firm made many	
'Spaniels' and 'Rockingham-type' dogs)	

Dudson, J. T.	J. DUDSON
1888–98, earthenwares	
and stonewares	J. DUDSON
'England' added 1891	ENGLAND
	impressed

Dudson Bros., Ltd.
1898–, earthenwares and
stonewares

DUDSON ENGLAND

printed mark, 1936–45

Dudson, Wilcox & Till, Ltd.
1902–26, earthenware
printed or impressed,
figure of Britannia also
used within double-ring
with full name of firm

Dura Porcelain Co. Ltd.
1919–21, porcelain

printed mark

Ellis, Unwin & Mountford
1860–61, earthenware

E.U. & M.
printed

Fancies Fayre Pottery
c. 1946, earthenware
Trade-name 'KNICK
KNACKS'
(now Bairstow & Co.)

STAFFORDSHIRE
F.F.
ENGLAND
printed or impressed

Fenton & Sons, Alfred
1887–1901, general
ceramics

A.F. & S.
impressed or printed
(also written within
circular crowned strap)

Fletcher, Thomas
c. 1786–1810, printer and
decorator

T. FLETCHER
SHELTON

Ford, Charles
1874–1904, porcelain

impressed
or printed

'Swan' mark, impressed
or printed, c. 1900–4

Ford, T. & C.
1854–71, earthenware
   impressed or printed
   marks

T. & C.F.

Ford, Thomas
1871–4, porcelain

   numerals indicate
   month and year, e.g.
   JULY, 1872

impressed or printed

Ford & Pointon Ltd.
1917–36, porcelain
(absorbed by Cauldon
c. 1921)

Furnival, Jacob & Thomas
c. 1843, earthenware

J. & T.F.
printed under
Royal Arms

Furnival & Co., Thomas
c. 1844–6, earthenware

T.F. & CO.
printed

Futura Art Pottery Ltd.
1947–56, earthenware

FUTURA
ART POTTERY LTD.
printed

Gelson Bros.
1867–76, earthenware

GELSON BROS.
HANLEY
printed

Glass, John
c. 1784–1838, earthenware
and stoneware

GLASS HANLEY
J. GLASS HANLEY
impressed

Glass, Joseph
c. 1700, slipwares

JOSEPH GLASS

Goldscheider (Staffordshire) Pottery Ltd.
1946–59, figures in
pottery and porcelain

Goldscheider
printed

Gray & Co. Ltd., A. E.
1912–61, earthenware
(known as 'Portmeirion
Potteries Ltd.' from 1962)
moved to Stoke in 1934

various printed marks
depicting ships with
factory name

printed mark
1934–61

Grimwade Bros.
1886–1900, earthenware

G. Bros.
on star within
circle

Grimwades Ltd.
1900–, earthenware
  printed mark, *c.* 1900–

STOKE POTTERY

many various fully named marks including
name or trade-name:
'WINTON' *c.* 1906, 'RUBIAN ART' *c.* 1906–,
'VITRO HOTEL WARE' *c.* 1930, 'ROYAL
WINTON IVORY' *c.* 1930, 'ATLAS' *c.* 1934–9

Hackwood & Co.
1807–27, earthenware and
stoneware

H. & CO.
HACKWOOD & CO.
impressed

Hackwood, William
1827–43, earthenware
  impressed or printed

W.H.
HACKWOOD
printed or impressed

Hackwood & Keeling
1835–6, earthenware

H. & K.
printed

Hall, Samuel
c. 1840–56, earthenware

HALL
impressed

Hall & Read
1883–8, earthenware
  'H. & R.' also probably
  used

HALL & READ
HANLEY
printed

Hammersley, J. & R.　　　　　　J.R.H.
1877–1917, general ceramics　　printed

Hanley Porcelain Co.
1892–99, porcelain

printed

Hanley China Co.　　　　　　　H
1899–1901, porcelain　　　　　C C°.
　printed　　　　　　　　　　in knot

Harrop & Burgess
1894–1903, earthenware

printed

Heath, J.　　　　　　　　　　I.H.
c. 1770–1800, earthenware

　　　　　　　　　　　　　　HEATH
　　　　　　　　　　　　　impressed

Heath, Joshua　　　　　　　JOSHUA HEATH
c. 1740, earthenware　　　　　incised

Hollins, T. J. & R.　　　　　T.J. & R. HOLLINS
c. 1818–22, earthenware　　　impressed

Johnson Bros. (Hanley) Ltd.　JOHNSON BROS.
1883–, earthenware　　　　　　ENGLAND
　impressed or printed
　name with various
　coat-of-arms, crowns,
　etc.　　　　　　　　　　Johnson Bros
(now part of Wedgwood Group)　England.

Jones & Son
c. 1826–8, earthenware

JONES & SON
printed

Keeling, Joseph
c. 1802–8, earthenware and
stoneware

JOSEPH KEELING
impressed

Keeling & Co., Samuel
1840–50, earthenware

S.K. & CO.

S. KEELING & CO.
printed

Keeling, Toft & Co.
1805–26, stonewares
in Wedgwood style

KEELING & TOFT

KEELING, TOFT & CO.
impressed

Kensington Fine Art Pottery Co.
1892–9, earthenware

printed or impressed

Lancaster & Sons
1900–44, earthenware
  '& Sons' & 'Ltd.' added
  c. 1906
  c. 1920–

L. & SONS LTD.
HANLEY. ENG.

'ROYALL & LANSAN' 1930–
'BRITISH CROWN WARE', *c.* 1935–
'CROWN DRESDEN WARE', *c.* 1935–

c. 1934–44

LANCASTERS LTD.
HANLEY. ENGLAND

Lancaster & Sandland Ltd.
1944–1968, earthenware

BRITISH
CROWN WARE

many various printed
marks including name
'SANDLAND'

CROWN DRESDEN WARE

SANDLAND
STAFFORDSHIRE
ENGLAND

Langdale Pottery Co. Ltd.
1947–58, earthenware
  printed

Langdale
MADE IN ENGLAND

Lear, Samuel
1877–86, general ceramics

LEAR
impressed

Livesley, Powell & Co.
1851–66, earthenware
and stoneware

LIVESLEY POWELL
& CO.
L.P. & CO.
impressed or printed

Powell & Bishop
1867–1878, general
ceramics

P. & B.
POWELL & BISHOP
printed or impressed

Powell, Bishop & Stonier
1878–91, general
ceramics

P.B. & S.
printed or impressed

  'Chinaman' mark first
  registered 1880, but
  continued by Bishop
  & Stonier

Bishop & Stonier
1891–1939, general ceramics
   full name printed in
   various designs, 1899–1936
   'Bishop' only used 1936–9

B. & S.

BISHOP & STONIER

Lloyd, J. & R.
c. 1834–52, 'Staffordshire
figures'

LLOYD SHELTON
impressed

Lockett, Baguley &
Cooper, 1855–60, porcelain

LOCKETT BAGULEY
& COOPER

Lockitt, William H.
1901–19, earthenware
   'DURA-WARE' 1913–19

W.H.L.
H
printed in crescent

Mann & Co.
1858–60, general ceramics

MANN & CO.
HANLEY
printed

Manzoni, Carlo
c. 1895–8, studio pottery

   incised mark including
   date

Mayer, Elijah
c. 1790–1804, various
Wedgwood-type wares

E. MAYER
impressed

Mayer & Son, Elijah
1805–34
Wedgwood-type wares

E. MAYER & SON
impressed or printed

Mayer & Co., Joseph
c. 1822–33, earthenware

JOSEPH MAYER & CO.
HANLEY

MAYER & CO.

Meakin, Charles
1883–9, earthenware

CHARLES MEAKIN
HANLEY
under Royal Arms

Meakin (Ltd.), J. & G.
1851–, earthenwares
(now part of Wedgwood
Group)
　1890–

J. & G. MEAKIN
impressed or printed

　'ENGLAND' added from
　1891
　'Sun-face' marks from
　1912–
　'PASTEL VITRESOL'
　'STUDIO WARE' and 'SOUTH
　SEAS' recent trade-names

printed

Meigh, Job
c. 1805–34, earthenware
　'Son' added *c.* 1812

MEIGH
impressed
OLD HALL
impressed or printed
J.M. & S.

Meigh, Charles	CHARLES MEIGH
1835–49, earthenware and	impressed
stonewares	G.M.
	printed with device
	and pattern name

printed or impressed marks of various
bodies and styles of decoration include:
'Indian Stone China', 'French China',
'Improved Stone China', 'Enamel Porcelain'

Meigh, Son & Pankhurst,	C.M.S. & P.
Charles, 1850–51, earthenware	printed

Meigh & Son, Charles	C.M. & S.
1851–61, earthenware	

many of the marks	M. & S.
used by this firm	
include the Royal	C. MEIGH & SON
Arms	
	MEIGH'S
	CHINA

printed or impressed	OPAQUE
	PORCELAIN

Old Hall Earthenware Co Ltd.
1861–86

	O.H.E.C.
printed	O.H.E.C.(L.)

printed or impressed

mark registered in 1884 and
continued by Old Hall
Porcelain Works Ltd.
printed

Old Hall Porcelain Works   (as above)
Ltd., 1886–1902, general
ceramics

Mills, Henry   H. MILLS
c. 1892, earthenware   printed

Moore & Co.   M. & CO.
1898–1903, earthenware   printed with name
                              of pattern

Morley & Co., Francis   F.M.
1845–58, earthenware

late form of Masons'   F.M. & CO.
Ironstone mark used
from 1845   F. MORLEY & CO.
                       printed with many
                     various backstamps

Morley & Ashworth   M. & A.
1859–62, earthenware   MORLEY &
  impressed or printed   ASHWORTH
  with pattern name   HANLEY

Neale & Co., James
c. 1776–*c.* 86, all manner
of wares in Wedgwood
style
   '& Co.' added *c.* 1778

N   NEALE
I. NEALE
I. NEALE. HANLEY

NEALE & CO.
impressed

Neale & Bailey
c. 1790–1814, earthenware

NEALE & BAILEY
printed or impressed

Neale, Harrison & Co.
1875–85, general ceramics

N.H. & CO.
printed

Neale & Palmer
c. 1769–76, earthenwares
in Wedgwood style

NEALE & PALMER
impressed

Neale & Wilson
c. 1784–95, earthenware
and Wedgwood-type wares

NEALE & WILSON

NEALE & CO.
impressed

New Hall Porcelain Works
1781–1835, hard-paste
porcelain 1781–*c.* 1812
bone-china, *c.* 1812–35

printed on bone-china

New Hall Pottery Co. Ltd.
1899–1956, earthenware

printed, *c.* 1930–51

165

New Pearl Pottery Co. Ltd.
1936–41, earthenware,
'Royal Bourbon Ware'

PEARL POTTERY CO.
printed

Palmer, Humphrey
c. 1760–78, earthenware
and Wedgwood-type
stonewares

PALMER

impressed

Pankhurst & Co., J. W.
1850–82, earthenware
    '& Co.' added *c.* 1852

J.W.P.

J. W. PANKHURST

Pearl Pottery Co. Ltd.
1894–1936, earthenware
    1894–1912

PP

printed or impressed

    printed in various
    forms, 1912–36

P.P. CO. LTD.

Physick & Cooper
1899–1900, earthenware

P. & C.
over crown

Art Pottery Co.
1900–11, earthenware

ART POTTERY CO.
over crown

Coopers Art Pottery Co.
c. 1912–58, earthenware

printed as above

166

Podmore China Co.
1921–41, porcelain

'P.C. CO.' monogram
under crown

Pointon & Co. Ltd.
1883–1916, porcelain

POINTONS
STOKE-ON-TRENT
printed with coat-
of-arms

Poole, Richard
1790–5, earthenware

R. POOLE
impressed

Ratcliffe, William
c. 1831–40, earthenware

R
HACKWOOD
printed or impressed

printed in underglaze blue

Ridgway, Job
c. 1802–8, earthenware

R   J.R.
printed
(J.R. also used by
John Ridgway)

Ridgway & Sons, Job
c. 1808–14, earthenware

RIDGWAY & SONS
impressed or printed

Ridgway, John & William
1814–*c.* 1830

J.W.R.   J. & W.R.
J. & W. RIDGWAY
printed or impressed

Ridgway & Co., John *c.* 1830–55, general ceramics	JOHN RIDGWAY J.R. JHN RIDGWAY
printed or impressed marks usually including name of pattern	I. RIDGWAY '& CO.' added *c.* 1841
Ridgway, Bates & Co., J. 1856–58, general ceramics	J.R.B. & CO. printed
Bates, Brown-Westhead & Moore, 1859–61, general ceramics	B.B.W. & M. printed or impressed
Brown-Westhead, Moore & Co. 1862–1904, general ceramics	*see p.* 149
Cauldon Ltd. 1905–20, general ceramics	*see p.* 150
Cauldon Potteries Ltd. 1920–62, general ceramics	*see p.* 151
Ridgway & Robey *c.* 1837–9, figures marks very rare	RIDGWAY & ROBEY HANLEY STAFFORDSHIRE POTTERIES
Ridgway, Morley, Wear & Co., 1836–42 earthenware	R.M.W. & CO. RIDGWAY, MORLEY WEAR & CO. printed

168

Ridgway & Morley
1842–44, earthenware

R. & M.
RIDGWAY & MORLEY
printed

Ridgway & Abington
c. 1835–60, earthenware

E. RIDGWAY & ABINGTON
HANLEY
impressed

Ridgway, Son & Co.,
William, *c.* 1838–48

W.R.S. & CO.
W. RIDGWAY, SON
& CO. HANLEY
printed

Ridgway, Sparks & Ridgway
1873–79, earthenware

R.S.R.
also printed in
'Staffordshire knot'

Ridgways
1879–20
  mark of 1880–

'RIDGWAYS' and 'ENGLAND' in various
marks from *c.* 1905–20
RIDGWAYS (BEDFORD WORKS) LTD.
1920–52, earthenware
'RIDGWAYS' and/or 'BEDFORD' in variety
of marks used from 1920–52
This firm became 'Ridgway & Adderley Ltd.'
in 1952, Ridgway, Adderley, Booths &
Colcloughs Ltd.' from 1955 and in same year
'Ridgway Potteries Ltd.'
(part of Allied English Potteries, Ltd.
from 1952, now Royal Doulton Group)

name of American firm, John R. Roth & Co. seen on some Ridgway exports, *c.* 1930–56	JONROTH J.H.R. & CO. monogram printed
Rigby & Stevenson 1894–1954, earthenware	R. & S. printed
Rivers, William *c.* 1818–22, earthenware	RIVERS impressed
Robinson & Wood 1832–6, earthenware	R. & W. printed
Salt, Ralph *c.* 1820–46, earthenware	'SALT' impressed on scroll
Sandlands & Colley, Ltd. 1907–1910, general ceramics	full name & 's.c.' monogram printed under crown
Scrivener & Co., R. G. 1870–83, general ceramics	R.G.S.
printed or impressed	R.G.S. & CO.
Sherwin & Cotton 1877–30, tiles impressed	
Shorthose & Co. *c.* 1817–1822	SHORTHOSE & CO. written impressed or printed

Shorthose & Heath
c. 1795–1815, earthenware

SHORTHOSE &
HEATH
impressed or printed

Shorthose, John
1807–23, earthenware

S

　impressed marks

SHORTHOSE

Sneyd & Hill
c. 1845, earthenware
　printed

SNEYD & HILL
HANLEY
STAFFORDSHIRE
POTTERIES

Sneyd, Thomas
1846–7, earthenware

T. SNEYD
HANLEY
impressed

Stevenson, William
c. 1802, earthenware
　rare impressed mark

W. STEVENSON
HANLEY

Swinnertons Ltd.
1906–71, earthenware
(Allied English Potteries)
Ltd.), mark printed
　c. 1906–17, later marks all include
　full-name of firm

SWINNERTONS
HANLEY

Sylvan Pottery Ltd.
1946–, earthenware

　'B' included in mark
　prior to 1948

Studio Szeiler, Ltd.
c. 1951–, earthenware printed or impressed

Taylor, George G. TAYLOR
c. 1784–1811, earthenware GEO. TAYLOR
impressed or incised

Taylor, Tunnicliffe & Co. T.T.
1868–, general ceramics T.T. & CO.
(now electrical & printed
industrial wares only)

Thomas & Co., Uriah
1888–1905, earthenware

printed or impressed

Toft, James (*b.* 1673) James Toft
Ralph (*b.* 1638), Ralph Toft
Thomas (*d.* 1689), slipware Thomas Toft

Unwin, Mountford & U.M. & T.
Taylor, *c.* 1864, earthenware printed

Unwin, Holmes & U.H. & W.
Worthington, *c.* 1865–8 printed
earthenware

Upper Hanley Pottery Co. U.H.P. CO.
c. 1895–1902, then at ENGLAND
Cobridge until 1910
earthenware impressed or printed
  'Ltd.' from 1900

172

Wardle & Co.
1871–1910, earthenware
Wardle Art Pottery Co. Ltd.
1910–1935, earthenware

     WARDLE
impressed

    printed, *c.* 1885–90

    printed, *c.* 1890–1935

Wardle & Ash
1859–62, earthenware

    W. & A.
    impressed

Weatherby & Sons, Ltd.
1891–, earthenware
    c. 1925–

    J.H.W. & SONS

    FALCON WARE

    c. 1936–, (trade-name)

    WEATHERBY WARE
    printed

Wellington Pottery Co.
1899–1901, earthenware

printed or impressed

Westminster Pottery Ltd.
1948–56, earthenware

    1952–, (trade-name)

    CASTLECLIFFE WARE

Whittaker & Co.
1886–92, earthenware

W. & CO.
printed

Whittaker, Heath & Co.
1892–8, earthenware

W.H. & CO.
printed

Wilson, Robert
1795–1801, earthenware

WILSON

impressed marks

Wilson, David
c. 1802–18, general ceramics

WILSON
impressed

Winkle & Wood
1885–90, earthenware

printed

Worthington & Harrop
1856–73, earthenware

W. & H.
printed

Wulstan Pottery Co. Ltd.
c. 1940–58, earthenware

printed

Yates, John
c. 1784–1835, earthenware

J.Y.

printed or impressed

LANE DELPH (Staffordshire)
Edge, William & Samuel
1841–8, earthenware

W. & S.E.
printed

Harrison, George
c. 1790–5, earthenware

G. Harrison
impressed

Mason, William
c. 1811–24, earthenware

W. MASON
printed

Mason, Miles
c. 1792–1816, porcelain
   marks impressed *c.* 1800–16

M. MASON
   MILES MASON

   printed mark on
   chinoiserie patterns

Mason, G. M. & C. J.
1813–29, earthenware
(ironstone)

G.M. & C.J. MASON

G. & C.J.M.

   impressed marks
   c. 1813–25

MASON'S PATENT
IRONSTONE CHINA

   patented in 1813

PATENT IRONSTONE
CHINA

   standard mark of
   c. 1820, continued by
   Ashworth (*c.* 1862)
'Mason's Ironstone China
Ltd.' from 1968–
(a Division of Josiah
Wedgwood & Sons Ltd., 1974)

printed mark with
pattern number *c.* 1825–

Mason & Co., Charles
James, 1829–45,
earthenware, (ironstone)
printed

FENTON
STONE WORKS
C.J.M. & CO.
GRANITE CHINA

printed

C.J. MASON & CO.
LANE DELPH

c. 1840–

'MASON'S CAMBRIAN ARGIL',
'MASON'S BANDANA WARE'
impressed or printed
c. 1825–40

Mason, Charles James
c. 1845–8, earthenware
(ironstone), also at
Longton, 1851–4

printed

Morley & Co., Francis
1845–58, earthenware
(Hanley)

F.M.
F.M. & CO.
F. MORLEY & CO.

Morley & Ashworth
1859–62, earthenware
(Hanley)

M. & A.
impressed or printed

176

Myatt, late 18th- early 19th centuries, earthenware	MYATT impressed
Pratt, William *c.* 1780–99, earthenware	PRATT
LANE END (Staffordshire) Abbott, Andrew *c.* 1781–3, earthenware	ABBOTT POTTER impressed
Abbott & Mist 1787–1810, earthenware	ABBOTT & MIST impressed or painted
Aynsley, John 1780–1809, engraver of prints for earthenwares	'*J. Aynsley Lane End*' printed
Barker, John, Richard & William, *c.* 1800 earthenware	BARKER impressed
Batkin, Walker & Broadhurst, 1840–5, earthenware	B.W. & B. printed
Booth & Sons 1830–5, earthenware	BOOTH & SONS impressed
Bott & Co. *c.* 1810–11, earthenware	BOTT & CO. impressed

Carey, Thomas & John *c.* 1823–42, earthenware	CAREYS impressed or printed with anchor
Chesworth & Robinson 1825–40, earthenware	C. & R. printed
Chetham & Woolley 1796–1810, earthenware	CHETHAM & WOOLLEY LANE END incised

Cyples, Joseph
c. 1784–1840
   (initials of various
   potters in this family
   rarely used)
	CYPLES
	
	I. CYPLES
	impressed

Deakin & Son 1833–41, earthenware printed mark	
Everard, Glover & Colclough, *c.* 1847– general ceramics	E.G. & C. printed
Floyd, Benjamin *c.* 1843, earthenware	B.F. printed
Goodwin, Bridgwood & Orton, 1827–9 earthenware	G.B.O. G.B. & O.

Goodwin, Bridgwood & Harris   G.B.H.
1829–31, earthenware

Goodwins & Harris   GOODWINS &
c. 1831–8, earthenware   HARRIS
printed

Griffiths, Beardmore &   G.B. & B.
Birks, 1830, earthenware   printed

Harley, Thomas   HARLEY
1802–8, earthenware   T. HARLEY
impressed

printed or written

T. HARLEY
LANE END

Harvey, Bailey & Co.   H.B. & CO.
1833–5, earthenware   printed

Heathcote & Co., Charles   C. HEATHCOTE & CO.
1818–24, earthenware   printed

Hilditch & Son
1822–30, general ceramics

printed in various
surrounds

Hulme & Sons, John   HULME & SONS
c. 1828–30, earthenware   printed

179

Lockett, J. & G.   J. & G. LOCKETT
c. 1802–5, earthenware   impressed

Lockett, John   J. LOCKETT
1821–58, earthenware   impressed

Lockett & Co., J.   J. LOCKETT & CO.
c. 1812–89, earthenware   impressed
(also at Longton 1882–   or
1960, and 1960– Burslem)   printed

Lockett & Hulme   L. & H.
1822–6, earthenware   L.E.
                                    printed

Mayer & Newbold   M. & N.
c. 1817–33, general ceramics

marks painted or   MAY^R & NEWB^D
printed

Plant, Benjamin
c. 1780–1820, earthenware
marks incised

Plant, Thomas
1825–50, earthenware

                                    painted

Ray, George, modeller   G. RAY
early 19th century   Lane End

180

Turner, John (also
entered under Longton)
c. 1762–1806, earthenware
and porcelain
  early impressed marks

TURNER
I. TURNER

  printed or impressed
  from 1784 after Turner
  was potter to the
  Prince of Wales

TURNER

  impressed, *c.* 1780–6
  1803–6

TURNER & CO.

  painted on earthenwares
  1800–5

Turner's Patent

Turner & Abbott
c. 1783–7 (Abbott
probably only agent)
earthenwares and
stoneware in Wedgwood
style

TURNER & ABBOTT
impressed

LONGPORT (Staffordshire)

Bodley & Son, E. F.
1881–98, earthenware

E.F.B. & SON

  trade-mark, 1883–98

181

Bourne, Edward   E. BOURNE
1790–1811, earthenware   impressed

Corn, W. & E.   W. & E.C.
1864–1904, earthenware
(also at Burslem *c.* 1864–   W.E.C.
1904, nearly all marks
   are late and include 'ENGLAND' (post-1891)

Davenport & Co., W.
c. 1793–1887, general
ceramics; 1798–1815   Davenport

c. 1815–60   DAVENPORT
'Davenport' or 'DAVENPORT'
is impressed with or
without anchor

marks on 'Stone-China'
c. 1815–30

19th century mark to
about 1860, including
last two numerals of
year
   anchor mark alone *c.* 1820–40

many printed wares of 1820–60 bear
name of pattern and 'DAVENPORT'

printed on porcelain   DAVENPORT
c. 1815–   LONGPORT
three numerals denote month and last
two numerals of year made
'Manufacturers of China to His Majesty
and the Royal Family' on porcelain
c. 1830–37

                                        DAVENPORT
impressed *c.* 1850–70   PATENT

printed in underglaze-blue
c. 1850–70
(sometimes in enamel
colours prior to 1830)

This mark was used   DAVENPORT
from *c.* 1830–45 in puce   LONGPORT
and from *c.* 1870–87   STAFFORDSHIRE
in red   printed under crown

printed on earthenware   DAVENPORTS LTD.
c. 1881–7

Liddle, Elliott & Son   L.E. & S.
1862–71, general   impressed or printed
ceramics

Mayer & Elliott
1858–61, earthenware
    number of month and
    last two numerals of year   printed
                6
impressed, e.g. — = June, 1859
               59

Phillips, Edward & George   PHILLIPS
1822–34, earthenware   LONGPORT

  printed marks   E. & G.P.

Phillips, George   PHILLIPS
1834–48, earthenware
  name with or without knot,
  sometimes 'Longport' also

Rogers, John & George   ROGERS
c. 1784–1814, earthenware

                       J.R.
  impressed marks   L.

Rogers & Son, John   as above and
c. 1814–36, earthenware

                       J.R.S.
                ROGERS & SON

Smith, Ltd., W. T. H.   W.T.H. SMITH & CO.
1898–1905, earthenware   LONGPORT
               printed with 'globe'

Wood & Son (Longport)   ARTHUR WOOD
Ltd., 1928–, earthenware   full name printed in
  'ROYAL BRADWELL   variety of marks
  ART WARE' trade-name

Wood, Arthur   A.W.
1904–28, earthenware   L
  mark impressed or   ENGLAND
  printed

LONGTON HALL (Staffordshire)
  c. 1749–60, porcelain
    rare marks painted in
    underglaze blue

LONGTON (Staffordshire)

Adams & Co. Harvey
1870–85, general ceramics

H.A. & CO.
over crown
printed

Adams & Cooper
1850–77, porcelain

A. & C.
printed

Adderleys Ltd.
1906–, general ceramics

  printed mark 1906–26
  many other marks all
  including full name of firm

Adderley, J. Fellows
1901–5, porcelain

J.F.A.

  printed marks

Adderley, William Alsager
1876–1905

W.A.A.

W.A.A. & CO.

  and 'sailing-ship' trade-
  mark as above

Adderley Floral China Works
1945– bone-china
decorative wares
  printed mark
(Royal Doulton Group
from 1973)

Aldridge & Co.
1919–49, earthenware

ALDRIDGE & CO.
LONGTON
impressed

Allerton & Sons, Charles
1859–1942, general
ceramics
  printed or impressed
  marks, *c.* 1890–1942
  Many other fully named
  marks also used

C.A. & SONS

CHAS. ALLERTON &
SONS
ENGLAND

Alton China Co. Ltd.
1950–7, bone-china

ALTON
BONE CHINA
printed

Amison, Charles
1889–1962, porcelain
  impressed initials, 1889–

  printed mark of 1906–30
  '& Co.' added 1916
  '& Co. Ltd.', 1930

  further late marks include
  'Stanley' and 'Staffordshire
  Floral Bone China'

C.A.
L.

Anchor Porcelain Co. Ltd.   A.P. CO.
1901–18, porcelain
   impressed marks   A.P. CO. L.

impressed or printed
'anchor-mark', 1901–15
'ROYAL WESTMINSTER CHINA' printed
with 'A.P. CO. L.', 1915–18

Aristocrat Florals & Fancies
1958–, bone-china decorative
wares (Wedgwood Group
from 1973)

Asbury & Co.   ASBURY
1875–1925, general ceramics   LONGTON
   printed marks

A. & CO.

Avon Art Pottery
1930–69, earthenware
   recent mark, printed
(seemingly merged with
Elektra Porcelain Co., 1962)

Aynsley & Co., H.   H.A. & CO.
1873–, earthenware   L.
   'Ltd.' added 1932
   late marks include
   name in full

187

Aynsley & Sons, John   AYNSLEY
1864–, porcelain   impressed
    various later marks include full name and
    'ENGLAND' added from 1891
(now Aynsley China Ltd.–Waterford Glass Co.
Ltd.)

Baddeley, William   EASTWOOD
1802–22, earthenware   impressed
(Wedgwood-type)

Baggerley & Ball   B. & B.
1822–36, earthenware   L.
    printed in blue
    within oval frame

Bailey & Sons, William
1912–14, earthenware
    printed mark

Bailey & Batkin   BAILEY & BATKIN
1814–*c.* 27, earthenware
including lustreware
    marks impressed or moulded   B. & B.

Bailey & Harvey   BAILEY & HARVEY
1834–5, earthenware   impressed
including lustre

Balfour China Co. Ltd.   BALFOUR
1947–52, bone-china   ROYAL CROWN
(then known as: POTTERY
Trentham Bone China   printed with crown
Ltd.)

Barker Bros. Ltd.   B.B.
1876–, general ceramics   impressed
  large variety of other printed marks
  including such trade names as:
  MEIR CHINA, MEIR WARE, TUDOR WARE
  and ROYAL TUDOR WARE
(Alfred Clough Ltd.)

Barlow & Son Ltd., T. W.   B.   B. & S.
1882–1940, earthenware   rare impressed
                                  marks
  marks used from about 1928 include
  'CORONATION WARE'

Barlow, Thomas   B.
1849–1882, general ceramics   impressed

Barlows (Longton) Ltd.   B. Ltd.
1920–52, earthenware   impressed
  later marks include 'MELBAR WARE'

Baxter, Rowley & Tams   B.R. & T.
1882–5, porcelain   impressed

Beardmore & Edwards   B. & E.
1856–8, earthenware   printed

Bentley & Co. Ltd., G. L.   G.L.B. & CO.
1898–1912, porcelain   LONGTON
  'Ltd.' added from 1904

Beswick & Son
1916–30, porcelain
'ALDWYCH CHINA', trade-name also used by
Bridgett & Bates, former prop's.

B. & S.
printed or impressed

Beswick Ltd., John
1936–, earthenware
(Royal Doulton Group 1973)

BESWICK
ENGLAND
printed

Blackhurst & Hulme
1890–1932, porcelain
early mark of printed
initials, later full
mark used from *c.* 1914

B. & H.

THE BELGRAVE
CHINA
B. & H.
L
ENGLAND

Blair & Co.
1880–1930, porcelain
'Ltd.' added *c.* 1912
(LONGTON) added *c.* 1923
early impressed 'B'
up until about 1900
'BLAIRS CHINA, ENGLAND'
impressed or printed
c. 1900–
printed mark of *c.* 1900–

Blyth Porcelain Co. Ltd.
c. 1905–35, porcelain
'DIAMOND CHINA'
also used from *c.* 1913

B.P. CO. LTD.
printed in
varying forms

190

Boulton & Co.   B . & CO.   B . & CO.
1892–1902, porcelain   L
                                  printed or impressed

Bradbury, Anderson & Bettanny B.A. & B.
1844–52, general ceramics   printed

Bradley, F. D.   BRADLEY
1876–96, porcelain   impressed

Bradleys (Longton) Ltd.   BRADLEYS
1922–41, porcelain   LONGTON
   mark printed with crown   MADE IN
                                   ENGLAND

Bridgett & Bates   B. & B.
1882–1915, porcelain   impressed or printed
   'ALDWYCH CHINA' trade-name from *c.* 1912

Bridgett, Bates & Beech
1875–82
   printed or impressed mark

Bridgwood & Son Ltd.,   BRIDGWOOD & SON
Sampson, 1805–, earthenware
(porcelain until *c.* 1887)

                                S. BRIDGWOOD &
   impressed or printed marks   SON
   from *c.* 1850–

                                   S.B. & S.

other various printed marks include
full name of firm or initials

'Parisian Granite' mark
c. 1870–, printed

Britannia China Company
1895–1906, porcelain

B.C. CO.
impressed

other fully-named marks
also used
1904–6

printed or impressed

British Anchor Pottery Co. Ltd.
1884–, earthenware
(from 1971, Hostess Tableware Ltd.)
  printed or impressed
  1884–*c.* 1913

other various marks include full
names and such trade names as:
REGENCY, MONTMARTRE, RICHMOND,
HOSTESS and TRIANON

British Pottery Ltd.
c. 1930–, agents only

B.P. LTD.
printed

Brough & Blackhurst
1872–95, earthenware

BROUGH &
BLACKHURST
printed or impressed

Burgess Bros.
1922–39, earthenware
  'Burgess Ware' also
  used

"BURCRAFT"
BURGESS BROS.
MADE IN ENGLAND
printed

Capper & Wood
1895–1904, earthenware

C. & W.
printed or impressed

Cara China Co.
1945–, porcelain

CARA CHINA
printed

Cartlidge & Co., F.
1889–1904, porcelain
  '& Co.' added *c.* 1892

F.C.
F.C. & CO.
printed or impressed

Cartwright & Edwards, Ltd.
c. 1857–
(Alfred Clough Ltd.)
  printed mark of 1912–
  'Ltd.' added *c.* 1926–
  trade names of 'Norville'
  & 'Baronian' ware used
  with 'C. & E.' from *c.* 1930–

C. & E.
printed or impressed

Chapman & Sons, David
1889–1906, porcelain
  'Atlas' mark of 1889–1906

Chapmans Longton Ltd.
1916–*c.* '67 porcelain
  printed 1916–30
(now Paragon China Ltd.)

STANDARD CHINA
crown
ENGLAND

various other marks including trade-names of:
'ROYAL STANDARD' and 'ROYAL
MAYFAIR', (from 1973 part of Royal Doulton
Group)

Chetham 1810–34, earthenware '& Son' added 1818	CHETHAM impressed
Chetham, Jonathan Lowe 1841–62, earthenware	J.L.C. printed
Chetham, J. R. & F. 1846–69, earthenware	J.R. & F.C. printed
Chetham & Robinson 1822–37, earthenware	C. & R. printed
Chew, John 1903–4, porcelain	J.C. L impressed

Clare China Co. Ltd.
1951–, decorators
  printed mark, possibly
  taken over by Taylor &
  Kent
	BONE CHINA
	CLARE
	MADE IN ENGLAND
	with crown

Clough's Royal Art
Pottery, 1961–69,
earthenware
  mark also used by
  Alfred Clough Ltd.
	'ROYAL ART POTTERY'
	ENGLAND
	with crown
	printed

(Royal Art Pottery), 1951–61
Transferred to Alfred Clough, Ltd., Longton
under name of Barker Bros. Ltd. in 1968

Coggins & Hill
1892–8, porcelain

C. & H.
printed or impressed

Colclough & Co.
1887–1928, general ceramics
  printed marks

R.S. monogram

'ROYAL STANLEY WARE'

Colclough, H. J.
1897–1937, general ceramics
  various marks including 'H.J.C.' and/or
  'VALE CHINA'

H.J.C.
L

Colclough China Ltd.
1937–48, porcelain

  late printed marks

Colclough
GENUINE
BONE CHINA
MADE IN ENGLAND

Collingwood Bros. Ltd.
1887–1957, porcelain

COLLINGWOOD
early impressed mark

  initials used with crown
  c. 1887–1912
  later marks fully named

C.B.
L

Collingwood & Greatbatch
1870–1887, porcelain

  printed or impressed
  (crown also used
  alone)

C. & G.

Cone Ltd., Thomas
1892–*c.* 1967
earthenware
  mark of 1892–1912
(moved to Meir in 1964)
    printed 1912–35
    'Alma Ware' 1935–
    'ROYAL ALMA' 1946–68

T.C.
L

T.C. monogram

T.C.
LONGTON
printed or impressed

Conway Pottery Co. Ltd.
1930–, earthenware
  mark printed from 1945–

CONWAY
POTTERY
ENGLAND

Cooke & Hulse
1835–55, porcelain

COOKE & HULSE
printed

Cooper & Dethick
1876–88, earthenware

C. & D.
printed

Co-operative Wholesale Society Ltd.
1922, porcelain and
from 1946 also earthenware
  printed mark on porcelain
  from *c.* 1946, also
  'Clarence Bone-China'

'Crown Clarence'
earthenware from 1946–
also 'Balmoral'
(from 1971–, Jon Anton Ltd.)

J. H. Cope & Co. Ltd.
1887–1947, porcelain

C. & CO.
impressed or printed

printed with 'back-stamps'   J.H.C. & CO.
from *c.* 1900
'WELLINGTON CHINA' with crown *c.* 1906–
'WELLINGTON CHINA' and profile of Duke
c. 1924–1947

Cotton & Barlow   C. & B.
1850–5, earthenware   printed

Cyples & Barker   CYPLES & BARKER
1846–7, earthenware   impressed

Day, George   STAFFORDSHIRE
1882–9, earthenware
  printed mark

Day & Pratt   DAY & PRATT
1887–8, porcelain   printed or impressed

Decoro Pottery Co.   TUSCAN
1933–49, earthenware   DECORO
  various fully-named   POTTERY
  printed marks

Denton China (Longton) Ltd.   DENTON
1945–, porcelain   CHINA
(Aynsley China Ltd.)

Dewes & Copestake   D. & C.
1894–1915, earthenware   L
  various printed marks
  including initials

Diane Pottery Co.
1960–, now closed,
porcelain
   various printed marks
   with full name

DIANE
POTTERY
LONGTON
STAFFORDSHIRE

Dinky Art Pottery Co. Ltd.
1931–47, earthenware
   printed mark

MADE IN
DINKY WARE
ENGLAND

Dixon & Co., R. F.
1916–29, ceramic retailers
and importers

various marks
include 'D.C.'
for Dixon & Co.

Dresden Floral Porcelain Co. Ltd.
1945–56, porcelain
   printed mark

Dresden Porcelain Co.   D.P. CO.   D.P. CO.
1896–1904, porcelain   L

                   printed or impressed

   printed mark 1896–1903

Edwards & Brown   E. & B.
1882–1933, porcelain   L
   impressed or printed mark 1882–1933
   'E. & B.L.' with 'DUCHESS CHINA', 1910–33

Elektra Porcelain Co Ltd.
1924–71, earthenware
  printed mark of 1924–
(now Allied English Potteries)
  similar mark 'VULCAN WARE' *c.* 1940–

Elkin, Samuel
1856–64, earthenware

S.E.
printed

Elkin & Newbon
c. 1844–5, earthenware

E. & N.

Fell & Co., J. T.
1923–57, earthenware

EMBOSA WARE

  printed or impressed

MADE BY CYPLES
OLD POTTERY
1793

Finney & Sons Ltd., A. T.
1947, porcelain
  trade-name in a variety
  of styles

DUCHESS
BONE CHINA
printed

Flacket, Toft & Robinson
1857–8, earthenware

F.T. & R.
printed

Floral China Co. Ltd.
1940–51, porcelain
  printed mark

Forester & Co., Thomas
1888–, earthenware
  printed mark

Forester & Sons, Thomas
1883–1959, general ceramics
   'Ltd.' added 1891
   printed, 1891–1912
   later marks include
   'PHOENIX CHINA'

T.F. & S.

Gallimore, Robert
1831–40, earthenware

R.G.
impressed

Gallimore & Co. Ltd.,
1906–34, earthenware
   mark impressed or printed

Gladstone China (Longton)
Ltd., 1939–1952,
porcelain
   printed mark until
   1961 after firm became:
Gladstone China
1952–, porcelain

GLADSTONE
BONE   CHINA

MADE IN ENGLAND
various marks with
'Gladstone Bone China'

Green & Clay
1888–91, earthenware
   printed or impressed

Grove & Stark
1871–85, earthenware
   printed or impressed
   'G.S.' impressed
   monogram also used

G. & S.
printed

GROVE & STARK
LONGTON

Hallam & Day
1880–85, earthenware

H. & D.
printed, often with
Royal Arms

Hammersley & Co.
1887–1932, porcelain
(Hammersley & Co., Longton) Ltd.
from 1932–present
  crown mark used without
  initials, 1887–1912
  many various fully-named marks from 1912–
(now Carborundum Group)

H. & C.   H. & CO.

H. & C₀
CHINA

Hammersley & Asbury
1872–5, earthenware

H. & A.
printed, sometimes
with 'Prince of Wales'
feathers

Hampson & Broadhurst
1847–53, earthenware

H. & B.
printed

Harvey, C. & W. K.
1835–53, general ceramics
  name also printed with
  Royal Arms and 'REAL
  IRONSTONE CHINA'

C. & W.K.H.

HARVEY
printed

Hawley, Webberley & Co.
1895–1902, earthenware
  printed mark

Hewitt & Leadbeater
1907–19, porcelain
then Hewitt Bros. until
c. 1926

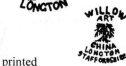

printed

Hibbert & Boughey
1889, general ceramics

H. & B.
printed with crown

Hill & Co.
1898–1920, porcelain

H. & CO.
impressed or printed

Holdcroft, Joseph
1865–1940, general ceramics
(Holdcrofts Ltd., *c.* 1906–,
later Cartwright & Edwards Ltd.)
   mark of 'H.J.' monogram on globe from
   1890–1939

printed or
impressed
1865–1906

Holland & Green
1853–82, earthenware

H. & G.
LATE HARVEY
printed or impressed

Holmes & Son
1898–1903, earthenware
   other marks include
   full name

H. & S.
LONGTON
impressed or printed

Hudden, John Thomas
1859–1885, earthenware

J.T.H.
J.T. HUDDEN
printed

Hudson, William
1889–1941, porcelain
   printed mark 1892–1912
   other later marks
   include 'SUTHERLAND
   CHINA'

W.H.
printed

202

Hudson & Middleton, Ltd.
1941–, porcelain
   various late marks
   include 'SUTHERLAND'
   and 'H.M.' with lion

Hulse & Adderley
1869–75, general
ceramics
   printed mark as
   used later by
   W. A. Adderley & Co.

H. & A.

Hulse, Nixon & Adderley   H.N. & A.
1853–68, earthenware   printed

Jackson & Gosling   J. & G.   J. & G.
1866–1968, porcelain   L
   'Ltd.' added *c.* 1930   impressed or printed
   variety of marks including trade-name of
   'Grosvenor China'

Jones (Longton) Ltd., A. E.
1905–46, earthenware
   printed or impressed
   c. 1908–36   ENGLAND
   other 'Palissy' mark continued by
Palissy Pottery, Ltd., now a subsidiary of
Royal Worcester, Ltd.

Jones & Co., Frederick   F. JONES LONGTON
1865–86, earthenware   impressed or printed

Jones & Sons, A. B.   A.B.J. & S.
1900–, porcelain   A.B.J. & SONS
(A. B. Jones from 1876)   A.B. JONES & SONS
   large variety of marks including
   initials, full name and/or trade-name of
   'GRAFTON' or 'ROYAL GRAFTON'
(acquired in 1966 by Crown House Glass Ltd.)

Jones, Shepherd & Co.   J.S. & CO.
1867–8, earthenware   printed

Jones, Josiah Ellis   J.E.J.
1868–72, earthenware   or full name
                     printed

Kent, James   JAMES KENT
1897–, general ceramics   ENGLAND
   'Ltd.' added 1913   with Royal Arms &
   printed mark of   'ROYAL SEMI CHINA'
   1897–1915
   various shield or 'globe' marks with full name
   or J.K.L. or J.K., from 1897–present, when
   'Old Foley' is used

Lawrence (Longton) Ltd., Thomas
1892–1964, earthenware
   printed or impressed
   marks include name
   'Falcon Ware'

Leadbeater, Edwin
1920–24, porcelain
  printed or impressed mark

Ledgar, Thomas P.   T.P.L.
1900–5, general ceramics
  impressed or printed mark

Lockett & Sons, John   J. LOCKETT & SONS
1828–35, earthenware   impressed

Longton New Art Pottery Co.   KELSBORO'
Ltd., 1932–66, earthenware   WARE
  various printed marks

Longton Porcelain Co. Ltd.   L.P. CO.
1892–1908, porcelains   monogram

Longton Pottery Co. Ltd.   L.P. CO. LTD.
1946–55, earthenware   printed

Lowe, William
1874–1930, porcelain

                printed or impressed
  also full name or initials with trade-names
  'ROYAL SYDNEY WARE', 'COURT CHINA'

Lowe, Ratcliffe & Co.
1882–92, earthenware
  printed or impressed

Mackee, Andrew
1892–1906, general ceramics
A.M.
L.
impressed or printed

Malkin, Walker & Hulse
1858–64, earthenware
M.W. & H.
printed

Martin, Shaw & Cope
c. 1815–24, general ceramics
MARTIN SHAW
& COPE
IMPROVED CHINA
printed

Mason, Holt & Co.
1857–84, porcelain
M.H. & CO.
printed or impressed

Massey, Wildblood & Co.
1887–9, porcelain
M.W. & CO.
printed

Matthews & Clark
c. 1902–6, general ceramics
printed mark in frame
M. & C.
L.

Mayer & Sherratt
1906–41, porcelain
M. & S.
L.
under crown
also other printed marks including trade-name
of 'MELBA CHINA'

McNeal & Co. Ltd.
1894–1906, earthenware
printed

Middleton & Co., J. H.
1889–1941, porcelain
  various printed marks
  with trade-name of
  'DELPHINE'

Moore Bros.
1872–1905, porcelain

MOORE

printed or impressed

  'Bros.' added 1872–1905

MOORE BROS.

  printed from *c.* 1880

MOORE (with globe)

  printed mark, 1902–5
Bernard Moore
continued at Stoke
until 1915

Morris, Thomas
1892–1941, porcelain

  early printed mark, from
  c. 1912 trade-name of
  'CROWN CHELSEA CHINA' used

New Chelsea Porcelain Co. Ltd.
  from 1913 many marks used
  including anchor and
  'Chelsea', 'New Chelsea'
  or 'Royal Chelsea'

New Chelsea China Co. Ltd.
1951–61, porcelain

New Park Potteries Ltd.
1935–57, earthenware
   initials or factory-
   name printed in
   varying frames

N.P.P. LTD.
NEW PARK
POTTERIES
LONGTON
NEW PARK

Osborne China Co. Ltd.
1909–40, porcelain

'Osborne China'
with torch

Palissy Pottery Ltd.
1946–, earthenware
(subsidiary of Royal
Worcester Ltd.)
   variety of printed marks include,
   'Palissy Pottery' or 'Palissy Ware', etc.

Paragon China Ltd.
1920–, porcelain
   large variety of marks
   include 'Royal Arms'
   and 'Paragon'
(now an Allied English
Potteries Ltd. company)

Pattison, J.
c. 1818–30, earthenware

JOHN PATTISON
incised

Plant, Benjamin
c. 1780–1820, earthenware

*B Plant
Lane End.*

incised

Plant & Co., R. H.
1881–98, porcelain

'R.H.P. & CO.'
in knot under a
winged crown

Plant, Ltd., R. H. & S. L.
c. 1898–1970, porcelain
   numerals under
   mark indicate last
   two numerals of year
   made. From 1973:

'TUSCAN CHINA'
trade-name in
many various
forms
'WEDGWOOD–ROYAL
TUSCAN DIVISION'

Plant & Sons, R.
1895–1901, earthenware

P. & S.
L
printed

Poole, Thomas
1880–1952, general ceramics

   impressed or printed
crown, 1880–1912
(common mark)
early form of 'ROYAL
STAFFORD CHINA' used
from 1912–

Poole & Unwin
1871–6, earthenware

P. & U.
printed or impressed

Proctor & Co., J. H.
1857–84, earthenware

WARRANTED
P
printed or impressed
under crown

Procter, John
1843–6, earthenware

J.P.
L
printed or impressed

Procter & Co. Ltd., G.
1891–1940, porcelain
with or without 'L'
for Longton
'GLADSTONE CHINA'
from 1924–40

G.P. & CO.
L
printed

trade-name

Ratcliffe & Co.
1891–1914, earthenware

printed

Redfern & Drakeford Ltd.
1892–1933, porcelain
printed or impressed
mark, 'BALMORAL
CHINA' added in
1909–33

Regency China Ltd.
1953–, porcelain

Reid & Co.
1913–46, porcelain

  'PARK PLACE CHINA'
  c. 1913–24

  'ROSLYN CHINA'
  c. 1924–46
  (SEE ROSLYN CHINA)   all printed

Riddle & Bryan   RIDDLE & BRYAN
c. 1835–40, earthenware   Longton
                                              printed

Robinson, W. H.   W.H. ROBINSON
1901–4, porcelain   LONGTON
   printed mark in   BALTIMORE CHINA
   circle under crown

Robinson & Son   R. & S.
1881–1903, porcelain   L.

   'Foley' is a name   FOLEY CHINA
   used by several potters

Roper & Meredith   R. & M.
1913–24, earthenware   LONGTON

Roslyn China
1946–63, porcelain
   printed mark also
   used by Reid & Co.

Rowley & Newton Ltd.   R. & N.
1896–1901, general ceramics   printed or impressed
'R. & N.' often with lion 'rampant'

Royal Albion China Co.   ROYAL ALBION CHINA
1921–48, porcelain   L
   printed marks   ENGLAND
                  with crown

Royal Stafford China   variety of marks
1952–, porcelain   with
   printed marks   'ROYAL STAFFORD'

Salisbury Crown China Co.
(Salisbury China Co. from
1949)
c. 1927–61, porcelain

   printed mark of *c.* 1952

Salt & Nixon, Ltd.   S. & N.
1901–34, porcelain   L
   various marks with initials
     & 'SALON CHINA'   printed

Shaw & Sons (Longton) Ltd., John
1931–63, general ceramics

   printed mark of *c.* 1949
   various other marks,
   include 'Burlington'

Shaw & Copestake
1901–, earthenware
  various printed or impressed
  marks with trade-name of 'SYLVAC'

Shelley Potteries, Ltd.
1925–67, porcelain
(now Royal Albert Ltd.)
  various printed marks
  with 'SHELLEY' (Royal Doulton Group)

Shepherd & Co., Alfred   A. SHEPHERD & CO.
1864–70, earthenware   printed

Shore & Co., J.   J.S. & CO.
1887–1905, porcelain   printed

Shore, Coggins & Holt   S.C.H.
1905–10, general ceramics   L
  initials printed under   *ENGLAND*
  crown

Shore & Coggins
1911–*c.* 67, porcelain
  mark of *c.* 1930, other
  marks include trade-name
  'Bell China' (now Royal Doulton Group)

Smith, Sampson   S.S.
c. 1846–1963, general   impressed
ceramics

'S.S.' monogram used in a variety of
marks during this century and 'WETLEY
CHINA' or 'OLD ROYAL CHINA'

Stanley & Lambert   S. & L.
c. 1850–4, earthenware   printed

Stanley Pottery Ltd.
1928–31, general ceramics

   same printed marks as
   used by Colclough & Co.

Star China Co.   S.C. CO.
1900–19, porcelain   printed with crown
                                 or star with
                           'THE PARAGON CHINA'

Stevenson, Spencer & Co. Ltd.
1948–60, porcelain
   fully named marks
   with 'WILLOW' or
   'ROYAL STUART'

Sutherland & Sons, Danial   S. & S.
1865–75, general   impressed or
ceramics   printed

Swift & Elkin   S. & E.
1840–3, earthenware   printed

Tams, John
c. 1875–, earthenware
  printed marks

J.T.
(or as monogram)

'& Son' added 1903–12
'LTD.' from 1912, with trade-marks:
'NANKIN WARE', 'ELEPHANT BRAND',
'TAMS REGENT' and 'CHININE'

J. Tams
J.T. & S.

Tams & Lowe
1865–74, earthenware

T. & L.
printed

Taylor & Kent
1867–, porcelain

T. & K.
L
printed or impressed

variety of named or initialled marks
with 'KENT' or 'ELIZABETHAN'

Thorley China Ltd.
1940–70, decorative
porcelain
(last six years in Fenton)

THORLEY CHINA
LTD.
printed under crown

Tomkinson & Billington
1868–70, earthenware

T. & B.
printed

Townsend, George
c. 1850–64, earthenware

G. TOWNSEND
printed

Trentham Bone China Ltd.
1952–7, porcelain
  printed

Turner, John
c. 1762–1806, Wedgwood-
type earthenwares and
stonewares

TURNER
impressed

TURNER.

printed or impressed
from 1784

impressed *c.* 1780–6,
1803–6
painted mark on
'ironstone' type ware
1800–5

TURNER & CO.

Turner & Abbott
c. 1783–7, Wedgwood-
type wares

TURNER & ABBOTT
impressed

Universal Pottery (Longton) Ltd.
1949–62, *general ceramics*
various printed marks
with 'Universal Ware'

Unwin, Joseph
1877–1926, *earthenware*
figures, etc.

UNWIN
moulded in
relief

Wagstaff & Brunt
1880–1927, *general*
ceramics

W. & B.
LONGTON
printed

Wain & Sons, Ltd., H. A.
1946–, earthenware

Waine & Co., Charles
1891–1920, porcelain
   printed, 1891–1913
   'Ltd.' from 1913

C.W.
or as monogram

Walker & Carter
1866–72, earthenware
(at Stoke 1872–89)

W. & C.
printed

Walton, J. H.
1912–21, porcelain

   printed or impressed

J. H. W.

LONGTON

Warrilow, George
1887–1940, porcelain
   '& S.' or '& Sons'
   and 'Ltd.' added
   from 1928

G.W.

G.W. & S.

G.W. & S. LTD.

Rosina China Co. Ltd.
1941–
   various marks with
   trade-names 'Rosina'
   or 'Queen's' China

ROSINA

CHINA
ENGLAND

Wayte & Ridge
c. 1864, general
ceramics & figures

W. & R.
L
printed

217

Wedgwood & Co. Ltd., H.F.　　H.F.W. & CO. LTD.
c. 1954–9, general　　　　　　ISLINGTON
ceramics　　　　　　　　　　　printed

Wild Bros.　　　　　　　　　　J.S.W.
1904–27, porcelain　　　or in monogram
　　　　　　　　　　　　　　W. Bros.

Wild & Co., Thomas C.　　　T.W. & CO.
1896–1904
　printed or impressed　　T.C.W. with crown

Wild, Thomas C.
1905–17, porcelain
　printed mark, 1905–7

Wild & Sons (Ltd.), Thomas C.
1917–*c.* 72, porcelain
　various printed marks
　with trade-name
　'Royal Albert', now Royal Doulton Group

Wild & Adams　　　　　　W. & A.
1909–27, earthenware　　printed or impressed
　'Ltd.' from 1923
　various marks with 'ROYAL CROWN'

Wildblood, Richard Vernon
1887–8, porcelain

　printed

Wildblood & Heath
1889–99, porcelain
printed

Wildblood, Heath & Sons
1899–1927, porcelain

'Ltd.' added from 1915

Williamson & Sons, H. M.
c. 1879–1941, porcelain

various marks of 'W. & Sons',
'H.M.W.' or 'Heathcote
China'
printed mark of *c.* 1908–

Winterton Pottery (Longton) 'WINTERTON'
Ltd., 1927–54, earthenware printed over crown

'Bluestone Ware'

Wood & Co., J. B.
1897–1926, earthenware

late printed or impressed
mark

Woolley, Richard WOOLLEY
1809–14, earthenware impressed

Yale & Barker Y. & B.
1841–53, earthenware printed

MIDDLEPORT (Staffordshire) FIVE TOWNS CHINA
Five Towns China Co. Ltd. CO. LTD.
1957–67, porcelain ENGLAND
  name with various
  printed marks

SHELTON (Staffordshire) ASTBURY
Astbury, mid-18th incised or impressed
century, earthenware

Astbury, Richard Meir R.M.A.
1790–, earthenware impressed

Baddeley, John & Edward B
1784–1806, earthenware I.E.B.
  impressed initials I.E.B.
then: W
Hicks & Meigh HICKS & MEIGH
1806–22, earthenware impressed or
and 'Ironstone' printed
then:
Hicks, Meigh & Johnson H.M.J.
1822–35, earthenware
and 'Ironstone' H.M. & J.
  printed with
  Royal Arms

then:

Ridgway, Morley, Wear & Co., 1836–42, earthenware	R.M.W. & CO.
	RIDGWAY, MORLEY WEAR & CO. printed
then: Ridgway & Morley 1842–44	R. & M.
various printed marks (backstamps) with names of pattern	RIDGWAY & MORLEY
Baddeley, Ralph & John 1750–95, earthenware marks impressed	BADDELEY
	R. & J. BADDELEY
Bairstow & Co., P. E. 1954–. earthenware and porcelain	Fancies Fayre England
Bentley, Wear & Bourne 1815–23, decorators printed mark (Bentley & Wear 1823– 33)	BENTLEY, WEAR & BOURNE
Birch, Edmund John 1796–1814, Wedgwood- type wares	BIRCH
	E.I.B. impressed
Birch & Whitehead 1796, Wedgwood-type	B. & W. impressed

Cockson & Harding
1856–62, earthenware
   marks printed or
   impressed
	C. & H.
	
	C. & H.
	LATE HACKWOOD

Cutts, James *c.* 1834–70, engraver and designer	J. CUTTS signature on prints
Dakin, Thomas early 18th century earthenware	THOMAS DAKIN sliptrailed
Hackwood & Son, Wm. 1846–9, earthenware	W.H. HACKWOOD printed
Harding, W. J. 1862–72, earthenware	W. & J.H. printed

Hicks & Meigh
1806–22, earthenware
   'Stone-China' & Royal
   Arms also used
	HICKS & MEIGH
	impressed or
	painted

Hicks, Meigh & Johnson
1822–35, earthenware
   'Stone-China' and
   Royal Arms also used
	H.M.J.
	
	H.M. & J.
	printed

Hollins, Samuel *c.* 1784–1813	S. HOLLINS

'Wedgwood-type' ware

HOLLINS
impressed

Hollins, T. & J.
c. 1795–1820, earthenware

T. & J. HOLLINS
impressed

Howard Pottery Co.
1925–, earthenware
  printed mark of 1925–

Keeling, Charles
1822–5, earthenware

C.K.
printed

Meir John
late 17th – early 18th-
centuries, slipware

JOHN MEIR
sliptrailed

Meir, Richard
late 17th – early 18th-
centuries, slipware

RICHARD MEIR
sliptrailed

Phillips, Edward
1855–62, earthenware
  printed mark

EDWARD PHILLIPS
SHELTON
STAFFORDSHIRE

Read & Clementson
1833–5, earthenware

R. & C.
printed

Read, Clementson &
Anderson
c. 1836, earthenware

R.C. & A.
printed

Ridgway, John & William
1814–1830, general
ceramics

J.W.R.
J. & W.R.
J. & W. RIDGWAY
printed or impressed

Ridgway, William
c. 1830–54, earthenware
(also at Hanley from
c. 1838–48)
  '& Co.' added *c.* 1834
  'QUARTZ CHINA' used
  from *c.* 1830–50

W. RIDGWAY

W.R.
printed or impressed

W.R. & CO.

Tittensor, Charles
c. 1815–23, earthenware
including figures

TITTENSOR
impressed or
printed

Twemlow, John
1795–7, earthenware
and stoneware

J.T.

rare initials

Washington Pottery Ltd.
1946–, earthenware
(now Washington Pottery
(Staffordshire) Ltd.)

Worthington & Green
1844–64, earthenware
and Parianware

WORTHINGTON
&
GREEN
impressed

STOKE (Staffordshire)
Alton Towers Handcraft
Pottery (Staffs.) Ltd.
1953–, earthenware

printed or impressed

Arkinstall & Sons (Ltd.)　　A. & S.
1904–24, bone-china　　printed, 1904–12

   trade marks on　　ARCADIAN
   souvenir wares 1904–
   24　　　ARCADIAN CHINA
(under various other
firms from 1908)　　printed marks

Atlas China Co. Ltd.　'ATLAS CHINA' with
1906–10, china　　figure supporting
(name revived by　　　globe
Grimwades Ltd. 1930–6)　printed

Bennett & Co., George　　G.B. & CO.
1894–1902, earthenware　impressed or printed

Bilton (1912) Ltd.
1900–, earthenware
  current mark, printed
(now Biltons Tableware Ltd.)

Birks & Co., L. A.　　BIRKS
1896–1900, general　　impressed
ceramics

B. & CO.

Birks, Rawlins & Co. (Ltd.)
1900–33, bone-china
  other marks include
  trade-names of:
  SAVOY CHINA
  CARLTON CHINA

printed

Booth & Son, Ephraim
c. 1795, earthenware

E.B. & S.
impressed

Booth, Hugh
1784–9, earthenware
including creamware

H. BOOTH
impressed

Carlton Ware Ltd.
1958–, earthenware
(Arthur Wood & Son Group)

modern printed mark

Ceramic Art Co. (1905)
Ltd., 1905–19, earthenware

C.A. & CO. LTD.
printed or impressed

Close & Co.
1855–64, earthenware

CLOSE & CO. LATE
W. ADAMS & SONS
STOKE-UPON-TRENT
printed or impressed

Copeland & Garrett
Copeland, W. T., etc.
(*see under* Spode)

Coronation Pottery Co.
1903–54, earthenware

　'Ltd.' from 1947

printed or impressed

Crown China Crafts Ltd.
1946–58, general ceramics
　printed mark

Daniel, H. & R.　　　　　　H. & R. Daniel
1820–41, pottery and
porcelain　　　　　　　　　H. Daniels & Sons
　fully named printed
　marks also used　　　　　　written marks

Empire Porcelain Co.
1896–1967, earthenware
　printed mark, 1896–1912
(1958–67, Qualcast Group)

EMPIRE
ENGLAND　*Shelton Ivory*

late printed or impressed marks

Era Art Pottery Co.
1930–47, earthenware

　printed mark, 1936–

227

Featherstone Potteries
1949–50, earthenware
   marks impressed or
   printed

F.P.

F.N.P.

Fielding & Co., S.
1879–, earthenwares
(part of Crown Devon
Group)

FIELDING
impressed

S.F. & CO.
(over crown and
lion)
printed

   'Crown Devon' trade-
   mark from *c.* 1930

   date-mark:
   10th March 1954

FIELDING
10 M 54

Floyd & Sons, R.
1907–30, earthenware

printed or impressed

Folch, Stephen
1820–30, earthenware

FOLCH'S GENUINE
STONE CHINA
impressed

Goss, W. H.
1858–1944, pottery and
porcelain

W.H.G.

W.H. GOSS

   printed mark from
   c. 1862

Greta Pottery   G
1938–41, earthenware   P
                            printed or painted

Hamilton, Robert   HAMILTON
1811–26, earthenware   STOKE
                            impressed or printed

Hancock & Co., F.
1899–1900, earthenware
  printed mark

Hancock, B. & S.   B. & S.H.
1876–81, earthenware   printed

Hancock & Sons, Sampson   S.H.
1858–1937, earthenware
(at Tunstall prior   S. HANCOCK
to 1870)   printed

    printed 1891–1935   S.H. & S.

                                 S.H. & SONS

    printed 1900–12
From 1935–37:–
S. Hancock & Sons
(Potters) Ltd.

Hancock & Whittingham   H. & W.
1873–9, earthenware   printed

Heath, Job
early 18th century
earthenware

JOB HEATH
sliptrailed

Jones, George
1861–1951, general ceramics

'& Sons', added on
crescent from 1873

in relief, impressed
or printed

Keys & Mountford
1850–7, 'Parian' ware

K. & M.

S. KEYS
& MOUNTFORD
impressed

Kirkham, William
1862–92, earthenware

W. KIRKHAM
impressed

Kirkhams Ltd.
1946–61, earthenware
(now Portmeiron
Potteries Ltd.)

Mayer, Thomas
1836–8, earthenware
(last three years at
Longport)

T. MAYER
T. MAYER, STOKE
printed

Meigh, W. & R.
1894–9, earthenware
    printed mark

Minton
1793–, general ceramics
(Royal Doulton Group from 1973)
   Sèvres type mark used
   on porcelain *c.* 1800–30,
   sometimes with   in blue enamel
   pattern number

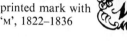

   printed mark with
   'M', 1822–1836

printed 1822–36

'M. & B.' for Minton &
Boyle partnership
1836–41, printed

'M. & Co.' Minton &
Co., 1841–73

'M. & H.', Minton &
Hollins partnership
1845–68

1862–71, 's' added in 1873	MINTON impressed

printed 1860–*c.* 69

impressed for 'BEST BODY' mid-19th century	B.B.

'Globe-mark', 1863–72 'S' added to Minton in 1871

impressed mark with year 1875, used from 1868–80

18
MINTON
75

printed mark from 1873, 'England' added from 1891, and 'Made in England' about 1910

impressed or moulded *c.* 1890–1910	MINTONS ENGLAND

'Globe-mark', *c.* 1912–50

standard factory-mark
adopted in 1951

'Ermine' mark used
from *c.* 1850 to identify
wares that had been
dipped in a soft-glaze
on which painting was
to be applied

relief mark of *c.* 1847–8
on 'Summerly's Art
Manufacturers' made
by Minton

Solon, Marc Louis, 1870–1904
decorator

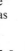

signature on 'Henri Deux'
reproductions   TOFT
Mussill, W. (*d.* 1906)
decorator in 1870s   W. Mussill

YEARLY MARKS OF MINTONS LTD., 1842–1942:

✳	△	☐	✕	⬭
1842	1843	1844	1845	1846
⌒	—	⟗	♣	∴
1847	1848	1849	1850	1851
V	♃	∿	✳	⚲
1852	1853	1854	1855	1856
◇	♈	♋	Ω	人
1857	1858	1859	1860	1861
⚇	⬦	Z	⋙	Ƴ
1862	1863	1864	1865	1866
⋈	G	⊡	Ⓜ	N
1867	1868	1869	1870	1871
⊗	⚒	↓	Ɛ	⊿
1872	1873	1874	1875	1876
◉	◮	◮	△	⊞
1877	1878	1879	1880	1881
⊗	◉	⊠	⋈	B
1882	1883	1884	1885	1886
♔	∞	S	T	⛉
1887	1888	1889	1890	1891

1892	1893	1894	1895	1896
1897	1898	1899	1900	1901
1902	1903	1904	1905	1906
1907	1908	1909	1910	1911
1912	1913	1914	1915	1916
1917	1918	1919	1920	1921
1922	1923	1924	1925	1926
1927	1928	1929	1930	1931
1932	1933	1934	1935	1936
1937	1938	1939	1940	1941
		1942		

At the commencement of 1943 the system of yearly date-marks that had operated from 1842 was discontinued, being replaced by figures denoting the year of production, preceded by a number allocated to the actual maker of the article, Number one was given to the factory's leading plate-maker, and plates he produces today have stamped in the clay 1–76, the last two digits representing the year.

Moore, Bernard
1905–15, art pottery and
porcelain, with
flambé glazes

BM
painted

    painted or printed

Mountford, G. T.
1888–98, earthenware

G.T.M.
STOKE
printed

Mountford, John
1857–9, 'Parian' ware

J. MOUNTFORD
STOKE
incised signature

Myott, Son & Co. Ltd.
1898–, earthenware
(now subsidiary of
Interpace Corporation)
(later Cobridge and
Hanley)

    late marks fully named

1898–1902

c. 1900–

Ollivant Potteries Ltd.   O.P.
1948–54, earthenware

                      O.P.L.

  printed marks, usually
  together with pattern   OLLIVANT

Plant & Co., J.   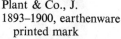
1893–1900, earthenware
  printed mark   STOKE POTTERY

Portmeirion Potteries Ltd.   PORTMEIRION
1962–, earthenware   POTTERY
                STOKE-ON-TRENT
  printed mark   MADE IN ENGLAND

Ridgway Potteries Ltd.
1955, earthenware
(an Allied English
Potteries Ltd., company)

      contemporary marks (1972)

Robinson & Leadbeater
1864–1924, 'Parian' ware
and bone-china   R & L
  'Ltd.' added to marks
  from *c.* 1905   impressed

Ruscoe, William
c. 1920– (to Exeter in
1944)
　full year-date added
　to initials from *c.* 1925

incised or painted

Shorter & Son, Ltd.
(member of Crown Devon
Group), 1905–
earthenware

late printed mark

Smith, James
1898–1924, general ceramics

JAMES SMITH

printed or impressed

printed

Spode, Josiah (*b.* 1733–
d. 1797) 1770–
earthenware
(Copeland & Garrett
from 1833)

Spode　SPODE
impressed or
in blue

　　c. 1784–1805

SPODE　S
impressed

painted marks with
pattern numbers, *c.* 1790–
1820

   c. 1805–

SPODE
printed

mark on stone-china,
in black *c.* 1805–15, in
blue *c.* 1815–30

S P O D E

Stone China
printed

painted

'Spode Stone China'

impressed 1810–15

SPODES
NEW STONE

printed *c.* 1805–33

N.S.

Spode's
Imperial

printed in puce enamel
on felspar porcelain
c. 1815–27

Spode

felspar
porcelain

painted, impressed
or printed *c.* 1797
to 1816

SPODE, SON
& COPELAND

Copeland & Garrett 1833–47, general ceramics	C. & G. painted or printed

COPELAND & GARRETT

printed in blue, with name of pattern, *c.* 1833–47

printed *c.* 1833–47   COPELAND & GARRETT
NEW
JAPAN STONE

Copeland & Sons, Ltd., W. T., 1847–
impressed or printed *c.* 1847–67

COPELAND, LATE
SPODE

printed on Parian figures *c.* 1847–55

COPELAND'S
PORCELAIN
STATUARY

printed, 1850–67

printed, *c.* 1847–51

printed, 1851–85

240

impressed on earthenware
1850–67

printed on porcelain
c. 1891–

SPODE
COPELANDS CHINA
ENGLAND

printed in various
colours on 'New Stone'
of this century

COPELAND   COPELAND

SPODE   SPODE

ENGLAND   ENGLAND New Stone

present-day mark

Spode
ENGLAND

Alcock, S., decorator
c. 1890–

S. Alcock

Hürten, C. F., designer
1859–1897

C.F.H.

Steele & Wood
1875–1892, tiles

printed or impressed

Tittensor, Jacob
1780–95, earthenware

Jacob Tittensor
signature

Turner, Hassall & Peake   T.H.P.
1865–9, general ceramics

                                printed or impressed

Turner & Wood   TURNER & WOOD
1880–8, general ceramics   STOKE
                                  impressed

Wiltshaw & Robinson Ltd.
1890–1957, general
ceramics
  printed mark, 1894–
  various marks include
  trade-mark 'CARLTON
  WARE'

Winkle & Co., F.   F.W. & CO.
1890–1931, earthenware   ENGLAND

  printed or impressed   F. WINKLE & CO.
  marks, 1890–1910
  'Ltd.' added in 1911

  printed, 1890–1925

  misleading mark used
  by Winkle & Co., 1908–25
  (the wares of the
  18th century potter,
  Thomas Whieldon, were
  not marked)

Wolfe, Thomas
1784–1800, earthenware
and later, *c.* 1811–18

WOLFE
impressed

Wolfe & Hamilton
c. 1800–11, earthenware

WOLFE & HAMILTON
STOKE
impressed or painted

TUNSTALL (Staffordshire)
Adams & Sons (Potters)
Ltd., William,

impressed, 1769–1800
(on creamware)

ADAMS & CO.

impressed, 1787–1864

ADAMS

on blue-printed wares
1804–40

impressed on earthenware
1810–25

impressed mark *c.* 1815

W. ADAMS & CO.

W. Adams & Sons
1819–64, printed

W.A. & S.

impressed on parian-
ware, 1845–64

ADAMS

printed, mid-19th century

W. ADAMS

printed as 'back-stamp'
with name of pattern,
1893–1917. 'ENGLAND'
added in 1891

W.A. & CO.

printed from 1879–

printed from 1896–
with varying names
of ceramic bodies
used, e.g. TITIAN
WARE, IMPERIAL
STONE WARE, etc.

impressed on Wedgwood-
type jasperwares
1896 with confusing
establishment date

ADAMS
ESTBD 1657
TUNSTALL
ENGLAND

printed mark, 1914–40

late impressed or printed mark	$\mathcal{C}alyx \ \mathcal{W}are$
late printed mark *c.* 1950–	W. Adams & Sons England under crown
Adams, Benjamin *c.* 1800–20, earthenware and stoneware	B. ADAMS impressed
Adams, W. & T. 1866–92, earthenware printed mark	W. & T. ADAMS TUNSTALL under coat-of-arms
Beech & Hancock 1857–76, earthenware	B. & H. printed
Blackhurst, Jabez 1872–83, earthenware	JABEZ BLACKHURST printed
Booth & Son, Thomas 1872–6, earthenware	T.B. & S. printed
Booth, Thomas, G. 1876–83, earthenware name of pattern on strap	
Booth, T. G. & F. 1883–91, earthenware	T.G. & F.B. printed

Booth (Limited)
1891–1948, earthenware
  printed, 1891–1906

  painted or printed on
earthenware reproductions
of Worcester porcelain, 1905–

  variety of marks used with 'Silicon China'
from about 1906. 'England' sometimes included

  late mark of 1930–48

Boulton, Machin & Tennant
1889–99, earthenware

  mark printed or impressed

Bourne, Nixon & Co.
1828–30, earthenware
  mark impressed

BOURNE NIXON
& CO.

  printed initials included
in backstamp

B.N. & CO.

Bowers & Co., G. F.
1842–68, pottery &
  porcelain
  other printed or
impressed marks
include full name

G.F. B.B.T.
printed

Breeze & Son, John
1805–12, pottery & porcelain
(other potters of this
name were operating from
late 18th century to *c.* 1826)

BREEZE
incised or
painted

British Pottery Ltd.
1920–26, earthenware

mark printed

Brougham & Mayer
1853–5, earthenware

BROUGHAM &
MAYER
printed

Brownhills Pottery Co.
1872–96, earthenware

B.P. CO.
printed or impressed

printed marks of
c. 1880–96

Butterfield, W. & J.
1854–61, earthenware

W. & J.B.
printed

Challinor, Edward
1842–67, earthenware

E.C.

E. CHALLINOR
printed

Christie & Beardmore   C.B.   C.B.
1902–3, earthenware   F.

printed initials with
various backstamps

Clews & Co. Ltd., George
1906–61, earthenware
   printed 'globe' mark from
   1906, other marks all
   include full name

Clive, J. H.   CLIVE
1802–11, earthenware   impressed

Clive, Stephen   S.C.   S.C. & CO.
1875–80, earthenware   printed

Colley & Co. Ltd., A.
1909–14, earthenware
   mark printed or impressed

Cumberlidge & Humphreys   C. & M.
1886–9; 1893–5
earthenware   C. & M.
   marks printed or impressed   TUNSTALL

Dean & Sons, Ltd., T.
1879–1947, earthenware
   printed 1896–1947

1937–47

Eardley & Hammersley
1862–6, earthenware

E. & H.
printed

Edge & Grocott
c. 1830, earthenware
figures

EDGE & GROCOTT

Elsmore & Forster
1853–71, general ceramics

ELSMORE & FORSTER
printed with
variety of backstamps

Elsmore & Son, T.
1872–87, earthenware

ELSMORE & SON
ENGLAND

Emberton, William
1851–69, earthenware

W.E.
printed

Emberton, T. I. & J.
1869–82, earthenware

T.I. & J.E.
printed

Ford, Challinor & Co.
1865–80, earthenware

F.C.　　　　F.C. & CO.
initials used with
various printed
marks

Gater & Co., Thomas
1885–94 (at Burslem)
earthenware

G.H. & CO.
later printed initials

Gater, Hall & Co.
1895–1943, earthenware
　printed mark of 1914–

printed mark from 1914–
(firm moved to Burslem
in 1907). Taken over
by:
Barratt's of Staffordshire
1943–. Some former
  marks continued:

  other marks include
full name of Barratt's.
'Delphatic' from 1957
(Barratt's now member of the manufacturing
division of G.U.S. Ltd.)

Gem Pottery Ltd.
1961–, earthenware
  printed mark

printed

Goodfellow, Thomas
1828–59, earthenware

T. GOODFELLOW
printed

Grenville Pottery Ltd.
1946–, earthenware

Grindley & Co. Ltd., W. H.
1880–, earthenware
  printed mark to 1914
  ('England' included from 1891)

printed from 1914–25
'Ltd.' included from 1925
other marks include full
name of firm

modern printed mark

(W. H. Grindley & Co.
now a subsidiary of
Alfred Clough Ltd.)

Grindley Hotel Ware Co. Ltd.
1908–, earthenware
   mark printed from *c.* 1946–

GRINDLEY HOTEL WARE
ENGLAND
VITRIFIED

Hall, Ralph
1822–49, earthenware
   printed in backstamp
   1822–41
   c. 1836

   1841–49

R. HALL

R. HALL & SON

R. HALL & CO.

R.H. & CO.

Heath & Co., Joseph
1828–41, earthenware

J. HEATH
printed

Heath, Joseph
1845–53, earthenware
   Note: the letter 'J' is
   often printed as 'I'

J. HEATH & CO.
printed
J.H. & CO.
printed

251

Holland, John   J. HOLLAND
1852–4, earthenware   printed

Hollingshead & Kirkham   H. & K.   H. & K.
1870–1956, earthenware   TUNSTALL
  1870–1900   printed or impressed

  mark of 1890 after   H. & K.
  take-over of Wedgwood   LATE WEDGWOOD
  & Co.   impressed

  printed mark, 1900–24

  later marks all include
  name or initials of
  firm

Ingleby & Co., Thomas   T.I. & CO.
c. 1834–5, earthenware   printed

Keele Street Pottery Co.   K.S.P.
1915–, earthenware
  other later printed marks include full name

Keeling, Anthony & Enoch   A. & E. KEELING
c. 1795–1811, general ceramics

                              A.E. KEELING

Kirkland & Co. (Etruria)   K. & CO.
1892–, earthenware
  printed on various   K. & CO.
  backstamps   E

other various printed marks include full name
of Kirkland & Co. or K. & Co./E.

'Kirklands (Etruria Ltd.)'
from *c.* 1938, printed
'Kirklands (Staffordshire)
Ltd.' from *c.* 1947

Knapper & Blackhurst   KNAPPER AND
1867–71, earthenware   BLACKHURST
                              impressed or printed

(1883–8 at Burslem)
initials also probably used   K. & B.

Lingard Webster & Co. Ltd.
1900–, earthenware

impressed or printed from
c. 1946–

Maudesley & Co., J.   STONE WARE
1862–4, earthenware   J.M. & CO.
  (J.M. & Co. was also
  used by other firms)

Mayer & Maudesley   M. & M.
1837–8, earthenware   printed

Meakin Ltd., Alfred   ALFRED MEAKIN
1875–, earthenware   impressed or printed

253

'Ltd.' added in 1897
and omitted from *c.* 1930
early mark *c.* 1875–97

ALFRED MEAKIN
LTD.

Firm re-named 'Alfred
Meakin (Tunstall) Ltd.'
in *c.* 1913

printed mark from *c.* 1891
when the word 'ENGLAND'
was added

later marks include 'M. IRONSTONE'
'BLEU DE ROI', 'GLO-WHITE' and
'TRADITIONAL IRONSTONE, LEEDS'

Meir, John
c. 1812–36, earthenware

J.M.   I.M.
printed

Meir & Son, John
1837–97, earthenware
    initials used in various
    printed or impressed
    marks
    Date codes sometimes
    used e.g. $\frac{9}{75}$: Sept. 1875

J.M. & S.
        I.M. & S.
J.M. & SON

J. MEIR & SON

MEIR & SON

Pitcairns Ltd.
1895–1901, earthenware
    printed mark

Podmore, Walker & Co. 1834–59, earthenware	P.W. & CO. printed in various backstamps

Podmore, Walker &
Wedgwood, *c.* 1856–9
    various printed marks
    included the confusing,
    name of 'Wedgwood'
    Enoch Wedgwood being
    a partner. Name of firm changed to
Wedgwood & Co. in *c.* 1860

P.W. & W.

WEDGWOOD

WEDGWOOD & CO.

Rathbone, Smith & Co.
1883–97, earthenware
then:
Smith & Binnall
1897–1900, earthenware
    printed
then:
Soho Pottery, Ltd.
1901–6, earthenware
(1906–44 at Cobridge)

R.S. & CO.
printed

    other later marks include full name of
    firm and various trade-names, e.g.
    'SOLIAN WARE', 'AMBASSADOR WARE',
    'QUEENS GREEN', 'CHANTICLEER' and
    'HOMESTEAD', etc.
then:
Simpsons (Potters) Ltd.
1944–, earthenware
(at Cobridge)

Simpsons (Potters) Ltd. of Cobridge continue
to use many of the Soho Pottery Ltd.
trade-names plus 'MARLBOROUGH',
'Ironstone' and 'CHINASTYLE'
e.g.

Rathbone & Co., T.　　　　T.R. & CO.
1898–1923, earthenware　　TUNSTALL

　　late printed mark:

Richardson, Albert G.　　A.G.R. & Co. Ltd.
1915–34, earthenware　　　　printed
(moved to Cobridge
in *c.* 1934)
　　various printed marks including trade-
　　name of 'Crown Ducal'

Salt Bros.　　　　　　　　　SALT BROS.
1897–1904, earthenware　　　TUNSTALL
(then 'taken-over' by　　　　ENGLAND
T. Till & Sons of　　　printed or impressed
Burslem)

Selman, J. & W.　　　　　　SELMAN
c. 1864–65, earthenware　　impressed
figures

Shaw, Anthony　　　　　ANTHONY SHAW
1851–1900, earthenware
　　　　　　　　　　A. SHAW　　　　A. SHAW
　'& Son' added to　　　　　　　　BURSLEM
　mark in c. 1882–c. 98
　　　　　　　　　　SHAWS　　　　SHAW
　'& Son' replaced by　　　　　　BURSLEM
　'& Co.' from c. 1898
Shaws taken over by A. J. Wilkinson Ltd.
in c. 1900

Simpson, William　　　　WILLIAM SIMPSON
late 17th- early 18th-　　　in slip-trailing
century, slip-trailed earthenware
(this name is also recorded at other
pottery towns in Staffs.)

Smith, Theophilus　　　　　T. SMITH
1790–c. 97, earthenware　　impressed

Smith & Binnall　　　　　(*see* Rathbone,
1897–1900, earthenware　　　Smith & Co.,
　　　　　　　　　　　　　Tunstall)

Soho Pottery Ltd.　　　　(*see* Rathbone,
1901–6, earthenware　　　　Smith & Co.,
　　　　　　　　　　　　　Tunstall)

Summerbank Pottery Ltd. 1952–, earthenware (now Summerbank Pottery (1970) Ltd.)	SUMMERBANK printed COOPERCRAFT MADE IN ENGLAND
Tunnicliff, Michael 1828–41, earthenware toys and figures	TUNNICLIFF TUNSTALL

Turner, Goddard & Co. 1867–74, earthenware 'ROYAL PATENT IRONSTONE'	TURNER, GODDARD & CO. printed
Turner & Tomkinson 1860–72, earthenware printed in various marks	TURNER & TOMKINSON T. & T.
Turner & Sons, G. W. 1873–95, earthenware various forms of initials used in a variety of backstamps sometimes in the form of a Royal Arms 'England' added in 1891	TURNERS G.W.T. & SONS G.W.T.S. G.W.T. & S. G.T. & S.

Walker, Thomas
1845–51, earthenware
  various printed
  backstamps include
  name

T. WALKER

THOS. WALKER

Wedgwood & Co.
(Enoch Wedgwood
(Tunstall) Ltd. from 1965)
  printed mark from *c.* 1862

'Ltd.' added from 1900

WEDGWOOD & CO.
impressed

variety of printed marks used with the
following trade-names: 'IMPERIAL
PORCELAIN', 'WACOLWARE', 'WACOL
IMPERIAL', 'EVERWARE', 'ROYAL
TUNSTALL' and 'VITRILAIN'. From 1965
renamed Enoch Wedgwood (Tunstall) Ltd.
also producing former patterns of
Furnivals, 'Quail', 'Old Chelsea' and
'Denmark'

Staffs. (Tunstall)	**England**	*Staffs. (Tunstall)*
Wood & Challinor 1828–43, earthenware		w. & c. printed
Wood, Challinor & Co. *c.* 1860–64, earthenware		w.c. & co. printed
Wood & Pigott 1869–71, earthenware		w. & p. printed
Wooliscroft, George 1851–3: 1860–4 earthenware		G. WOOLISCROFT or G. WOOLLISCROFT

FRESHWATER (I.o.W.)
  Island Pottery Studio
  Lester, Joe
  earthenware, 1956–

      'Freshwater' sometimes   printed or impressed
      added to mark

WHIPPINGHAM (I.o.W.)
  Isle of Wight Pottery
  Saunders, S. E., *c.* 1930–40
  earthenware
      (same monogram used at
      Carisbrooke Pottery Works, Newport, 1929–32)

CHANNEL ISLANDS

GUERNSEY (Channel Islands)
  The Guernsey Pottery Ltd.
  red ware, studio pottery
  1961–

JERSEY (Channel Islands)   JERSEY POTTERY
  Jersey Pottery Ltd., 1946–   C.I.
  earthenware   painted

      1946–   1951
impressed or printed marks
            261

ISLE OF MAN

Isle of Man Potteries, Ltd.
earthenware, 1963–

Isle of Man
Pottery
Handmade

NORTHERN IRELAND

PORTADOWN (Co. Armagh)
  Wade (Ireland) Ltd., 1947–
  porcelain, industrial
  and artware
  (subsidiary of Wade
  Potteries, Ltd.)

printed

SCOTLAND

AIRTH (Central Region)
  Dunmore Pottery Co.,
  1903–11, earthenware,
  c. 1860–1903
  (Dunmore Pottery)

PETER GARDNER
DUNMORE POTTERY
DUNMORE
impressed

BO'NESS (Central Region)
  McNay & Sons, Charles W.
  earthenware, 1887–1958
    'Dalmeny' trade-name

stick-on labels

Marshall & Co. Ltd., John
earthenware, 1854–99
'Ltd.' added in 1897

JOHN MARSHALL &
CO.
printed

COATBRIDGE (Strathclyde)
Crest Ceramics (Scotland)
earthenware souvenirs,
etc.

DUNOON (Strathclyde)
West Highland Pottery Co. Ltd.
earthenware, 1961–
trade-names: 'Flow' ware,
'Argyll', 'Cowal'
printed

EDINBURGH (Lothian)
Millar, John, 1840–82
retailer only

JOHN MILLAR
printed

GLASGOW (Strathclyde)
Bayley, Murray & Co.
earthenware, 1875–
1900 (Saracen
Pottery Co. from *c.* 1884)

B.M. & CO.
SARACEN POTTERY
printed or impressed

Britannia Pottery Co. Ltd.
earthenware, 1920–35
'HIAWATHA' trade-name
from *c.* 1925

printed

263

Campbellfield Pottery Co. Ltd.   C.P. CO.
earthenware, 1850–1905
  'Ltd.' added *c.* 1884

  printed or impressed   CAMPBELLFIELD
  marks

                               C.P. CO. LTD.

  printed mark of *c.* 1884–
  c. 1905

  or,
  'SPRINGBURN' with thistle

Cochran & Fleming   C. & F.   C. & F.
earthenware, 1896–   G
1920   ROYAL
                          IRONSTONE CHINA

     printed

PORCELAIN OPAQUE   COCHRAN & FLEMING
GLASGOW. BRITAIN   GLASGOW BRITAIN
FLEMING   printed

Cochran & Co., R.   R.C. & CO.
general ceramics   impressed
1846–1896

Geddes & Son, John
earthenware and porcelain
c. 1806–27
  '& Son' added in 1824

JOHN GEDDES
Verreville
Pottery
printed

Govancroft Potteries Ltd.
pottery, 1913–
  trade-names: 'Croft',
  'Hamilton', 'Lunar'
  1913–49

CROWN   GOVAN
printed or impressed

printed 1949–

Grosvenor & Son, F.
pottery, *c.* 1869–1926

printed mark from 1879

Kennedy & Sons Ltd., Henry
stoneware, 1866–1929

Lockhart & Arthur
earthenware, 1855–64
  marks impressed or
  printed

L. & A.

LOCKHART &
ARTHUR

Lockhart & Co., David
earthenware, 1865–98

D.L. & CO.
printed

Lockhart & Sons Ltd., David
earthenware, 1898–1953
  printed in backstamps

D.L. & SONS

Murray & Co. Ltd., W. F.
pottery, 1870–98
  mark impressed or
  printed

Nautilus Porcelain Co.
  porcelain, 1896–1913
  printed mark

North British Pottery
earthenware, 1869–75

J.M. CO.

printed marks

J.M. & CO.   I.M. & CO.

Port Dundas Pottery Co. Ltd.
stoneware, *c.* 1850–1932

PORT DUNDAS
GLASGOW POTTERY

  impressed or printed

Possil Pottery Co.
general ceramics,
1898–1901

printed

'Star Pottery'
stoneware and 'majolica'
1880–1907

STAR

impressed or printed

Thomson & Sons, John
c. 1816– late 19th century
'& Sons' added *c.* 1866

J.T.
ANNFIELD

J.T. & SONS
GLASGOW

Williamson, John
pottery, 1844–94

WELLINGTON
POTTERY

marks impressed or
printed

WILLIAMSON
WELLINGTON
POTTERY

GREENOCK (Strathclyde)
Clyde Pottery Co. Ltd.
earthenware, *c.* 1815–
1903
'Ltd.' used *c.* 1857–63

CLYDE

G.C.P. CO.

GREENOCK
impressed or printed

Greenock Pottery
earthenware, *c.* 1820–
60

GREENOCK
POTTERY

mark impressed or
printed

Shirley & Co., Thomas   T.S. & COY.
earthenware, *c.* 1840–57
                                    T.S. & C.
                         impressed

INVERDRUIE (Highland Region)
  Castlewynd Studios, Ltd.
  earthenware and stoneware
    trade-names, 'Castlewynd'
    'Aviemore'
  Started Edinburgh 1950
  moved to Gifford 1954
  (Castlewynd Studios
  (Highland China) 1974
  at Fort William)

                         printed

KIRKCALDY (Lothian)   R.H. & S.
  Heron & Son, Robert
  earthenware, *c.* 1850–
  1929
    Date of 1820 in mark
    is that of an earlier
    pottery taken over by Heron

                         printed

Methven & Sons, David   D.M. & S.
19th century–*c.* 1930
earthenware

                         METHVEN

                    D. METHVEN & SONS

NORTH BERWICK   Tantallon
(Lothian)   Ceramics
  Tantallon Ceramics   NORTH BERWICK
  earthenware, 1962–

                   268

PAISLEY (Strathclyde)
Brown & Co., Robert   BROWN PAISLEY
earthenware, 1876–1933

printed or impressed

PORTOBELLO (nr. Edinburgh, Lothian)
Buchan & Co. Ltd., A. W.
stoneware, 1867
trade-name: 'Thistle'
printed mark from 1949–

Gray & Sons, Ltd., W. A.   W.A. GRAY
pottery, *c.* 1857–1931   printed
'& Sons' from 1870, 'Ltd.'
from 1926

Milne Cornwall & Co.   MILNE CORNWALL
stoneware, *c.* 1830–40   & CO.
                            impressed

Rathbone & Co., Thomas   T.R. & CO.
earthenware, *c.* 1810–45

   marks printed or   T. RATHBONE
   impressed   P

Scott Brothers   SCOTT BROTHERS
earthenware, *c.* 1786–96

                   SCOTT BROS.   SCOTT
   marks impressed   P.B.

PRESTONPANS (Lothian)   FOWLER THOMPSON
Fowler, Thompson & Co.   & CO.
earthenware, *c.* 1820–40   printed or impressed

Gordon's Pottery earthenware, 18th century– 1832	GORDON impressed
initials in printed backstamps	G.G.
Watson's Pottery earthenware, *c*. 1750– 1840	WATSON impressed
	WATSON & CO.
mark of *c*. 1800–40	printed

WALES

CARDIFF AND SWANSEA
(Glamorgan)
    Primavesi & Son, F.
    retailers of earthenware
        c. 1850–1915 ('& Son'
        added *c*. 1860)
	F. PRIMAVESI & SON
	CARDIFF
	Full name in a
	variety of marks

CARDIGAN (Dyfed)
    Cardigan Potteries
    earthenware, *c*. 1875–90
        printed mark
	CARDIGAN
	POTTERIES
	WOODWARD & CO.
	CARDIGAN

CREIGIAU (nr. Cardiff)
    Creigiau Pottery, 1947–
    Southcliffe, R. G. & Co. Ltd.
    earthenware in copper
    lustre traditional style
	'Creigiau'

LLANDUDNO (Gwynedd)
Cambrian Ceramic Co. Ltd.
(formerly Cambrian Pottery
Co. Ltd.), earthenware
1958–

CAMBRIAN
STUDIO
WARE
impressed or printed

LLANELLY (Dyfed)
Guest & Dewsbury
earthenware, 1877–1927
printed initials in
backstamps

G. & D.L.

G.D.
L

South Wales Pottery
earthenware, *c.* 1839–58
Chambers & Co.
c. 1839–54
Coombs & Holland
c. 1854–58

CHAMBERS
LLANELLY

S.W.P.

printed or impressed

NANTGARW (Glamorgan)
Nantgarw China Works
porcelain, 1813–14; 1817–22
Billingsley, William &
Walker, Samuel
'C.W.' stands for 'China
Works' (transferred to
Swansea in 1814 until
1817)

NANT-GARW
C.W.
impressed
(painted and stencilled
marks used, but
also found on later
copies)

SWANSEA (Glamorgan)
Swansea Pottery, Cambrian Pottery
c. 1783–1870, earthenwares

c. 1783–, mark impressed　　SWANSEA

　　　　　　　　　　　　　CAMBRIAN POTTERY

impressed or printed　　　　CAMBRIA
marks, *c.* 1783–1810

impressed or printed　　DILLWYN & CO.
marks, *c.* 1811–17　　　　SWANSEA

　　　　　　　　　　　　D. & CO.

impressed from *c.* 1817–24　BEVINGTON & CO.

printed from *c.* 1847–50

impressed, *c.* 1847–50　　　CYMRO
　　　　　　　　　　　　　STONE CHINA

impressed, *c.* 1824–50　　　DILLWYN

Evans, David & Glasson
pottery, *c.* 1850–62
　impressed or printed

Evans, D. J. & Co.　　　D.J. EVANS & CO.
pottery, *c.* 1862–70

　　　　　　　　　　　　EVANS & CO.

printed, *c.* 1862–70

Swansea porcelain
impressed marks, 1814–22

SWANSEA

printed or written in red
enamel

SWANSEA

impressed, sometimes
with 'SWANSEA'

Swansea

DILLWYN & CO.

rare impressed mark
of *c.* 1820

BEVINGTON & CO.

Baker, Bevans & Irwin
Glamorgan Pottery
earthenware, 1813–38

BAKER BEVANS
& IRWIN
printed or impressed

example of printed mark

The name of Pellatt & Green, retailers
of St. Paul's Church Yard, London, is
sometimes seen on Welsh wares of *c.* 1805–30

Calland & Co., John F.   C. & CO.
Landore Pottery
earthenware, 1852–56   CALLAND SWANSEA

YNYSMEDW (nr. Swansea)   Y.M.P.   Y.P.
Ynysmedw Pottery
earthenware, *c.* 1850–70   impressed

IRELAND

BELLEEK (Co. Fermanagh)   BELLEEK
    porcelain, 1863–   CO. FERMANAGH
    McBirney, David &
    Armstrong, Robert   FERMANAGH
                         POTTERY
                         impressed

    impressed or printed
    mark of 1863–80

    early version of usual
    mark, 1863–91

    post-1891 version
    includes 'Ireland'
    and 'Co. Fermanagh'
    to comply with the
    McKinley Tariff Act

                     printed

CORK
   Carrigaline Pottery Ltd.
   earthenware, 1928–   CARRIG WARE
                                          CARRIGALINE
      printed marks   POTTERY

DUBLIN
   Chambers, John, *c.* 1730–
   c. 1745
   tin-glazed earthenware
      inscription painted on
      plate

   Delamain, Captain Henry (*d.* 1757)
   1752–*c.* 1771

   Donovan & Son, John   DONOVAN
   decorator of English
   pottery and porcelain   *DONOVAN*
   c. 1770–1829   *DUBLIN*
                                   painted
      'DONOVAN' impressed on
      wares made to order

   Vodrey's Pottery   VODREY DUBLIN
   earthenware, 1872–*c.* 85   POTTERY

                                  impressed

LIMERICK
  Stritch, John, *c.* 1760
  tin-glazed earthenware

Made by John Stritch
Limerick, 4th June 1761

inscription on plate

ADDENDUM OF RECENT MANUFAC-
TURERS, OTHER CHANGES, ETC.

BOURNEMOUTH (Dorset)
Purbeck Pottery Ltd.
stoneware, Dec. 1965–

printed marks

Purbeck
Pottery
England

BROADSTAIRS (Kent)
Broadstairs Pottery Ltd.
stoneware, 1966–
printed mark

BRUTON (Somerset)
Goddard Ltd., Elaine
earthenware, 1939–

mark printed label

CHESTERFIELD (Derbyshire)
Price, Powell & Co. Ltd.   No registered
earthenware, 1740–   trade mark
(Ltd. from 1961)
Now subsidiary of Pearsons of Chesterfield

CHURCH GRESLEY
(Derbyshire)
    Mason, Cash & Co. Ltd.
    Pool Potteries, 1901
    domestic earthenware
    (Ltd. Co. since 1941)

products
unmarked

DARTMOUTH (Devon)
    Britannia Designs, Ltd.
    earthenware, 1959
      mark an applied label
      used from 1971

ELKESLEY (Nottinghamshire)
    Aston, Christopher S.
    stoneware, 1968
    (moved to Elkesley
    from Bawtry in 1971)

applied label

FARNHAM (Surrey)
    Harris & Sons, A.
    earthenware, 1872
    (established in 1864
    at Elstead, Surrey)

No special mark
used

HINDHEAD (Surrey)
    Surrey Ceramic Co. Ltd.
    Kingswood Pottery
    earthenware and
    stoneware, 1956–

LIVERPOOL (Merseyside)
Prince William Pottery Co.
earthenware, 1953–

'PRINCE WILLIAM'

LONDON
Macbride, Kitty
(Brown & Muntzer)
earthenware figures of
mice. Trade-name:
'The Happy Mice of
Berkeley Square'
1960–

Kitty MacBride
England

PAIGNTON (Devon)
Barn Pottery, Ltd.
earthenware, 1964

Trade-name 'Barn' ware

REDRUTH (Cornwall)
Foster's Pottery Co.
earthenware, 1949–

FOSTER'S
POTTERY
REDRUTH

stamped mark

STOKE D'ABERTON (Surrey)
Everson, Ronald
porcelain and bone-china
1953
mark in the form of
a dated signature

Ronald Everson

HANLEY (Staffordshire)
   Mason's Ironstone China Ltd.
   earthenware, March 1968
   (from March 1974 name changed
   to: Mason's Ironstone, a Division
   of Josiah Wedgwood & Sons Ltd.)
     printed marks

LONGTON (Staffordshire)
   Anton Potteries, Ltd., Jon
   ironstone, 1974–
   (pottery established
   c. 1874, 'Crown Clarence'
   from *c.* 1953–1971
   Jon Anton Potteries
   1971–74)

   mark on bone-china

Blyth Pottery (Longton) Ltd.
earthenware (taken over by John Tams Ltd.
in April, 1973 and no longer trading on own
account)

LONGTON (Staffordshire)
  Hostess Tableware
  Thomas Poole &
  Gladstone China Ltd.
    'Royal Stafford' and
    'Hostess' bone china
    and 'Hostess' ironstone
    1971–

Hostess Tableware

FINE BONE CHINA
STAFFS, ENGLAND

& other full marks

Royal Albert Ltd.
(Royal Doulton Tableware
Ltd.) Ltd. added 1970
bone-china
    'Royal Albert' previously
    used by Thomas C.
    Wild & Sons Ltd.

ROYAL ALBERT
Bone China
ENGLAND

printed

Royal Grafton Bone China
(A. B. Jones & Sons, Ltd.
part of Crown Lynn Potteries
Group, N.Z. from 1971–)
bone-china from 1959–

Royal Tuscan
bone-china, *c.* 1962–
(Division of Wedgwood
Group from 1966)

STOKE (Staffordshire)
Baifield Productions Ltd.
(S. Fielding & Co. Ltd., Crown
Devon Group), 1963–

Blakeney Art Pottery
earthenware, 1968–
　'Flow Blue Victoria'
　printed ware, Kent
　Staffordshire figures
　and floral art containers.
M. J. Bailey & S. K. Bailey
Note the lion and harp
in coat-of-arms are in
reverse positions to the
authentic version

printed
backstamps in
blue

Similar Royal
Arms mark used,
with 'Romantic'
pattern

Blakeney Art Pottery (*cont.*)

IRONSTONE
STAFFORDSHIRE
ENGLAND

printed backstamp
in brown 'M.J.B.'
(Michael J. Bailey)

similar backstamp
used with:
FLO BLUE
T.M. STAFFORDSHIRE
ENGLAND

FLO BLUE
T.M. STAFFORDSHIRE
ENGLAND

Dorothy Ann Floral China
bone china floral
jewellery, 1946

STOKE ON TRENT
ENGLAND

TUNSTALL (Staffordshire)
　Wedgwood (Tunstall) Ltd., Enoch
　name changed from Wedgwood & Co. Ltd.
　in 1965 (see p. 259)

Patent Office Registration Mark

From 1842 until 1883 many manufacturers' wares are marked with the following 'diamond-mark', which is an indication that the design was registered with the British Patent Office; ceramics and glass are Classes IV and III, as indicated in the topmost section of the mark, and gave copyright protection for a period of three years (see Appendix B and Preface, page 11).

The date of the 'diamond mark' only indicates the time of registration, but a popular form of decoration was often produced for far longer than the three years. Printed marks usually refer to the applied pattern, whereas impressed or moulded applied versions are more likely to relate to the form of the ware.

When checking date to determine the name of the manufacturer it will sometimes be the case that the design was registered by retailers, wholesalers or even foreign manufacturers.

'Diamond-marks' impressed into bone-china can often be more accurately read when held before a strong artificial light.

Example of ceramic
design registered on
23rd May 1842

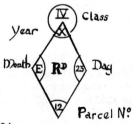

APPENDIX A

Index to letters for each year and month from 1842 *to*
1867:

Years

1842 X	1849 S	1856 L	1863 G
1843 H	1850 V	1857 K	1864 N
1844 C	1851 P	1858 B	1865 W
1845 A	1852 D	1859 M	1866 Q
1846 I	1853 Y	1860 Z	1867 T
1847 F	1854 J	1861 R	
1848 U	1855 E	1862 O	

Months

January	C	July	I	
February	G	August	R	For September 1857
March	W	September	D	query letter R used
April	H	October	B	from 1st–19th Sept.
May	E	November	K	For December 1860
June	M	December	A	query letter K used.

Index to letters for each year and month from 1868 *to*
1883:

Example of ceramic design,
registered on 6th January 1868

Years

1868 X	1872 I	1876 V	1880 J
1869 H	1873 F	1877 P	1881 E
1870 C	1874 U	1878 D	1882 L
1871 A	1875 S	1879 Y	1883 K

Months

Jan. C	April H	July I	Oct. B
Feb. G	May E	Aug. R	Nov. K
Mar. W	June M	Sept. D	Dec. A

For Registration marks brought in with W for the year, see below:

From 1st to 6th March, 1878, the following Registration Mark was issued:

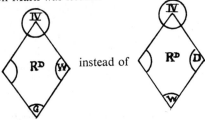

instead of

From 1884 this method of dating registrations ceased and the designs were numbered consecutively in the following manner: 'Rd. 12345' or 'Rd. No. 12345'. The following table gives a guide up until 1910 to the range of numbers used within a year:

Registered in January		Registered in January	
1	1884	90483	1888
19734	1885	116648	1889
40480	1886	141273	1890
64520	1887	163767	1891

185713	1892	368154	1901
205240	1893	385500	1902
224720	1894	402500	1903
246975	1895	420000	1904
268392	1896	447000	1905
291241	1897	471000	1906
311658	1898	494000	1907
331707	1899	519500	1908
351202	1900	550000	1909

Information concerning the work of the full members of the Craftsmen Potters Association (modern studio-potters) is well provided by an excellent directory, *Potters*, where the full particulars, including the mark and an illustration of the ware of 138 potters, are given. This directory may be obtained from the Craftsmen Potters Shop, William Blake House, Marshall Street, London, W.1., price 75p, plus postage.

The part of the Class IV Design Index in the Public Record Office that relates to pottery and porcelain is included in Appendix B, pages 288 to 392.

APPENDIX B

Index of Names and Dates of Manufacturers, Retailers, Wholesalers and others who registered designs from 1842 to 1883

(See Appendix A, page 284, and Preface, page 12)

Date	Parcel No.	Patent No.	Factory, Retailer Wholesaler, etc	Place
1842				
Sept 22	1	1694	James Dixon & Sons	Sheffield
Nov 2	1	2152	Joseph Wolstenholme	Sheffield
3	1	2163	idem	Sheffield
26	3	2503–4	Henry Hunt	London
Dec 2	3	2599–00	Joseph Clementson	Shelton
30	2	3346	James Edwards	Burslem
1843				
Jan 24	2	4296–7	John Ridgway & Co.	Shelton
Feb 3	4	4462	T. Woodfield	London
21	1	5266–70	Samuel Alcock & Co.	Burslem
Mar 21	5	5993–4	Josiah Wedgwood & Sons	Etruria
31	6	6266	Samuel Alcock & Co.	Burslem
May 2	4	6978	Josiah Wedgwood & Sons	Etruria
5	1	7037	W. S. Kennedy	Burslem
11	2	7074	idem	Burslem
13	4	7122	Jones & Walley	Cobridge
June 14	5	7503–5	Samuel Alcock & Co.	Burslem
Aug 30	8	9678–80	James Edwards	Burslem
Oct 6	2	10370	idem	Burslem
Nov 10	3	11292	Minton & Co.	Stoke
28	5	11690	Thos. Dimmock & Co.	Shelton
Dec 14	10	12331	G. F. Bowers & Co.	Tunstall

APPENDIX B

Date	Parcel No.	Patent No.	Factory, Retailer Wholesaler, etc	Place
1844				
Feb 15	9	16264–5	Samuel Alcock & Co.	Burslem
20	4	16374–5	idem	Burslem
Mar 1	6	16687	Hamilton & Moore	Longton
5	3	16831	Mellor, Venables & Co.	Burslem
7	4	16871	J. & T. Lockett	Lane End
Apr 3	3	17566–72	Thos. Edwards	Burslem
11	4	17714	Hilditch & Hopwood	Lane End
May 7	4	18207	Thos. Dimmock & Co.	Shelton
June 29	3	19182	idem	Shelton
July 20	5	19977–9	John Ridgway & Co.	Shelton
30	2	20332–4	Herbert Minton & Co.	Stoke
Aug 15	3	20779	King, Knight & Elkin	Stoke
21	7	21069–73	Herbert Minton & Co.	Stoke
Sept 9	7	21450	Cyples, Barlow & Cyples	Lane End
19	4	21700–1	Jn. Ridgeway & Co.	Shelton
21	2	21715	Henry Hunt	London
30	7	21960	Charles Meigh	Hanley
Oct 14	4	22158	Copeland & Garrett	Stoke
17	3	22192	Clementson, Young & Jameson	Shelton
30	4	22394–6	Herbert Minton & Co.	Stoke
Nov 6	4	22424	idem	Stoke
11	5	22490	James Edwards	Burslem
13	4	22499–500	John Ridgway & Co.	Shelton
22	4	22834	Thos. Dimmock & Co.	Shelton
26	3	22883	Ray & Wynne	Longton
Dec 2	3	22919–20	Copeland & Garrett	Stoke
7	4	23207–10	Thos. Edwards	Burslem
16	6	23593	Willm. Ridgway, Son & Co.	Hanley
24	2	23843	John Meir & Son	Tunstall
1845				
Jan 11	6	24846	George Phillips	Longport

289

APPENDIX B

Date	Parcel No.	Patent No.	Factory, Retailer Wholesaler, etc	Place
15	2	24996	Clementson, Young & Jameson	Shelton
21	6	25199	T. J. & J. Mayer	Longport
27	5	25273	John Rose & Co.	Coalport
Feb 26	5	26532–3	W. S. Kennedy	Burslem
27	3	26543	George Phillips	Longport
Mar 5	1	26608	Copeland & Garrett	Stoke
6	5	26617	Herbert Minton & Co.	Stoke
17	10	26939	idem	Stoke
20	1	26949	idem	Stoke
31	4	27034	Thos. Pearce	London
Apr 10	1	27202	idem	London
25	2	27350	Copeland & Garrett	Stoke
26	1	27352	George Pearce	London
26	3	27354	T. & R. Boote, Walley & Jones	Burslem, Cobridge and Hanley
30	2	27383	Jacob Furnival & Co.	Cobridge
May 8	2	27451	Herbert Minton & Co.	Stoke
10	3	27482	Walley & T. & R. Boote	Cobridge and Burslem
31	1	27800	Francis Morley	Shelton
June 19	1	28150	George Phillips	Longport
26	3	28296	Minton & Co.	Stoke
July 5	1	28668–71	George Phillips	Longport
5	2	28672	Enoch Wood	Burslem
26	1	29173	William Adams & Sons	Stoke
Aug 28	3	29993	Joseph Clementson	Shelton
Sept 4	3	30161–3	Copeland & Garrett	Stoke
11	2	30286	Thos. Phillips & Son	Burslem
19	1	30383	Minton & Co.	Stoke
Oct 6	1	30543–4	H. Minton & Co.	Stoke
21	1	30699	Copeland & Garrett	Stoke

APPENDIX B

Date	Parcel No.	Patent No.	Factory, Retailer Wholesaler, etc	Place
22	2	30701	Clementson & Young	Shelton
Nov 15	2	31128	Bayley & Ball	Longton
22	2	31329	Minton & Co.	Stoke
Dec 4	4	31670–3	John Ridgway	Shelton
27	2	32553	James Edwards	Burslem
29	2	32555	Joseph Clementson	Shelton
30	3	32601	Furnival & Clark	Hanley
1846				
Jan 7	2	32698	Joseph Clementson	Shelton
24	2	33319	Jacob Furnival & Co.	Cobridge
Feb 26	5	34031	T. J. & J. Mayer	Longport
Mar 2	4	34108	Minton & Co.	Stoke
11	2	34281–5	W. S. Kennedy	Burslem
Apr 7	1	34564–66	idem	Burslem
17	3	34684	Copeland & Garrett	Stoke
May 21	3	35030–1	H. Minton & Co.	Stoke
26	2	35116–7	idem	Stoke
June 6	1	35219	W. Chamberlain & Co.	Worcester
26	2	35777	H. Minton & Co.	Stoke
30	3	35795	John Goodwin	Longton
July 11	1	36047	J. K. Knight	Longton
16	1	36167	Ridgway, Son & Co.	Hanley
17	1	36263	John Ridgway & Co.	Shelton
21	1	36278	F. Morley & Co.	Shelton
Aug 1	2	36447–8	Josiah Wedgwood & Sons	Etruria
3	1	36450	idem	Etruria
3	2	36451–2	H. Minton & Co.	Stoke
Sept 3	2	37170	G. Phillips	Longport
3	3	37171–2	F. Morley & Co.	Shelton
14	4	37254	Copeland & Garrett	Stoke
26	2	37419–21	John Ridgway & Co.	Shelton
29	3	37586	T. J. & J. Mayer	Longport
Oct 26	1	37806	F. Morley & Co.	Shelton
26	5	37864	J. Edwards	Burslem

APPENDIX B

Date	Parcel No.	Patent No.	Factory, Retailer Wholesaler, etc	Place
Nov 3	1	37935	Ridgway & Abington	Hanley
5	2	37986	G. Phillips	Longport
12	3	38068	C. Meigh	Hanley
16	2	38113	H. Minton & Co.	Stoke
21	2	38291–2	Thos. Furnival & Co.	Hanley
Dec 3	4	38606	Ridgway & Abington	Hanley
4	2	38610	H. Minton & Co.	Stoke
10	3	38786	Joseph Clementson	Shelton
14	3	39480	James Edwards	Burslem
14	4	39481	Minton & Co.	Stoke
16	1	39519	John Goodwin	Longton
17	2	39544–5	Copeland & Garrett	Stoke
26	5	39614	Henry Hunt	London
29	2	39703	Edward Challinor	Tunstall
31	3	39746	Josiah Wedgwood & Sons	Etruria
1847				
Jan 9	4	40104–5	John Ridgway & Co.	Shelton
9	7	40110	Copeland & Garrett	Stoke
Feb 2	7	41213	T. & R. Boote	Burslem
8	5	41266–7	T. J. & J. Mayer	Longton
15	4	41459–60	Copeland & Garrett	Stoke
Mar 17	3	42044	John Wedge Wood	Tunstall
17	6	42047–8	John Ridgway & Co.	Shelton
22	2	42233	Bailey & Ball	Longton
23	7	42279	Herbert Minton & Co.	Stoke
30	1	42363	James Edwards	Burslem
Apr 3	6	42435	Samuel Alcock & Co.	Burslem
27	1	42804	idem	Burslem
May 12	4	43154	Copeland & Garrett	Stoke
14	1	43170–1	Herbert Minton & Co.	Stoke
June 11	4	43536	James Edwards	Burslem
11	6	43557	Joseph Alexander	Norwich
21	5	43728	John Rose & Co.	Coalport
25	2	43780	James Edwards	Burslem

APPENDIX B

Date	Parcel No.	Patent No.	Factory, Retailer Wholesaler, etc	Place
July 5	5	43916–7	Mellor, Venables & Co.	Burslem
15	1	44014–5	idem	Burslem
16	5	44036–9	James Edwards	Burslem
27	3	44398	T. J. & J. Mayer	Longport
Aug 3	3	44872	John Rose & Co.	Coalport
16	2	45088	James Edwards	Burslem
17	2	45091–2	W. T. Copeland	Stoke
19	3	45175	H. Minton & Co.	Stoke
26	2	45367	James Edwards	Burslem
Sept 9	3	45730	William Taylor Copeland	Stoke
16	3	45822	idem	Stoke
25	5	45992	John Wedge Wood	Tunstall
Oct 1	4	46130	Thos. Peake	Tunstall
2	5	46192–4	John Ridgway & Co.	Shelton
4	3	46232	H. Minton & Co.	Stoke
8	4	46265	John Wedge Wood	Tunstall
13	1	46299	W. T. Copeland	Stoke
23	2	46516–8	H. Minton & Co.	Stoke
27	1	46529	John Ridgway & Co.	Shelton
Nov 11	4	46886	H. Minton & Co.	Stoke
23	4	47183	J. Wedgwood & Co.	Etruria
Dec 1	2	47417–20	John Rose & Co.	Coalport
10	3	47562–3	Minton & Co. & John Bell	Stoke
15	4	48130	Minton & Co.	Stoke
1848				
Jan 1	4	48540–2	Barker & Till	Burslem
6	4	48717	Geo. Grainger	Worcester
18	2	49040	W. T. Copeland	Stoke
Feb 11	3	49780–1	H. Minton & Co.	Stoke
29	12	50473	Minton & Co.	Stoke
Mar 4	4	50549	Minton & Co.	Stoke
7	1	50635–6	Ridgway & Abington	Hanley
14	2	50798	W. T. Copeland	Stoke
15	2	50803	idem	Stoke

Date	Parcel No.	Patent No.	Factory, Retailer Wholesaler, etc	Place
20	7	50994	Wood & Brownfield	Cobridge
27	8	51185–91	J. & S. Alcock Jnr.	Cobridge
Apr 15	4	51542	John Ridgway & Co.	Shelton
17	6	51599	Frederick Harrison	London
22	3	51661	Josiah Wedgwood & Sons	Etruria
27	4	51763	idem	Etruria
28	5	51768	Giovanni Franchi	London
May 30	3	52162	Thos. Peake	Tunstall
June 20	4	52402	G. F. Bowers & Co.	Tunstall
30	2	52529	W. T. Copeland	Stoke
30	3	52530	Ridgway & Abington	Hanley
Aug 10	3	53782	Geo. Grainger	Worcester
16	8	53876	Thos. Pinder	Burslem
23	2	54018	John Wedge Wood	Tunstall
26	2	54067	John Meir & Son	Tunstall
Sept 15	3	54438	W. T. Copeland	Stoke
18	4	54487	Charles Meigh	Hanley
25	4	54578–9	Giovanni Franchi	London
30	7	54662	John Ridgway & Co.	Shelton
Oct 17	3	54901	T. & R. Boote	Burslem
Nov 4	2	55174	W. T. Copeland	Stoke
13	4	55337	idem	Stoke
21	5	55456–7	Minton & Co.	Stoke
27	2	55766	John Ridgway & Co.	Shelton
Dec 16	3	56631–3	James Edwards	Burslem
28	2	56845	John Ridgway	Shelton
1849				
Jan 3	2	56978	William Adams & Sons	Stoke
20	2	57506–8	W. Davenport & Co.	Longport
Feb 2	4	58069	Mellor, Venables & Co.	Burslem
16	5	58461	Minton & Co.	Stoke
16	11	58474	Ridgway & Abington	Hanley
26	2	58578	John Rose & Co.	Coalport
Mar 13	2	58874	Joseph Clementson	Shelton

Date	Parcel No.	Patent No.	Factory, Retailer Wholesaler, etc	Place
26	5	59232	Minton & Co.	Stoke
27	2	59245	Cope & Edwards	Longton
31	2	59286	John Ridgway & Co.	Shelton
Apr 2	5	59308	Podmore, Walker & Co.	Tunstall
10	4	59400	W. T. Copeland	Stoke
16	6	59571	C. J. Mason	Longton
May 24	1	60081	Mr. Wedge Wood	Tunstall
June 7	3	60265	T. J. & J. Mayer	Longport
July 16	2	61347	Ridgway & Abington	Hanley
Aug 11	4	61865	W. T. Copeland	Stoke
15	2	61986	H. Minton & Co.	Stoke
17	2	62003	W. T. Copeland	Stoke
27	5	62316	Mellor, Venables & Co.	Burslem
Sept 14	6	62498	F. & R. Pratt & Co.	Fenton
28	6	62690–4	J. Ridgway	Shelton
Oct 10	2	62883	idem	Shelton
12	4	62914	Minton & Co.	Stoke
26	5	63267	J. Hollinshead	Shelton
Nov 8	6	63490	John Cliff Quince	London
9	4	63523	W. T. Copeland	Stoke
17	2	63718	Minton & Co.	Stoke
22	2	64319	W. T. Copeland	Stoke
30	5	64627	John Rose & Co.	Coalport
Dec 6	3	64739	W. T. Copeland	Stoke
15	4	64982	T. J. & J. Mayer	Longport
1850				
Jan 3	1	65884	W. Davenport & Co.	Longport
14	4	66266–7	J. Ridgway	Shelton
26	6	66862	G. Grainger	Worcester
Feb 13	1	67398	idem	Worcester
13	3	67413	J. & M. P. Bell & Co.	Glasgow
27	4	67783	G. Grainger	Worcester
Mar 9	3	67987	W. T. Copeland	Stoke
30	9	68489	John Rose & Co.	Coalport

APPENDIX B

Date	Parcel No.	Patent No.	Factory, Retailer Wholesaler, etc	Place
Apr 4	4	68623	T. J. & J. Mayer	Longport
8	1	68720	J. Clementson	Shelton
13	7	68797	Minton & Co.	Stoke
18	11	68959	John Rose & Co.	Coalport
24	3	69142	William Pierce	London
25	3	69149	Minton & Co.	Stoke
June 4	1	69679	J. & M. P. Bell & Co.	Glasgow
5	3	69685	Barker & Son	Burslem
21	4	69884	E. Walley	Cobridge
July 2	2	70088	T. J. & J. Mayer	Longport
16	5	70364	C. & W. K. Harvey	Longton
Sept 9	5	71843	Thomas Till	Burslem
16	8	71952	J. & M. P. Bell & Co.	Glasgow
16	9	71953–4	J. Ridgway	Shelton
19	2	71989	W. T. Copeland	Stoke
21	1	72057	Mellor, Venables & Co.	Burslem
Oct 9	2	72395–6	Minton & Co.	Stoke
17	6	72544	W. T. Copeland	Stoke
Nov 4	4	73327	J. Wedgwood & Sons	Etruria
20	7	73693	F. Morley & Co.	Shelton
22	3	73719	John Rose & Co.	Coalport
Dec 5	3	74138	F. Morley & Co.	Shelton
19	5	74785	John Rose & Co.	Coalport
19	6	74786	T. J. & J. Mayer	Longport
20	6	75148	W. T. Copeland	Stoke
1851				
Jan 20	4	75883–4	James Green	London
Feb 10	9	76664	William Brownfield	Cobridge
Mar 17	13	77481–91	J. Ridgway & Co.	Shelton
31	4	77986	J. & M. P. Bell & Co.	Glasgow
Apr 9	2	78268	Thos. Till & Son	Burslem
11	4	78309–10	J. & M. P. Bell & Co.	Glasgow
11	6	78312	W. S. Kennedy	Burslem
14	7	78398–401	J. & M. P. Bell & Co.	Glasgow

APPENDIX B

Date	Parcel No.	Patent No.	Factory, Retailer Wholesaler, etc	Place
26	3	78634	E. Walley	Cobridge
May 30	4	79085	W. T. Copeland	Stoke
June 7	4	79164	J. Ridgway & Co.	Shelton
11	2	79183	W. T. Copeland	Stoke
11	3	79184	Ralph Scragg	Hanley
19	5	79300	W. T. Copeland	Stoke
July 10	3	79588	R. Britton & Co.	Leeds
14	3	79684	W. T. Copeland	Stoke
21	7	79750–3	T. & R. Boote	Burslem
24	2	79782	Thos. Till & Son	Burslem
26	3	79802	C. Collinson & Co.	Burslem
Aug 16	2	80184	Ridgway & Abington	Hanley
Sept 2	4	80365	T. J. & J. Mayer	Longport
19	3	80629–30	T. & R. Boote	Burslem
29	4	80815–16	James Edwards	Burslem
30	3	80826	idem	Burslem
Oct 1	1	80827	W. T. Copeland	Stoke
7	3	80887	Chamberlain & Co.	Worcester
10	4	80910–1	W. Brownfield	Cobridge
10	6	80913	T. & R. Boote	Burslem
14	4	80980	Thos. Till & Son	Burslem
16	4	80989	W. Brownfield	Cobridge
17	3	80997	George Bowden Sander	London
21	3	81057	Wm. Ridgway	Shelton
Nov 1	5	81225–6	Geo. B. Sander	London
10	4	81492	Ralph Scragg	Hanley
12	6	81510–12	Minton & Co.	Stoke
13	2	81518	Charles Meigh & Son	Hanley
14	4	81558	Geo. B. Sander	London
Dec 2	2	81815	T. J. & J. Mayer	Burslem
4	3	81843–4	Minton & Co.	Stoke
5	5	81864	John Ridgway & Co.	Shelton
8	8	81960	W. T. Copeland	Stoke
15	6	82052	Geo. B. Sander	London

APPENDIX B

Date	Parcel No.	Patent No.	Factory, Retailer Wholesaler, etc	Place
1852				
Jan 27	1	83342	W. & G. Harding	Burslem
Feb 17	1	83826	Venables & Baines	Burslem
Mar 4	2	84133–4	Wm. Brownfield	Cobridge
13	3	84239	Wm. Ridgway	Shelton
22	7	84385	Ralph Scragg	Hanley
24	3	84406	James Edwards	Burslem
24	4	84407	Minton & Co.	Stoke
25	1	84410	John Milner	Cobridge
26	3	84471	J. & M. P. Bell & Co.	Glasgow
Apr 1	1	84541	Thos. Till & Son	Burslem
8	4	84615	idem	Burslem
21	4	84837	George Ray	Longton
May 5	5	85001–2	J. M. Blashfield	London
6	5	85008	Geo. Bowden Sander	London
7	2	85010–3	J. M. Blashfield	London
14	5	85081	W. T. Copeland	Stoke
18	1	85102	Minton & Co.	Stoke
June 1	2	85224–5	J. M. Blashfield	London
5	5	85248	Minton & Co.	Stoke
14	4	85354	W. T. Copeland	Stoke
21	2	85404	J. & T. Lockett	Longton
July 5	3	85619	J. Pankhurst & Co.	Hanley
23	3	85803–4	Minton & Co.	Stoke
Aug 4	3	86070–1	W. T. Copeland	Stoke
13	5	86126	Thos. Till & Son	Burslem
25	4	86318	Chas. Meigh & Son	Hanley
25	5	86319	Geo. Bowden Sander	London
Sept 3	7	86473	Minton & Co.	Stoke
15	5	86649	Thos. Till & Son	Burslem
16	1	86657	Minton & Co.	Stoke
24	1	86815	idem	Stoke
27	3	86857	Warburton & Britton	Leeds
Oct 1	6	86931	W. T. Copeland	Stoke
7	5	87040	Ralph Scragg	Hanley

Date	Parcel No.	Patent No.	Factory, Retailer Wholesaler, etc	Place
23	4	87219	Davenports & Co.	Longport
25	2	87228	Wm. Brownfield	Cobridge
30	3	87464	Marple, Turner & Co.	Hanley
Nov 4	5	87541	John Holland	Tunstall
11	3	87633	Minton & Co.	Stoke
22	3	87883	J. Pankhurst & J. Dimmock	Hanley
25	4	88037	Keys & Mountford	Stoke
Dec 16	4	88350	John Rose & Co.	Coalport
27	1	88693	Warburton & Britton	Leeds
1853				
Jan 3	3	88808–9	W. T. Copeland	Stoke
12	6	88978	Thos. Goodfellow	Tunstall
14	3	88987	Davenports & Co.	Longport
18	2	89050	idem	Longport
Feb 4	9	89469	J. Pankhurst & J. Dimmock	Hanley
10	2	89626	Geo. Wooliscroft	Tunstall
11	6	89646	Thos. Worthington & J. Green	Shelton
12	3	89661–3	Minton & Co.	Stoke
17	4	89722–3	W. S. Kennedy & Co.	Burslem
26	5	89958	W. T. Copeland	Stoke
Mar 10	2	90253	J. & M. P. Bell & Co.	Glasgow
17	5	90360	J. W. Pankhurst & Co.	Hanley
19	2	90372	Minton & Co.	Stoke
Apr 4	6	90610	John Rose & Co.	Coalport
23	2	90876	Wm. Adams & Sons	Stoke
May 7	5	91121–4	John Alcock	Cobridge
June 7	3	91329	Geo. Wood & Co.	Shelton
14	2	91405–6	Livesley, Powell & Co.	Hanley
22	3	91469	Pankhurst & Dimmock	Hanley
24	3	91487	Geo. Wooliscroft	Tunstall
24	11	91512–3	Ridgway & Co.	Shelton

APPENDIX B

Date	Parcel No.	Patent No.	Factory, Retailer Wholesaler, etc	Place
July 18	4	91737	John Edwards	Longton
20	2	91749–50	J. H. Baddeley	Shelton
Aug 8	1	92001	Anthony Shaw	Tunstall
10	2	92018	Holland & Green	Longton
Sept 3	2	92340	T. & R. Boote	Burslem
6	3	92364	F. Morley & Co.	Shelton
21	2	92631–2	James Edwards	Burslem
Oct 5	2	92768–70	Venables, Mann & Co.	Burslem
10	3	92859	Barrow & Co.	Fenton
11	5	92864	Ralph Scragg	Hanley
12	3	92867	James Edwards	Burslem
12	4	92868–9	Livesley, Powell & Co.	Hanley
19	4	92952	Minton & Co.	Stoke
22	1	93008–9	T. J. & J. Mayer	Longport
Nov 24	2	93438–9	Thos. Till & Son	Burslem
26	2	93452	W. T. Copeland	Stoke
30	5	93483	Wm. Adams & Sons	Stoke
Dec 6	4	93536	J. Alcock	Cobridge
24	3	93706–7	Samuel Moore & Co.	Sunderlnd
24	4	93708	J. Alcock	Cobridge
1854				
Jan 10	4	94326	W. & G. Harding	Burslem
13	1	94343–4	Deaville & Baddeley	Hanley
14	3	94632	Samuel Moore & Co.	Sunderlnd
21	3	94727	J. & M. P. Bell & Co.	Glasgow
30	4	94815	Samuel Alcock & Co.	Burslem
Feb 23	3	95163	W. T. Copeland	Stoke
Mar 11	4	95275	Samuel Alcock & Co.	Burslem
20	1	95388	Thos. Till & Son	Burslem
22	2	95397	James Edwards & Son	Longport
24	3	95420	Minton & Co.	Stoke
27	3	95448	Geo. Baguley	Hanley
27	6	95451	J. Deaville	Hanley
31	1	95469	Holland & Green	Longton

APPENDIX B

Date	Parcel No.	Patent No.	Factory, Retailer Wholesaler, etc	Place
Apr 1	4	95510	Wm. Brownfield	Cobridge
4	3	95523	Woollard & Hattersley	Cambdge
5	3	95542	Ralph Scragg	Hanley
6	3	95553	Samuel Alcock & Co.	Burslem
10	3	95575	J. Deaville	Hanley
10	4	95576	Samuel Alcock & Co.	Burslem
11	5	95587–8	Pearson, Farrall & Meakin	Shelton
15	1	95611	Geo. Baguley	Hanley
21	3	95646	Warburton & Britton	Leeds
May 4	3	95733	John Ridgway & Co.	Shelton
8	3	95751	Wm. Brownfield	Cobridge
June 3	2	96003	Thos. Till & Son	Burslem
9	2	96039	Chas. Meigh & Son	Hanley
21	5	96085–6	T. & R. Boote	Burslem
July 18	2	96296	idem	Burslem
18	4	96298	Alcock & Co.	Burslem
Sept 5	3	96773	Samuel Alcock & Co.	Burslem
12	2	96826	W. T. Copeland	Stoke
Oct 2	3	96980	Wm. Brownfield	Cobridge
6	4	97141	Davenports & Co.	Longport
9	4	97160	T. J. & J. Mayer	Longport
31	2	97508	Geo. Ray	Longton
Nov 10	5	97659	John Ridgway & Co.	Shelton
Dec 27	3	98640	Samuel Alcock & Co.	Burslem
27	4	98641	Pankhurst & Dimmock	Hanley
29	1	98648	F. & R. Pratt & Co.	Fenton
1855				
Jan 4	2	98696	Worthington & Green	Shelton
6	4	98786	Samuel Alcock & Co.	Burslem
15	2	99042	Pinder, Bourne & Hope	Burslem
15	4	99051	Brougham & Mayer	Tunstall
19	3	99086	Pankhurst & Dimmock	Hanley
30	1	99188	John Edwards	Longton

301

Date	Parcel No.	Patent No.	Factory, Retailer Wholesaler, etc	Place
Feb 3	4	99231	J. & M. P. Bell & Co.	Glasgow
5	7	99282	Coomb(e)s & Holland	Llanelly
7	2	99310	John Alcock	Cobridge
17	3	99394	Pratt & Co.	Fenton
26	3	99488	Lockett, Baguley & Cooper	Shelton
28	4	99528	J. Ridgway & Co.	Shelton
Mar 1	5	99538–40	Minton & Co.	Stoke
5	3	99579	Elsmore & Forster	Tunstall
13	4	99653	Warburton & Britton	Leeds
17	1	99679	Wm. Baker	Fenton
Apr 7	7	99814	W. T. Copeland	Stoke
17	4	99876	Stephen Hughes & Son	Burslem
26	1	99972–4	Wm. Brownfield	Cobridge
28	7	100008	Venables, Mann & Co.	Burslem
May 10	5	100094	Beech, Hancock & Co.	Burslem
14	3	100116	Minton & Co.	Stoke
June 7	4	100246–7	John Alcock	Cobridge
11	3	100299	Saml. Alcock & Co.	Burslem
July 4	5	100624	J. Thompson	Staffs.
24	1	100816	Chas. Meigh & Son	Hanley
Aug 6	1	101019	James Dudson	Shelton
8	5	101026	J. Edwards & Son	Longport
11	1	101082	Geo. Grainger & Co.	Worcester
20	3	101127	Thos. Ford	Shelton
27	2	101229–31	Barrow & Co.	Fenton
Sept 27	4	101623–4	Saml. Bevington & Son	Shelton
Oct 3	2	101681	Geo. Mayor & Co.	London
3	3	101682	Minton & Co.	Stoke
17	8	101932	John Williamson	Glasgow
25	3	102325	D. Chetwynd	Cobridge
29	6	102355	G. W. Reade	Burslem
Nov 1	3	102415	Josiah Wedgwood & Sons	Etruria
22	4	102744	J. & M. P. Bell & Co.	Glasgow
28	3	102785	Wm. Brownfield	Cobridge

APPENDIX B

Date	Parcel No.	Patent No.	Factory, Retailer Wholesaler, etc	Place
1856				
Jan 5	3	103103	J. Edwards	Longton
15	4	103404	James Pankhurst & Co.	Hanley
23	3	103506	J. Roberts	Kent (Upnor)
23	4	103507	Minton & Co.	Stoke
31	4	103616	Josiah Wedgwood & Sons	Etruria
Mar 11	1	104078	Davenports & Co.	Longport
12	3	104090	Pratt & Co.	Fenton
Apr 7	2	104313–16	A. Shaw	Tunstall
7	3	104317	J. & M. P. Bell & Co.	Glasgow
18	2	104392	Wm. Beech	Burslem
18	3	104393	Ralph Scragg	Hanley
18	6	104396	E. Walley	Cobridge
18	7	104397	Ridgway & Abington	Hanley
30	3	104602–3	Wm. Brownfield	Cobridge
May 8	2	104694	Minton & Co.	Stoke
22	1	104762	idem	Stoke
June 13	3	105059	Chas. Meigh & Son	Hanley
28	3	105223	Worthington & Green	Hanley
30	7	105258	J. Clementson	Shelton
July 28	3	105492	E. Challinor	Tunstall
30	5	105702	J. Edwards & Son	Longport
Aug 12	2	105871	F. & R. Pratt & Co.	Fenton
19	5	105926	idem	Fenton
22	4	105955–9	T. & R. Boote	Burslem
Sept 1	3	106161	W. T. Copeland	Stoke
Oct 2	3	106477	H. Baggaley	Hanley
16	2	106671–2	Minton & Co.	Stoke
22	3	106770	W. T. Copeland	Stoke
Nov 7	6	106950	F. & R. Pratt & Co.	Fenton
14	9	107038	Davenports & Co.	Longport
27	3	107708	idem	Longport
27	6	107714	Wm. Brownfield	Cobridge
29	1	107783–5	E. Walley	Cobridge

APPENDIX B

Date	Parcel No.	Patent No.	Factory, Retailer Wholesaler, etc	Place
Dec 11	4	107955	W. T. Copeland	Stoke
18	2	108052	Mayer & Elliott	Longport
23	4	108105	idem	Longport
1857				
Jan 15	5	108605	F. & R. Pratt & Co.	Fenton
26	7	108785	J. Edwards	Longport
Feb 4	5	108854–5	John Meir & Son	Tunstall
9	4	108930	Minton & Co.	Stoke
17	3	109063	idem	Stoke
23	9	109180	Podmore, Walker & Co.	Hanley
Mar 20	4	109427	John Alcock	Cobridge
Apr 16	1	109738	John Alcock	Cobridge
29	1	109810	W. T. Copeland	Stoke
June 5	3	110096–7	Wm. Brownfield	Cobridge
19	1	110160	W. T. Copeland	Stoke
19	2	110161	Wilkinson & Rickhuss	Hanley
25	1	110247	J. & M. P. Bell & Co.	Glasgow
July 30	2	110780	Ridgway, Bates & Co.	Shelton
Aug 4	5	110806	Taylor, Pears & Co.	Fenton
11	3	110862	Kerr & Binns	Worcester
Sept 7	2	111105	W. T. Copeland	Stoke
Oct 3	3	111495–6	Doulton & Watts	London
5	5	111515–6	idem	London
14	1	111585	Ridgway & Abington	Hanley
17	1	111642	Mayer Bros. & Elliott	Longport
17	2	111643–4	T. & R. Boote	Burslem
22	1	111677	Pratt & Co.	Fenton
Nov 3	3	111831–2	Maw & Co.	Broseley
28	2	112263	Kerr & Binns	Worcester
Dec 4	4	112350	Minton & Co.	Stoke
9	2	112354	Wm. Brownfield	Cobridge

APPENDIX B

Date	Parcel No.	Patent No.	Factory, Retailer Wholesaler, etc	Place
1858				
Jan 29	3	112875	Cockson & Harding	Hanley
29	4	112876	E. & W. Walley	Cobridge
Mar 25	2	113290	Kerr & Binns	Worcester
Apr 9	2	113387	idem	Worcester
17	4	113456	Ridgway & Abington	Hanley
22	5	113565	T. & R. Boote	Burslem
30	5	113631	Minton & Co.	Stoke
May 6	4	113668	J. Edwards	Longton
25	4	113864	A. Shaw	Burslem
31	1	113900	Holland & Green	Longton
31	4	113903	Wm. Adams	Tunstall
June 2	1	113905–6	Wm. Brownfield	Cobridge
23	6	114048	Samuel Alcock & Co.	Burslem
July 13	2	114214	Mayer & Elliott	Longport
29	4	114532	Samuel Alcock & Co.	Burslem
Aug 24	2	114763	Wm. Brownfield	Cobridge
Sept 3	2	115120	Sharpe Bros. & Co.	Swadlncte
6	5	115197	James Edwards	Longport
10	3	115217	John Edwards	Longton
10	6	115343	Bridgwood & Clarke	Burslem
Oct 5	2	115901	Minton & Co.	Stoke
5	3	115902	Wm. Brownfield	Cobridge
7	1	115953	Ridgway & Abington	Hanley
18	3	116176	Minton & Co.	Stoke
29	2	116468	B. Green	Fenton
Nov 3	8	116585	James Stiff	London
5	5	116607	Wm. Savage	Winchstr
11	2	116737	E. & W. Walley	Cobridge
Dec 8	11	117336–8	T. & R. Boote	Burslem
8	12	117339	J. Clementson	Hanley
17	6	117443	W. T. Copeland	Stoke
23	2	117516	J. Clementson	Hanley
23	9	117530	W. T. Copeland	Stoke
27	4	117559	J. Clementson	Hanley

APPENDIX B

Date	Parcel No.	Patent No.	Factory, Retailer Wholesaler, etc	Place
1859				
Jan 25	4	118119	W. T. Copeland	Stoke
Feb 2	3	118294	T. & R. Boote	Burslem
3	2	118303–4	Davenports & Co.	Longport
8	6	118415	Leveson Hill (Excrs. of)	Stoke
Mar 19	1	118827	Alsop, Downes, Spilsbury & Co.	London
21	7	118891	T. & R. Boote	Burslem
29	7	119137	idem	Burslem
May 7	1	119721–2	E. & W. Walley	Cobridge
10	2	119760	Samuel Alcock & Co.	Burslem
20	1	119968	Wm. Brownfield	Cobridge
26	1	120096	Lockett, Baguley & Cooper	Hanley
July 2	2	120560	W. T. Copeland	Stoke
Aug 6	7	121140	F. & R. Pratt & Co.	Fenton
27	6	121724	Samuel Alcock & Co.	Burslem
Sept 1	3	121833	James Edwards & Son	Longport
Oct 12	4	122959	Wm. Adams	Tunstall
14	4	123116	W. T. Copeland	Stoke
25	1	123389–91	Minton & Co.	Stoke
28	1	123604	Davenports & Co.	Longport
Nov 2	3	123738–40	Elsmore & Forster	Tunstall
5	4	123816	Wm. Brownfield	Cobridge
17	4	124140–3	Minton & Co.	Stoke
23	4	124274	idem	Stoke
Dec 10	5	124653	Josiah Wedgwood & Sons	Etruria
14	2	124716	E. & W. Walley	Cobridge
15	3	124725	Minton & Co.	Stoke
1860				
Jan 10	4	125365	W. T. Copeland	Stoke
23	7	125863	Mayer & Elliott	Longport
Feb 14	9	126446–7	W. T. Copeland	Stoke

Date	Parcel No.	Patent No.	Factory, Retailer Wholesaler, etc	Place
Mar 1	2	126950	Bates, Brown-Westhead & Moore	Hanley
27	1	127513	idem	Hanley
Apr 5	1	127766	Geo. Grainger & Co.	Worcester
12	4	127965	Minton & Co.	Stoke
May 2	2	128476	John Meir & Son	Tunstall
19	9	129129	Lockett, Baguley & Cooper	Hanley
30	10	129578	Edward Corn	Burslem
June 6	4	129680–2	Wm. Brownfield	Cobridge
22	2	130106	Minton & Co.	Stoke
28	2	130135	Minton & Co.	Stoke
Aug 21	2	131943	John Wedge Wood	Tunstall
Sept 24	3	133411	Minton & Co.	Stoke
29	7	133788	idem	Stoke
Oct 13	5	134204	B. Green	Fenton
18	4	134519–20	Bates, Brown–Westhead & Moore	Hanley
19	4	134555–7	J. Clementson	Shelton
19	5	134558–9	Holland & Green	Longton
29	3	134936	Minton & Co.	Stoke
29	9	134968	Wm. Brownfield	Cobridge
Nov 23	9	136032	T. & R. Boote	Burslem
Dec 3	3	136285–6	Bates, Brown–Westhead & Moore	Hanley
12	3	136643	Bates & Co.	Hanley
1861				
Jan 8	6	137217	T. & R. Boote	Burslem
21	7	137529	Wedgwood & Co.	Tunstall
Feb 15	3	138356	J. Furnival & Co.	Cobridge
27	5	138535	James Edwards & Son	Longport
Mar 7	7	138861–2	Turner & Tomkinson	Tunstall
19	3	139053	W. T. Copeland	Stoke
19	4	139054–5	W. H. Kerr & Co.	Worcester

APPENDIX B

Date	Parcel No.	Patent No.	Factory, Retailer Wholesaler, etc	Place
Apr 5	3	139360	Pinder, Bourne & Hope	Burslem
6	1	139369–72	Minton, Hollins & Co.	Stoke
12	3	139714–5	Davenports & Co.	Longport
18	5	139881	T. & R. Boote	Burslem
20	6	139945	F. & R. Pratt	Fenton
25	2	140200	James Dudson	Hanley
May 3	8	140367	W. T. Copeland	Stoke
6	3	140478	The Hill Pottery Co.	Burslem
6	5	140480–1	The Old Hall Earthenware Co.	Hanley
9	3	140578–9	Bates, Brown–Westhead & Moore	Hanley
13	7	140679	Minton & Co.	Stoke
14	2	140683	W. H. Kerr & Co.	Worcester
25	2	141055	idem	Worcester
31	3	141114	Cork, Edge & Malkin	Burslem
June 4	1	141214	Bates, Brown–Westhead & Moore	Hanley
7	5	141288	The Hill Pottery Co.	Burslem
11	2	141326–7	W. T. Copeland	Stoke
13	6	141369	Minton & Co.	Stoke
July 4	2	141715	Lockett & Cooper	Hanley
5	2	141727	Beech & Hancock	Tunstall
6	2	141732	Wm. Brownfield	Cobridge
18	4	141869–70	Josiah Wedgwood & Sons	Etruria
Aug 19	7	142755	T. & R. Boote	Burslem
22	7	142847	Wedgwood & Co.	Tunstall
23	2	142850	G. W. Reade	Cobridge
Sept 6	6	143313	Wm. Brownfield	Cobridge
12	6	143400	J. & J. Peake	Newcastle
17	2	143702	W. T. Copeland	Stoke
18	7	143769	Wm. Beech	Burslem
26	7	144179	John Cliff & Co.	London
Oct 10	5	144757	W. H. Kerr & Co.	Worcester
11	3	144767	Mountford & Scarratt	Fenton

APPENDIX B

Date	Parcel No.	Patent No.	Factory, Retailer Wholesaler, etc	Place
15	3	144896	Leveson Hill (Excrs of)	Stoke
18	3	145157	W. T. Copeland	Stoke
24	5	145499	Hulse, Nixon & Adderley	Longton
28	7	145686–7	Bates, Brown–Westhead & Moore	Hanley
Nov 15	3	146352–4	J. Clementson	Hanley
29	5	146924	Josiah Wedgwood & Sons	Etruria
Dec 4	7	147309–10	Wm. Brownfield	Cobridge
5	5	147322	Till, Bullock & Smith	Hanley
20	7	147820	Lockett & Cooper	Hanley
20	9	147823	Wedgwood & Co.	Tunstall
1862				
Jan 11	5	148517	Wm. Brownfield	Cobridge
25	3	148870	idem	Cobridge
Feb 1	4	149090	Elliot Bros.	Longport
10	6	149290	W. H. Kerr & Co.	Worcester
10	8	149292	Minton & Co.	Stoke
27	4	149673–4	James Dudson	Hanley
Mar 1	6	149716	T. & R. Boote	Burslem
13	6	149938	W. T. Copeland	Stoke
13	7	149939	Wm. Adams	Tunstall
14	8	149955	J. Knight	Fenton
14	9	149956	Wedgwood & Co.	Tunstall
14	10	149957–8	Wm. Brownfield	Cobridge
21	6	150100	Thompson Bros.	Burton-on-Trent
22	9	150152	T. & R. Boote	Burslem
27	1	150241	J. & M. P. Bell & Co.	Glasgow
28	5	150301–3	idem	Glasgow
29	3	150322	Minton & Co.	Stoke
Apr 1	5	150377	Josiah Wedgwood & Sons	Etruria
4	2	150455	Minton & Co.	Stoke
4	5	150458	J. & T. Furnival	Cobridge

309

APPENDIX B

Date	Parcel No.	Patent No.	Factory, Retailer Wholesaler, etc	Place
7	12	150515	Geo. Grainger & Co.	Worcester
9	3	150538	The Old Hall Earthenware Co. (Ltd.)	Hanley
17	5	151029–30	Thompson Bros.	Burton
24	2	151141	Turner & Tomkinson	Tunstall
May 1	7	151351	Eardley & Hammersley	Tunstall
3	3	151378	G. L. Ashworth Bros.	Hanley
5	5	151456	John Cliff	London
9	9	151568–9	Brown–Westhead, Moore & Co.	Hanley
14	3	151672–3	Geo. Jones & Co.	Stoke
27	3	151995	E. Challinor	Tunstall
29	5	152013	J. Furnival & Co.	Cobridge
June 24	5	152709	T. C. Brown–Westhead, Moore & Co.	Hanley
July 2	4	152859	Minton & Co.	Stoke
4	8	152963	J. Clementson	Hanley
12	4	153112	idem	Hanley
14	2	153127	Beech & Hancock	Tunstall
19	6	153366	J. Clementson	Hanley
31	3	153476	Jones & Ellis	Longton
31	4	153477	Minton & Co.	Stoke
Aug 16	5	153821	Richard Edwards	Longport
16	7	153823	J. H. Baddeley	Hanley
18	4	153827	Hulse, Nixon & Adderley	Longton
19	4	153844	G. L. Ashworth & Bros.	Hanley
25	3	154143–4	E. F. Bodley & Co.	Burslem
30	3	154220	Thos. Fell & Co.	Newcastle upon Tyne
30	4	154221	T. & R. Boote	Burslem
Sept 6	2	154401	Malkin, Walker & Hulse	Longton
11	3	154678	Minton & Co.	Stoke
12	2	154693	Thos. Cooper	Longton

Date	Parcel No.	Patent No.	Factory, Retailer Wholesaler, etc	Place
17	6	154812	Hope & Carter	Burslem
22	7	155103	Minton & Co.	Stoke
26	1	155220–2	Hope & Carter	Burslem
Oct 1	7	155263–4	Thos. Fell & Co.	Newcastle upon Tyne
9	3	155550	Hill Pottery	Burslem
15	2	156190	Turner & Tomkinson	Tunstall
23	8	156715–7	Wm. Baker & Co.	Fenton
Nov 11	3	157274	E. F. Bodley & Co.	Burslem
19	5	157547	Geo. Wooliscroft	Tunstall
28	4	157907	Minton & Co.	Stoke
Dec 3	5	158052–3	T. C. Brown–Westhead Moore & Co.	Hanley
5	2	158091	Wm. Brownfield	Cobridge
9	5	158221	Thomas Cooper	Hanley
17	5	158480	The Old Hall Earthenware Co. (Ltd.)	Hanley
18	3	158498	Geo. Jones	Stoke
1863				
Jan 12	6	159083	Davenport, Banks & Co.	Etruria
16	2	159123	Minton & Co.	Stoke
16	8	159153	Liddle, Elliot & Sons	Longport
29	1	159551	Josiah Wedgwood & Sons	Etruria
30	3	159573	T. & R. Boote	Burslem
Feb 2	3	159613	Minton & Co.	Stoke
17	4	159972	T. & R. Boote	Burslem
24	5	160110	James Stiff & Sons	London
Mar 6	2	160319	G. L. Ashworth & Bros.	Hanley
13	2	160456	Hope & Carter	Burslem
13	3	160457	Wilkinson & Sons	Hanley
20	8	160752	Worthington & Green	Hanley
20	9	160753–4	John Pratt & Co.	Fenton
21	2	160759	Beech & Hancock	Tunstall

APPENDIX B

Date	Parcel No.	Patent No.	Factory, Retailer Wholesaler, etc	Place
21	4	160761	Hulse, Nixon & Adderley	Longton
21	5	160762	James Edwards & Son	Burslem
23	2	160791–2	Bodley & Harrold	Burslem
Apr 11	1	161404	J. Macintyre	Burslem
23	4	161852	T. C. Brown–Westhead Moore & Co.	Hanley
25	1	161861	Beech & Hancock	Tunstall
30	3	162021	Wilkinson & Son	Hanley
May 4	6	162122	Harding & Cotterill	Burton-on-Trent
11	3	162261–2	E. Pearson	Cobridge
12	1	162267	Bodley & Harrold	Burslem
15	10	162304	Harding & Cotterill	Burton-on-Trent
22	4	162618–9	W. T. Copeland	Stoke
26	9	162765	T. C. Brown–Westhead, Moore & Co.	Hanley
·June 4	5	162976	The Old Hall Earthenware Co. (Ltd.)	Hanley
8	15	163188	Minton & Co.	Stoke
8	16	163189	Wm. Brownfield	Cobridge
July 14	2	164213	Turner & Tomkinson	Tunstall
15	3	164221	H. Venables	Hanley
20	3	164353	Wm. Brownfield	Cobridge
24	3	164468–9	W. T. Copeland	Stoke
28	6	164635	Minton & Co.	Stoke
Aug 11	3	165045–7	Turner & Tomkinson	Tunstall
12	4	165171	Hancock, Whittingham & Co.	Burslem
21	1	165317	J. Clementson	Hanley
28	5	165448	H. Venables	Hanley
Sept 7	6	165720	T. & R. Boote	Burslem
28	4	166439	H. Venables	Hanley
28	6	166441–2	James Edwards & Son	Longport

APPENDIX B

Date	Parcel No.	Patent No.	Factory, Retailer Wholesaler, etc	Place
Oct 2	5	166625	H. Venables	Hanley
6	5	166775	Thompson Bros.	Burton
14	7	167289	Wm. Brownfield	Cobridge
15	2	167299	F. Brewer & Son	Longton
17	1	167374	T. & R. Boote	Burslem
22	5	167536	Eardley & Hammersley	Tunstall
24	5	167560	Josiah Wedgwood & Sons	Etruria
26	7	167594–5	The Old Hall Earthenware Co. (Ltd.)	Hanley
28	8	167715	George Jones & Co.	Stoke
31	3	167761–3	Edmund T. Wood	Tunstall
Nov 3	5	168132	John Meir & Son	Tunstall
4	7	168188	T. & R. Boote	Burslem
6	1	168234–5	Geo. Jones & Co.	Stoke
16	10	168765	Wm. Kirkham	Stoke
26	12	169553	Wm. Brownfield	Cobridge
27	3	169561	Bodley & Harrold	Burslem
Dec 2	5	169774	J. W. Pankhurst	Hanley
2	6	169775	T. & R. Boote	Burslem
18	4	170294	F. & R. Pratt & Co.	Fenton
23	2	170418	Wm. Brownfield	Cobridge
30	1	170590	T. C. Brown–Westhead Moore & Co.	Hanley
1864				
Jan 5	2	170759	Wm. Brownfield	Cobridge
11	5	170883	Malkin, Walker & Hulse	Longton
Feb 2	5	171421	Josiah Wedgwood & Sons	Etruria
5	5	171520	Hope & Carter	Burslem
6	3	171536	Thos. Goode & Co.	London
13	6	171673	W. T. Copeland	Stoke
22	7	171970	Cork, Edge & Malkin	Burslem
25	6	172060	Liddle, Elliot & Son	Longport
29	6	172183	J. & D. Hampson	Longton
Mar 3	4	172212	Geo. L. Ashworth & Bros.	Hanley

APPENDIX B

Date	Parcel No.	Patent No.	Factory, Retailer Wholesaler, etc	Place
12	5	172559	Cork, Edge & Malkin	Burslem
18	1	172648	T. C. Brown–Westhead, Moore & Co.	Hanley
22	3	172815–6	Minton & Co.	Stoke
23	4	172876	Burgess & Leigh	Burslem
Apr 9	4	173200	Josiah Wedgwood & Sons	Etruria
15	4	173659	Geo. Jones	Stoke
18	5	173671	Minton & Co.	Stoke
21	4	173785	T. C. Brown–Westhead Moore & Co.	Hanley
21	8	173799	Liddle, Elliot & Son	Longport
23	11	173996	Geo. L. Ashworth & Bros.	Hanley
26	3	174112	Bodley & Harrold	Burslem
27	4	174138	Hope & Carter	Burslem
29	2	174168	Wm. Brownfield	Cobridge
May 9	3	174424	R. T. Boughton & Co.	Burslem
10	5	174455–8	Geo. Jones & Co.	Stoke
11	3	174475	R. H. Grove	Barlaston
18	5	174795	Geo. Ray	Longton
21	1	174817	J. & D. Hampson	Longton
June 9	7	175330	Minton & Co.	Stoke
16	3	175500	Hope & Carter	Burslem
30	4	175927	Wm. Brownfield	Cobridge
30	10	175935	The Worcester Royal Porcelain Co. Ltd.	Worcester
July 2	3	175959	Wood & Sale	Hanley
9	5	176164	Pinder, Bourne & Co.	Burslem
11	8	176235–6	idem	Burslem
18	6	176597	Bodley & Harrold	Burslem
18	7	176598	Evans & Booth	Burslem
19	4	176701	Hope & Carter	Burslem
19	8	176706	Wood & Sale	Hanley
28	4	176916	Holland & Green	Longton
Aug 10	2	177455	James Fellows	W/hmptn
20	10	177912	Geo. Jones & Co.	Stoke

Date	Parcel No.	Patent No.	Factory, Retailer Wholesaler, etc	Place
26	5	178037	T. C. Brown–Westhead Moore & Co.	Hanley
Sept 6	5	178264	W. T. Copeland	Stoke
10	1	178410	Minton & Co.	Stoke
12	2	178433	idem	Stoke
14	4	178521	Bodley & Harrold	Burslem
16	6	178597–8	Geo. L. Ashworth & Bros.	Hanley
19	1	178680–1	Josiah Wedgwood & Sons	Etruria
21	1	178693–4	Minton & Co.	Stoke
22	6	178823–7	Josiah Wedgwood & Sons	Etruria
Oct 4	2	179445	Geo. Jones & Co.	Stoke
12	4	179656	Wm. Brownfield	Cobridge
27	4	180444	Evans & Booth	Burslem
28	2	180449	The Worcester Royal Porcelain Co. Ltd.	Worcester
28	4	180453	Bodley & Harrold	Burslem
28	9	180483	Minton & Co.	Stoke
29	2	180486	Chas. Collinson & Co.	Burslem
31	3	180569	Cork, Edge & Malkin	Burslem
Nov 1	7	180695	W. T. Copeland	Stoke
4	3	180713	Livesley, Powell & Co.	Hanley
10	2	181214–5	Elsmore & Forster	Tunstall
10	3	181296	Hope & Carter	Burslem
10	10	181286	Geo. Jones & Co.	Stoke
24	5	181722	T. C. Brown–Westhead Moore & Co.	Hanley
29	1	181843	Hope & Carter	Burslem
Dec 9	1	182203	Wm. Kirkham	Stoke
10	8	182249	Hope & Carter	Burslem
31	6	182699	Geo. Jones & Co.	Stoke
1865				
Jan 6	3	182806	Hope & Carter	Burslem
6	4	182807	Minton & Co.	Stoke
14	4	183331	Geo. Jones & Co.	Stoke

APPENDIX B

Date	Parcel No.	Patent No.	Factory, Retailer Wholesaler, etc	Place
Feb 1	1	183650–2	Minton & Co.	Stoke
2	4	183706–7	Geo. L. Ashworth & Bros.	Hanley
13	7	183940	F. & R. Pratt & Co.	Fenton
14	4	183945	Liddle, Elliot & Son	Longport
27	4	184220	Livesley, Powell & Co.	Hanley
Mar 31	3	185473	Hope & Carter	Burslem
Apr 1	4	185520	Wm. Brownfield	Cobridge
3	4	185613	Minton & Co.	Stoke
22	5	186266	Thos. Till & Sons	Burslem
22	7	186273	James Edwards & Son	Burslem
26	5	186325	idem	Burslem
28	4	186349	Hope & Carter	Burslem
28	7	186354	Henry Alcock & Co.	Cobridge
29	3	186361	The Worcester Royal Porcelain Co. (Ltd.)	Worcester
May 2	8	186477	Livesley, Powell & Co.	Hanley
15	2	186841	J. T. Hudden	Longton
17	2	186901	Minton & Co.	Stoke
June 6	6	187358–9	J. T. Hudden	Longton
9	4	187403	The Worcester Royal Porcelain Co. (Ltd.)	Worcester
13	5	187533	idem	Worcester
14	6	187574	The Hill Pottery Co. Ltd.	Burslem
15	2	187576	J. T. Hudden	Longton
16	1	187583	Evans & Booth	Burslem
17	5	187633	The Worcester Royal Porcelain Co. (Ltd.)	Worcester
29	2	187847–8	Ed. F. Bodley & Co.	Burslem
30	4	187861	The Hill Pottery Co. Ltd.	Burslem
July 3	7	187972	T. C. Brown–Westhead, Moore & Co.	Hanley
12	3	188167	James Edwards & Son	Burslem
Aug 21	6	189155	J. Furnival & Co.	Cobridge
23	5	189283	Josiah Wedgwood & Sons	Etruria
Sept 11	4	189700	R. T. Boughton & Co.	Burslem

Date	Parcel No.	Patent No.	Factory, Retailer Wholesaler, etc	Place
11	5	189701	Thos. Cooper (Excrs of)	Hanley
14	2	189718	T. C. Brown–Westhead, Moore & Co.	Hanley
18	6	189782	Liddle, Elliot & Son	Longport
28	4	190200	Minton & Co.	Stoke
30	4	190656	S. Barker & Son	Swinton
Oct 13	8	190903	T. C. Brown–Westhead, Moore & Co.	Hanley
24	4	191292	Edward Johns	Staffs.
30	4	191407–8	Wm. Brownfield	Cobridge
Nov 10	4	192236	Pinder Bourne & Co. & Anthony Shaw	Burslem
23	10	192793	The Old Hall Earthenware Co. Ltd.	Hanley
29	8	192963	James Edwards & Son	Burslem
Dec 2	3	193061	The Worcester Royal Porcelain Co. (Ltd.)	Worcester
23	3	193844	James Dudson	Hanley
1866				
Jan 2	4	194063	Pratt & Co.	Fenton
3	6	194194	J. T. Close & Co.	Stoke
13	2	194450	Ed. F. Bodley & Co.	Burslem
17	4	194537	Burgess & Leigh	Burslem
24	1	194696	Minton & Co.	Stoke
31	5	194840	James Edwards & Son	Burslem
Feb 2	7	194949	W. T. Copeland	Stoke
Mar 2	2	195644	Ford, Challinor & Co.	Tunstall
10	1	195841	The Old Hall Earthenware Co. (Ltd.)	Hanley
Apr 14	6	196551	Walker & Carter	Longton
14	7	196552–4	Geo. L. Ashworth & Bros.	Hanley
16	8	196619	The Old Hall Earthenware Co. (Ltd.)	Hanley
18	4	196651	James Edwards & Son	Burslem

317

APPENDIX B

Date	Parcel No.	Patent No.	Factory, Retailer Wholesaler, etc	Place
20	7	196672–3	Wm. Brownfield	Cobridge
May 1	4	196987–8	J. Furnival & Co.	Cobridge
25	1	197705–6	Hope & Carter	Burslem
June 4	4	197857	James Broadhurst	Longton
12	1	198135–7	John Edwards	Fenton
21	4	198383–4	Pinder, Bourne & Co.	Burslem
30	4	198589	Thos. Minshall	Stoke
July 19	5	199186	J. T. Hudden	Longton
25	3	199295	Geo. Jones	Stoke
Aug 17	3	200006	Morgan, Wood & Co.	Burslem
29	4	200324	Ed. F. Bodley & Co.	Burslem
Sept 6	4	200599	F. & R. Pratt & Co.	Fenton
13	9	201040	T. & C. Ford	Hanley
15	8	201089	Geo. L. Ashworth & Bros.	Hanley
20	8	201495	Anthony Keeling	Tunstall
Oct 8	3	202103–5	Minton & Co.	Stoke
13	3	202493	Thos. Furnival	Cobridge
Nov 3	6	203173	Minton & Co.	Stoke
12	3	203538	W. T. Copeland	Stoke
14	8	203817	T. C. Brown–Westhead, Moore & Co.	Hanley
15	4	203912	Geo. Grainger & Co.	Worcester
Dec 13	4	204764	Liddle, Elliot & Son	Longport
14	8	204794	Samuel Barker & Son	Swinton
15	5	204863	T. C. Brown–Westhead, Moore & Co.	Hanley
19	5	205088	John Meir & Son	Tunstall
24	2	205201	J. T. Hudden	Longton
1867				
Jan 8	5	205372	James Edwards & Son	Burslem
17	3	205596	Ed. F. Bodley & Co.	Burslem
23	2	205759	The Worcester Royal Porcelain Co. (Ltd.)	Worcester
Feb 9	1	206033	Ed. F. Bodley & Co.	Burslem

Date	Parcel No.	Patent No.	Factory, Retailer Wholesaler, etc	Place
23	5	206275	Worthington & Harrop	Hanley
Mar 2	7	206422	Josiah Wedgwood & Sons	Etruria
4	4	206497	T. C. Brown–Westhead, Moore & Co.	Hanley
5	6	206517	Powell & Bishop	Hanley
6	4	206522	The Old Hall Earthenware Co. (Ltd.)	Hanley
9	3	206564	John Edwards	Fenton
11	2	206662	Josiah Wedgwood & Sons	Etruria
14	1	206718	Davenport Banks & Co.	Etruria
15	7	206762–6	Wm. Brownfield	Cobridge
18	5	206867–8	Cockson & Chetwynd & Co.	Cobridge
19	5	206881	James Edwards & Son	Burslem
20	2	206887	Josiah Wedgwood & Sons	Etruria
21	10	206971	James Edwards & Son	Burslem
25	3	206994	Josiah Wedgwood & Sons	Etruria
26	4	207024–5	Minton & Co.	Stoke
Apr 3	5	207163	idem	Stoke
4	2	207165	Josiah Wedgwood & Sons	Etruria
4	9	207201	Elsmore & Forster	Tunstall
17	1	207564	Chas. Hobson	Burslem
23	3	207616	Adams, Scrivener & Co.	Longton
24	2	207636	W. T. Copeland	Stoke
May 6	3	207938	J. & M. P. Bell & Co.	Glasgow
7	4	207977	John Meir & Son	Tunstall
8	6	208002	T. C. Brown–Westhead Moore & Co.	Hanley
18	7	208394	Wm. McAdam	Glasgow
22	6	208434–5	Clementson Bros.	Hanley
June 6	3	208750	Josiah Wedgwood & Sons	Etruria
11	6	208819	Clementson Bros.	Hanley
11	7	208820	Cockson, Chetwynd & Co.	Cobridge
13	3	208891	W. & J. A. Bailey	Alloa
21	4	209057	Wm. Brownfield	Cobridge

APPENDIX B

Date	Parcel No.	Patent No.	Factory, Retailer Wholesaler, etc	Place
21	8	209062	E. & D. Chetwynd	Hanley
24	4	209087	idem	Hanley
July 1	7	209290	Joseph Ball	Longton
4	5	209362	E. J. Ridgway	Hanley
8	3	209431	Geo. L. Ashworth & Bros.	Hanley
12	5	209530	Geo. Jones	Stoke
15	2	209556	Josiah Wedgwood & Sons	Etruria
17	2	209601	E. & D. Chetwynd	Hanley
25	3	209726	Hope & Carter	Burslem
Aug 28	10	210598	The Worcester Royal Porcelain Co. Ltd.	Worcester
Sept 16	7	211275	Thos. Goode & Co.	London
17	3	211290	Wedgwood & Co.	Tunstall
21	1	211536	Geo. L. Ashworth & Bros.	Hanley
25	9	211873–4	Powell & Bishop	Hanley
Oct 2	1	211995	Minton & Co.	Stoke
3	5	212054	Thompson Bros.	Burton-on-Trent
3	6	212055	Minton & Co.	Stoke
7	4	212078	idem	Stoke
10	1	212194	Thos. Booth	Hanley
24	5	212765	Ford, Challinor & Co.	Tunstall
26	1	212881	W. T. Copeland & Sons	Stoke
28	4	212956	idem	Stoke
29	3	212964	Josiah Wedgwood & Sons	Etruria
30	3	212974	J. T. Hudden	Longton
31	7	213065	Powell & Bishop	Hanley
Nov 6	7	213430	W. & J. A. Bailey	Alloa
7	4	213436	James Edwards & Son	Burslem
18	9	214000	Ford, Challinor & Co.	Tunstall
Dec 3	3	214618	W. T. Copeland & Sons	Stoke
12	6	214981	F. & R. Pratt & Co.	Fenton
20	3	215085	Josiah Wedgwood & Sons	Etruria
27	1	215314	J. & J. B. Bebbington	Hanley

APPENDIX B

Date	Parcel No.	Patent No.	Factory, Retailer Wholesaler, etc	Place
1868				
Jan 3	1	215481	Minton & Co.	Stoke
7	8	215636	Thompson Bros.	Burton-on-Trent
7	11	215642	Cockson, Chetwynd & Co.	Cobridge
8	5	215674	T. & R. Boote	Burslem
9	7	215698	Taylor, Tunnicliffe & Co.	Hanley
10	2	215705	Cork, Edge & Malkin	Burslem
11	2	215725	Wm. Brownfield	Cobridge
13	2	215735	Geo. L. Ashworth & Bros.	Hanley
16	13	215879	The Old Hall Earthenware Co. (Ltd.)	Hanley
25	3	216186	Hope & Carter	Burslem
30	6	216333	J. Furnival & Co.	Cobridge
31	8	216347	Josiah Wedgwood & Sons	Etruria
31	14	216363	T. & R. Boote	Burslem
Feb 5	4	216451	Adams, Scrivener & Co.	Longton
5	8	216470	E. Hodgkinson	Hanley
10	8	216676–8	Minton & Co.	Stoke
12	1	216699	Josiah Wedgwood & Sons	Etruria
14	10	216821	John Mortlock	London
18	1	216895	Josiah Wedgwood & Sons	Etruria
18	2	216896–7	T. C. Brown–Westhead, Moore & Co.	Hanley
20	9	216988	Minton & Co.	Stoke
25	6	217070	John Rose & Co.	Coalport
27	5	217100	Alcock & Digory	Burslem
28	7	217112	W. & J. A. Bailey	Alloa
Mar 5	12	217208	Thos. Goode & Co.	London
5	15	217212	Minton & Co.	Stoke
25	7	217615	W. T. Copeland & Sons	Stoke
25	8	217616–7	The Worcester Royal Porcelain Co. (Ltd.)	Worcester
26	3	217630	Walker & Carter	Longton
Apr 1	6	217727	Minton & Co.	Stoke

Date	Parcel No.	Patent No.	Factory, Retailer Wholesaler, etc	Place
6	6	217938–9	Pinder, Bourne & Co.	Burslem
16	7	218139	Geo. L. Ashworth & Bros.	Hanley
21	6	218285	Beech & Hancock	Tunstall
23	8	218387	R. Hammersley	Tunstall
28	7	218466	T. G. Green	Burton-on-Trent
May 13	1	218664	Adams, Scrivener & Co.	Longton
14	2	218764	Hope & Carter	Burslem
14	6	218773	Philip Brookes	Fenton
26	5	218951	T. C. Brown–Westhead Moore & Co.	Hanley
26	6	218952	Pinder, Bourne & Co.	Burslem
28	3	218967	Holdcroft & Wood	Tunstall
28	5	218969–71	Minton & Co.	Stoke
28	7	218973	J. & T. Bevington	Hanley
30	4	219042	T. & R. Boote	Burslem
June 8	4	219174	Burgess & Leigh	Burslem
12	5	219316–7	Wm. Brownfield	Cobridge
16	4	219344	W. P. & G. Phillips	London
22	5	219484	Minton & Co.	Stoke
July 10	3	219756	Josiah Wedgwood & Sons	Etruria
16	3	219833	Hackney & Co.	Longton
20	2	219942–3	Hope & Carter	Burslem
24	4	219997	W. T. Copeland & Sons	Stoke
30	6	220183	Adams, Scrivener & Co.	Longton
Aug 1	5	220236–7	T. & R. Boote	Burslem
13	1	220772	Josiah Wedgwood & Sons	Etruria
15	8	220821–4	James Edwards & Son	Burslem
17	2	220828	Ed. F. Bodley & Co.	Burslem
21	2	220906	Ralph Malkin	Fenton
31	7	221124	T. & R. Boote	Burslem
Sept 1	1	221125–6	James Wardle	Hanley
4	6	221203–4	Gelson Bros.	Hanley
5	3	221214	T. C. Brown–Westhead, Moore & Co.	Hanley

APPENDIX B

Date	Parcel No.	Patent No.	Factory, Retailer Wholesaler, etc	Place
5	6	221217–9	McBirney & Armstrong	Belleek
9	4	221311	Hope & Carter	Burslem
9	5	221312	F. Jones & Co.	Longton
9	6	221313	Wedgwood & Co.	Tunstall
9	9	221316	J. & T. Bevington	Hanley
12	3	221521–2	Minton & Co.	Stoke
14	4	221548	Thos. Booth & Co.	Burslem
17	4	221688	T. C. Sambrook & Co.	Burslem
21	4	221814–7	George Ash	Hanley
25	4	221881–2	Minton & Co.	Stoke
25	13	222083–4	T. C. Brown–Westhead, Moore & Co.	Hanley
Oct 8	7	222460	Minton & Co.	Stoke
9	2	222476	J. Holdcroft	Stoke
9	3	222477	Hope & Carter	Burslem
9	5	222482–4	Davenports & Co.	Longport
14	8	222736	Geo. Jones	Stoke
17	4	223063	Minton & Co.	Stoke
21	8	223308	W. P. & G. Phillips	London
22	1	223309	McBirney & Armstrong	Belleek
22	5	223314–5	James Edwards & Son	Burslem
Nov 3	5	223817–8	Minton & Co.	Stoke
3	6	223819	T. C. Brown–Westhead, Moore & Co.	Hanley
6	13	224090	Powell & Bishop	Hanley
9	5	224172	Josiah Wedgwood & Sons	Etruria
16	3	224382	Knapper & Blackhurst	Tunstall
17	1	224389	Moore Bros.	Cobridge
21	5	224539	Minton & Co.	Stoke
24	5	224645	T. C. Brown–Westhead Moore & Co.	Hanley
25	4	224724	Cork, Edge & Malkin	Burslem
Dec 1	4	224953	T. C. Brown–Westhead, Moore & Co.	Hanley

Date	Parcel No.	Patent No.	Factory, Retailer Wholesaler, etc	Place
3	5	225073–4	The Worcester Royal Porcelain Co. (Ltd.)	Worcester
11	5	225410	Ed. T. Bodley & Co.	Burslem
12	4	225425	Wm. Brownfield	Cobridge
14	7	225441	Cockson, Chetwynd & Co.	Cobridge
23	5	225734	Minton & Co.	Stoke
23	6	225735	The Worcester Royal Porcelain Co. (Ltd.)	Worcester
31	6	225993	Geo. L. Ashworth & Bros.	Hanley
31	7	225994	R. Hammersley	Tunstall
1869				
Jan 1	8	226051	Geo. Jones	Stoke
4	4	226098	Minton & Co.	Stoke
7	6	226131	Thos. Goode & Co.	London
21	6	226527–8	Minton & Co.	Stoke
22	5	226570	Gelson Bros.	Hanley
22	13	226581	T. C. Brown–Westhead, Moore & Co.	Hanley
25	3	226625	Worthington & Son	Hanley
28	5	226738	Minton & Co.	Stoke
28	10	226747–8	George Ash	Hanley
Feb 1	7	226910	T. C. Brown–Westhead, Moore & Co.	Hanley
2	4	226928	Geo. Yearsley	Longton
9	5	227219	Minton & Co.	Stoke
11	10	227277	Geo. Jones	Stoke
15	1	227307	Thos. Booth & Co.	Burslem
19	2	227345	Josiah Wedgwood & Sons	Etruria
22	6	227403	idem	Etruria
22	11	227409	McBirney & Armstrong	Belleek
22	13	227411	Pinder, Bourne & Co.	Burslem
27	5	227518	Josiah Wedgwood & Sons	Etruria
Mar 1	8	227556–8	Worthington & Son	Hanley
3	8	227619	Thos. Till & Sons	Burslem

APPENDIX B

Date	Parcel No.	Patent No.	Factory, Retailer Wholesaler, etc	Place
6	8	227668	F. Primavesi	Cardiff
8	6	227696	F. & R. Pratt & Co.	Fenton
9	1	227743–4	Geo. Jones	Stoke
9	3	227746	idem	Stoke
10	10	227823	F. Primavesi	Cardiff
24	1	228141	J. F. Wileman	Fenton
Apr 1	1	228290	Wood & Pigott	Tunstall
2	6	228377	Wm. Brownfield	Cobridge
2	7	228378	Minton & Co.	Stoke
6	3	228430	Baker & Chetwynd	Burslem
7	2	228455	Minton & Co.	Stoke
7	4	228457	The Worcester Royal Porcelain Co. (Ltd.)	Worcester
12	4	228572	Taylor, Tunnicliffe & Co.	Hanley
12	5	228573	Liddle, Elliot & Son	Longport
20	5	228764	idem	Longport
28	13	228937	J. & T. Bevington	Hanley
May 11	1	229319	Adams, Scrivener & Co.	Longton
13	16	229405	James Edwards & Son	Burslem
21	1	229523	Worthington & Son	Hanley
26	4	229627	Thos. Booth	Hanley
27	8	229642–4	Davenport & Co.	Longport
June 3	6	229837	McBirney & Armstrong	Belleek
8	7	229959	W. P. & G. Phillips & Pearce	London
19	5	230183–4	Wm. Brownfield	Cobridge
25	4	230429	James Edwards & Son	Burslem
26	9	230455	Minton & Co.	Stoke
July 3	9	230707–8	Josiah Wedgwood & Sons	Etruria
6	3	230739	John Meir & Son	Tunstall
19	8	231101	James Wardle	Hanley
20	2	231124	Josiah Wedgwood & Sons	Etruria
21	6	231153–4	George Ash	Hanley
23	6	231215	Minton & Co.	Stoke
24	4	231222	W. T. Copeland & Sons	Stoke

Date	Parcel No.	Patent No.	Factory, Retailer Wholesaler, etc	Place
26	4	231241	Leveson Hill (Excrs of)	Stoke
27	4	231256	J. T. Hudden	Longton
Aug 2	6	231504	W. T. Copeland	Stoke
3	5	231602	John Edwards	Fenton
4	4	231613	Tomkinson Bros. & Co.	Hanley
11	13	231812	W. P. & G. Phillips & Pearce	London
19	6	232307	W. T. Copeland & Sons	Stoke
26	6	232474	idem	Stoke
31	6	232586–7	John Pratt & Co.	Lane Delph
31	12	232598	W. T. Copeland & Sons	Stoke
Sept 4	3	232822	Minton & Co.	Stoke
8	5	232878	W. T. Copeland & Sons	Stoke
8	6	232879	Pinder, Bourne & Co.	Burslem
9	3	232890	John Pratt & Co.	Lane Delph
10	4	232903	Minton & Co.	Stoke
21	7	233411	Gelson Bros.	Hanley
22	10	233527	W. & J. A. Bailey	Alloa
30	8	233864–6	T. C. Brown–Westhead Moore & Co.	Hanley
Oct 1	3	233923–4	Minton & Co.	Stoke
4	6	234016	idem	Stoke
14	3	234465	McBirney & Armstrong	Belleek
15	6	234486	Geo. Jones	Stoke
23	4	235012	idem	Stoke
26	2	235158	James Ellis & Son	Hanley
27	5	235168	McBirney & Armstrong	Belleek
29	3	235399–400	Minton & Co.	Stoke
29	4	235401–2	Powell & Bishop	Hanley
Nov 2	12	235589	Ed. Clarke	Tunstall
3	12	235691	T. C. Brown–Westhead, Moore & Co.	Hanley

Date		Parcel No.	Patent No.	Factory, Retailer Wholesaler, etc	Place
	8	1	235827–9	McBirney & Armstrong	Belleek
	8	2	235830	T. C. Brown–Westhead, Moore & Co.	Hanley
	9	11	235966	Tams & Lowe	Longton
	10	3	235974	Wm. Brownfield	Cobridge
	13	5	236184–5	McBirney & Armstrong	Belleek
	15	8	236203–7	Liddle, Elliot & Son	Longport
	18	5	236435	Alcock & Digory	Burslem
	19	12	236478	The Worcester Royal Porcelain Co. (Ltd.)	Worcester
	20	8	236533	Thos. Goode & Co.	London
	20	9	236534	John Mortlock	London
	23	1	236585	McBirney & Armstrong	Belleek
	24	4	236628	Minton & Co.	Stoke
	26	3	236653	idem	Stoke
Dec	1	3	236756	Geo. Jones	Stoke
	3	9	236829	Wm. Brownfield	Cobridge
	17	7	237224	Minton & Co.	Stoke
	18	2	237229	Powell & Bishop	Hanley
	18	3	237230	McBirney & Armstrong	Belleek
	20	8	237358	George Ash	Hanley
	22	7	237500	Geo. Jones	Stoke
	24	1	237552	Gelson Bros.	Hanley
	28	2	237565	John Pratt & Co.	Lane Delph
	31	2	237644	Minton & Co.	Stoke
1870					
Jan	1	5	237691	T. C. Brown–Westhead, Moore & Co.	Hanley
	3	4	237742	Geo. Jones	Stoke
	7	9	237899	Pellatt & Co.	London
	15	12	238147–8	Liddle, Elliot & Son	Longport
	27	8	238388	Chas. Hobson	Burslem
	29	3	238436	Minton & Co.	Stoke

APPENDIX B

Date	Parcel No.	Patent No.	Factory, Retailer Wholesaler, etc	Place
Feb 1	6	238527–8	T. C. Brown–Westhead, Moore & Co.	Hanley
3	13	238595–6	idem	Hanley
4	7	238603	Powell & Bishop	Hanley
7	5	238627	Wiltshaw, Wood & Co.	Burslem
7	6	238628	W. & J. A. Bailey	Alloa
9	2	238663	Josiah Wedgwood & Sons	Etruria
10	8	238688	Minton & Co.	Stoke
11	12	238761–2	W. P. & G. Phillips & Pearce	London
15	6	238898–9	T. C. Brown–Westhead Moore & Co.	Hanley
25	2	239139	Minton & Co.	Stoke
28	6	239239	idem	Stoke
Mar 2	4	239304	idem	Stoke
7	6	239422	Chas. Hobson	Burslem
8	1	239424–6	Geo. Jones	Stoke
10	1	239474	idem	Stoke
10	9	239510	Powell & Bishop	Hanley
11	8	239528	Leveson Hill (Excrs of)	Stoke
14	4	239548	T. C. Brown–Westhead, Moore & Co.	Hanley
15	6	239585	Thos. Till & Sons	Burslem
16	2	239590–1	Minton & Co.	Stoke
17	4	239610–1	McBirney & Armstrong	Belleek
17	7	239622	The Worcester Royal Porcelain Co. (Ltd.)	Worcester
17	9	239628	J. Mortlock	London
18	6	239642	Minton & Co.	Stoke
23	9	239793–4	J. Blackshaw & Co.	Stoke
25	4	239968	Hope & Carter	Burslem
25	5	239969–70	Minton & Co.	Stoke
26	1	240000–1	idem	Stoke
26	2	240002	Worthington & Son	Hanley

328

APPENDIX B

Date	Parcel No.	Patent No.	Factory, Retailer Wholesaler, etc	Place
28	9	240079	The Old Hall Earthenware Co. Ltd.	Hanley
Apr 7	9	240383	Cork, Edge & Malkin	Burslem
7	10	240384–5	Baker & Co.	Fenton
7	11	240386	Harvey Adams & Co.	Longton
9	1	240458	Minton & Co.	Stoke
11	3	240493	The Worcester Royal Porcelain Co. Ltd.	Worcester
13	4	240516	Thos. Goode & Co.	London
14	7	240570	Minton & Co.	Stoke
May 5	1	241231	James Oldham & Co.	Hanley
6	5	241264–5	McBirney & Armstrong	Belleek
10	4	241367–8	George Ash	Hanley
13	8	241474	T. C. Brown–Westhead, Moore & Co.	Hanley
17	7	241544	idem	Hanley
18	6	241567–8	Bates, Elliott & Co.	Longport
21	6	241649	The Old Hall Earthenware Co. Ltd.	Hanley
21	12	241666	James Edwards & Son	Burslem
25	7	241754	idem	Burslem
26	5	241960	Minton & Co.	Stoke
30	15	242077	Geo. Jones	Stoke
June 3	8	242154	F. & R. Pratt & Co.	Fenton
7	15	242233	Hope & Carter	Burslem
7	16	242234	Thos. Booth	Hanley
9	3	242391	T. C. Brown–Westhead, Moore & Co.	Hanley
10	1	242392–4	Wm. Brownfield	Cobridge
11	3	242439	James Edwards & Son	Burslem
17	7	242503–8	Minton, Hollins & Co.	Stoke
22	1	242634–5	Harvey Adams & Co.	Longton
22	3	242637–8	Minton, Hollins & Co.	Stoke
22	4	242639	The Worcester Royal Porcelain Co. Ltd.	Worcester

APPENDIX B

Date	Parcel No.	Patent No.	Factory, Retailer Wholesaler, etc	Place
27	1	242715	Geo. Jones	Stoke
July 5	5	242859	Baker & Co.	Fenton
8	7	243049–50	James Wardle	Hanley
13	8	243176	James Edwards & Son	Burslem
14	9	243197–9	Minton, Hollins & Co.	Stoke
14	10	243200	The Worcester Royal Porcelain Co. Ltd.	Worcester
15	1	243207	W. T. Copeland & Sons	Stoke
16	2	243235	James Wardle	Hanley
19	6	243352	F. & R. Pratt & Co.	Fenton
20	5	243368	Thos. Booth	Hanley
21	1	243378	idem	Hanley
22	1	243385	Cork, Edge & Malkin	Burslem
27	1	243480	Beech, Unwin & Co.	Longton
Aug 1	2	243555	R. G. Scrivener & Co.	Hanley
4	4	243646	James Wardle	Hanley
4	5	243647–8	J. Broadhurst	Longton
9	2	243807	Wm. Brownfield	Cobridge
22	4	244137–8	T. & R. Boote	Burslem
23	6	244173	Geo. Jones	Stoke
25	5	244223	T. & R. Boote	Burslem
Sept 7	7	244703	Bailey & Cooke	Hanley
10	9	244741	Minton & Co.	Stoke
16	5	244961	idem	Stoke
19	2	244976	Wm. Brownfield	Cobridge
27	4	245227	Elsmore, Forster & Co.	Tunstall
27	6	245229	W. P. & G. Phillips & D. Pearce	London
28	11	245265	Gelson Bros.	Hanley
Oct 4	7	245463	Joseph Holdcroft	Longton
4	8	245464	Minton & Co.	Stoke
6	4	245604	idem	Stoke
6	5	245605	James Broadhurst	Longton
7	3	245620	Minton & Co.	Stoke
8	9	245668	Powell & Bishop	Hanley

Date	Parcel No.	Patent No.	Factory, Retailer Wholesaler, etc	Place
	19	2	245985–6	Geo. Jones	Stoke
	22	2	246149	Wm. Brownfield	Cobridge
	25	6	246181	T. C. Brown–Westhead, Moore & Co.	Hanley
Nov 4	9	246927	idem	Hanley
	9	8	247047	John Meir & Son	Tunstall
	9	9	247048	Pellatt & Co.	London
	10	5	247071–3	Minton & Co.	Stoke
	10	10	247079–80	Wm. Brownfield	Cobridge
	12	3	247248	McBirney & Armstrong	Belleek
	12	8	247255	Minton, Hollins & Co.	Stoke
	22	3	247944	Geo. Jones	Stoke
	24	3	248041	Minton & Co.	Stoke
	24	8	248049	Bates, Elliott & Co.	Longport
	25	1	248051	Minton & Co.	Stoke
	25	2	248052	Turner, Goddard & Co.	Tunstall
	26	9	248114–6	T. & R. Boote	Burslem
Dec 1	7	248242	Wm. Brownfield	Cobridge
	2	11	248294	T. C. Brown–Westhead, Moore & Co.	Hanley
	5	4	248309–15	Minton, Hollins & Co.	Stoke
	16	5	248869	Bates, Elliott & Co.	Longport
	17	11	248899	idem	Longport
	19	9	248953	Harvey, Adams & Co.	Longton
	27	4	249104	James Edwards & Son	Burslem

1871

Date	Parcel No.	Patent No.	Factory, Retailer Wholesaler, etc	Place
Jan 2	2	249235	Gelson Bros.	Hanley
	6	3	249331	Minton & Co.	Stoke
	7	8	249356	Bates, Elliott & Co.	Longport
	9	4	249388–93	McBirney & Armstrong	Belleek
	10	7	249439	Geo. Jones	Stoke
	11	4	249464	J. Mortlock	London
	12	7	249479	McBirney & Armstrong	Belleek
	12	12	249490	Soane & Smith	London

APPENDIX B

Date	Parcel No.	Patent No.	Factory, Retailer Wholesaler, etc	Place
24	4	249811	idem	London
26	8	249903–6	Minton, Hollins & Co.	Stoke
27	9	249927	The Worcester Royal Porcelain Co. Ltd.	Worcester
30	2	249972	Gelson Bros.	Hanley
Feb 2	3	250020	James Edwards & Son	Burslem
6	5	250168–71	McBirney & Armstrong	Belleek
8	9	250231	James Macintyre & Co.	Burslem
11	9	250291	T. C. Brown–Westhead, Moore & Co.	Hanley
13	6	250366	Edge, Malkin & Co.	Burslem
13	7	250367	Worthington & Son	Hanley
13	9	250369	Powell & Bishop	Hanley
13	10	250370	Ed. F. Bodley & Co.	Burslem
15	7	250416–8	Powell & Bishop	Hanley
17	7	250440–1	Thos. Peake	Tunstall
20	2	250478–9	Elsmore & Forster	Tunstall
28	8	250657	The Watcombe Terra Cotta Clay Co. Ltd.	Devon
Mar 9	4	250865	J. & T. Bevington	Hanley
14	4	250954	John Pratt & Co.	Lane Delph
15	10	251013	Bates, Elliott & Co.	Longport
27	1	251246	Wm. Brownfield & Son	Cobridge
29	1	251329	Thos. Furnival & Son	Cobridge
Apr 4	4	251453	McBirney & Armstrong	Belleek
22	4	251966	John Pratt & Co.	Stoke
24	4	251988	Josiah Wedgwood & Sons	Etruria
26	12	252068	Minton, Hollins & Co.	Stoke
27	7	252093–4	Wood & Clarke	Burslem
27	8	252095–7	W. P. & G. Phillips & Pearce	London
28	1	252128	Wood & Clarke	Burslem
29	6	252156	idem	Burslem
29	7	252157	James Edwards & Son	Burslem

332

APPENDIX B

Date	Parcel No.	Patent No.	Factory, Retailer Wholesaler, etc	Place
May 1	9	252171–3	T. C. Brown–Westhead, Moore & Co.	Hanley
2	3	252176	Ambrose Bevington	Hanley
2	4	252177–80	Wm. Brownfield & Son	Cobridge
3	4	252188	John Jackson & Co.	Rother'm
6	1	252258	W. P. & G. Phillips & Pearce	London
9	9	252387	Liddle, Elliott & Co.	Longport
11	13	252487	Powell & Bishop	Hanley
13	6	252503	Elsmore & Forster	Tunstall
22	9	252709	McBirney & Armstrong	Belleek
24	10	252756	John Meir & Son	Tunstall
June 2	4	253017	T. C. Brown–Westhead, Moore & Co.	Hanley
7	7	253069	Grove & Stark	Longton
16	9	253335	John Twigg	Rother'm
17	3	253339–40	Minton & Co.	Stoke
19	9	253378–9	Pinder, Bourne & Co.	Burslem
22	1	253472	Thos. Till & Sons	Burslem
23	9	253571	Bates, Elliott & Co.	Longport
July 4	8	253796–8	W. T. Copeland	Stoke
14	6	254013	Taylor, Tunnicliffe & Co.	Hanley
15	2	254030	Thos. Booth	Hanley
19	2	254074	Ambrose Bevington	Hanley
22	8	254130–3	Haviland & Co.	London and Limoges
25	12	254239	Bates, Elliott & Co.	Longport
29	6	254344	Hope & Carter	Burslem
Aug 2	3	254429	Robinson & Leadbeater	Stoke
9	7	254757	Bates, Elliott & Co.	Longport
18	10	254899	Pratt & Co.	Fenton
28	5	255267	James Wardle	Hanley
29	2	255274	Geo. Jones	Stoke
30	4	255320	Thos. Barlow	Longton

APPENDIX B

Date	Parcel No.	Patent No.	Factory, Retailer Wholesaler, etc	Place
31	9	255333	J. H. & J. Davis	Hanley
Sept 15	7	255821	J. Bevington & Co.	Hanley
15	10	255825	Thos. Barlow	Longton
19	2	255849	Minton & Co.	Stoke
25	8	256079	T. C. Brown–Westhead, Moore & Co.	Hanley
28	5	256215	Thos. Booth & Co.	Tunstall
Oct 4	7	256357–60	Minton & Co.	Stoke
4	9	256362	Pinder, Bourne & Co.	Burslem
6	6	256427–9	Moore & Son	Longton
9	8	256538	E. J. Ridgway & Son	Hanley
10	3	256582	J. T. Hudden	Longton
10	6	256586	T. C. Brown–Westhead, Moore & Co.	Hanley
11	4	256598	McBirney & Armstrong	Belleek
14	6	256687	Thos. Booth & Co.	Tunstall
14	7	256688	Josiah Wedgwood & Sons	Etruria
14	8	256689	McBirney & Armstrong	Belleek
18	4	256853	Moore & Son	Longton
19	6	256907	W. T. Copeland & Sons	Stoke
24	3	257126	Robert Cooke	Hanley
31	5	257258	Minton & Co.	Stoke
31	6	257259	Edge, Hill & Palmer	Longton
Nov 3	4	257364–5	R. G. Scrivener & Co.	Hanley
3	5	257366	J. F. Wileman	Fenton
15	4	257728	John Thomson & Sons	Glasgow
23	6	257944–6	Thos. Ford	Hanley
Dec 1	6	258095	Geo. Jones	Stoke
15	5	258773	Robinson & Leadbeater	Stoke
16	7	258816	McBirney & Armstrong	Belleek
22	6	258949	F. & R. Pratt	Fenton
23	3	258956–7	Geo. Jones	Stoke
29	10	259053	T. C. Brown–Westhead, Moore & Co.	Hanley

Date		Parcel No.	Patent No.	Factory, Retailer Wholesaler, etc	Place
1872					
Jan	1	5	259076	Moore & Son	Longton
	1	6	259077	Edge Malkin & Co.	Burslem
	5	3	259264	McBirney & Armstrong	Belleek
	6	1	259271	Minton & Co.	Stoke
	18	6	259801	The Worcester Royal Porcelain Co. Ltd.	Worcester
	20	6	259854	Geo. Jones	Stoke
	30	7	260081	W. T. Copeland & Sons	Stoke
Feb	2	2	260187	Moore & Son	Longton
	2	11	260240–1	Turner & Tomkinson	Tunstall
	3	4	260255–6	Geo. Jones	Stoke
	7	3	260297	Ambrose Bevington	Hanley
	15	3	260463	Powell & Bishop	Hanley
	16	6	260503	McBirney & Armstrong	Belleek
	16	7	260504–6	Geo. Jones	Stoke
	19	6	260565	Wm. H. Goss	Stoke
	20	4	260578	The Worcester Royal Porcelain Co. Ltd.	Worcester
	22	3	260640	Minton & Co.	Stoke
Mar	4	3	260868	Geo. Jones	Stoke
	4	4	260869–70	Minton & Co.	Stoke
	4	6	260872	Minton, Hollins & Co.	Stoke
	7	7	260992–3	Harvey, Adams & Co.	Longton
	7	10	260998	Bates, Elliott & Co.	Burslem
	8	5	261006–8	Minton, Hollins & Co.	Stoke
	9	1	261016	McBirney & Armstrong	Belleek
	13	8	261120	Minton, Hollins & Co.	Stoke
	16	6	261190	Minton & Co.	Stoke
	18	6	261207	idem	Stoke
	20	10	261325	The Worcester Royal Porcelain Co. Ltd.	Worcester
	21	14	261379	R. M. Taylor	Fenton
	22	5	261391	J. Holdcroft	Longton

Date	Parcel No.	Patent No.	Factory, Retailer Wholesaler, etc	Place
22	8	261394	T. C. Brown–Westhead, Moore & Co.	Hanley
26	3	261453–4	Robinson & Leadbeater	Stoke
26	6	261458	Phillips & Pearce	London
Apr 5	4	261638	Wedgwood & Co.	Tunstall
5	5	261639	Minton & Co.	Stoke
6	1	261646–7	J. Holdcroft	Longton
9	6	261724	T. C. Brown–Westhead, Moore & Co.	Hanley
10	11	261749	Thos. Furnival & Son	Cobridge
17	13	261976	E. J. Ridgway & Son	Hanley
19	5	262013	Minton, Hollins & Co.	Stoke
24	5	262203	John Pratt & Co. Ltd.	Lane Delph
27	9	262354	Moore & Son	Longton
May 2	9	262425–6	Harvey Adams & Co.	Longton
2	11	262428–9	Thos. Furnival & Son	Cobridge
3	9	262471–2	Minton & Co.	Stoke
3	11	262474	Bates, Elliott & Co.	Burslem
6	3	262483–5	Moore & Son	Longton
6	8	262493	Bates, Elliott & Co.	Burslem
6	9	262494–5	Minton, Hollins & Co.	Stoke
10	1	262651	Moore & Son	Longton
11	4	262672	Thos. Booth & Sons	Hanley
27	1	262951	Geo. Jones	Stoke
27	3	262953	Minton, Hollins & Co.	Stoke
29	2	262990	Geo. Jones	Stoke
29	5	262993–4	Geo. Grainger & Co.	Worcester
30	1	262999–3000	Minton & Co.	Stoke
June 3	6	263106	The Watcombe Terra Cotta Clay Co. Ltd.	Devon
5	3	263134	Hope & Carter	Burslem
6	6	263162	Wm. Brownfield & Son	Cobridge
7	4	263191	Minton, Hollins & Co.	Stoke

APPENDIX B

Date	Parcel No.	Patent No.	Factory, Retailer Wholesaler, etc	Place
11	5	263315	Josiah Wedgwood & Sons	Etruria
11	12	263348	W. T. Copeland & Sons	Stoke
18	3	263496–7	Geo. L. Ashworth & Bros.	Hanley
18	4	263498–9	Minton, Hollins & Co.	Stoke
21	7	263541–2	idem	Stoke
22	5	263561	Minton & Co.	Stoke
22	8	263565	Wm. Brownfield & Son	Cobridge
27	1	263771	T. C. Brown–Westhead, Moore & Co.	Hanley
July 2	2	263883–4	Robinson & Leadbeater	Stoke
2	3	263885	Josiah Wedgwood & Sons	Etruria
13	5	264081	Gelson Bros.	Hanley
15	4	264194	Robinson & Leadbeater	Stoke
16	5	264206–7	Minton, Hollins & Co.	Stoke
19	5	264299–303	R. M. Taylor	Fenton
20	3	264306–7	Geo. Jones	Stoke
24	2	264490	W. & T. Adams	Tunstall
29	7	264613	J. Dimmock & Co.	Hanley
31	3	264636–7	Minton & Co.	Stoke
Aug 2	1	264685–6	E. J. Ridgway & Son	Stoke
14	4	265105	T. Booth & Co.	Tunstall
16	1	265167–8	Wm. Brownfield & Sons	Cobridge
19	4	265254	W. E. Cartlidge	Hanley
19	5	265255	W. & J. A. Bailey	Alloa
Sept 2	3	265666	McBirney & Armstrong	Belleek
2	8	265687	Bates, Elliott & Co.	Burslem
12	6	265969	Minton, Hollins & Co.	Stoke
25	9	266628–31	Minton, Hollins & Co.	Stoke
26	2	266633	F. Jones	Longton
26	5	266636	W. E. Cartlidge	Hanley
Oct 7	7	266959	T. C. Brown–Westhead, Moore & Co.	Hanley
11	5	267060–4	Josiah Wedgwood & Sons	Etruria
12	10	267103–4	Bates, Elliott & Co.	Burslem

APPENDIX B

Date	Parcel No.	Patent No.	Factory, Retailer Wholesaler, etc	Place
14	4	267112	Minton, Hollins & Co.	Stoke
17	8	267265	Josiah Wedgwood & Sons	Etruria
18	5	267317–9	Geo. Jones	Stoke
30	2	267523	J. F. Wileman	Fenton
30	5	267527	The Brownhills Pottery	Tunstall
30	9	267534	Maw & Co.	Broseley
Nov 2	6	267588–91	The Worcester Royal Porcelain Co. Ltd.	Worcester
4	3	267618	Geo. Grainger & Co.	Worcester
11	2	267806	W. E. Cartlidge	Hanley
12	4	267839	Minton & Co.	Stoke
14	13	267893–5	Wm. Brownfield & Son	Cobridge
14	14	267896	Moore Bros.	Longton
18	3	267972	Holland & Green	Longton
30	8	268309	Belfield & Co.	Preston-pans
Dec 2	5	268322	T. C. Brown–Westhead, Moore & Co.	Hanley
4	3	268388	John Pratt & Co. Ltd.	Lane Delph
10	2	268724–5	Minton & Co.	Stoke
11	8	268748–9	The Old Hall Earthenware Co. Ltd.	Hanley
14	5	268806–7	Wm. Brownfield & Son	Cobridge
24	1	269197	Cockson & Chetwynd	Cobridge
27	4	269269	John Adams (Excrs of)	Longton
27	5	269270	R. G. Scrivener & Co.	Hanley
27	8	269275	John Meir & Son	Tunstall
1873				
Jan 10	1	269585	Geo. Jones	Stoke
13	4	269621	W. T. Copeland & Sons	Stoke
14	8	269686	J. Defries	London
15	2	269690	Worthington & Son	Hanley

Date	Parcel No.	Patent No.	Factory, Retailer Wholesaler, etc	Place
29	1	269993–70001	Minton, Hollins & Co.	Stoke
29	2	270002–4	Moore Bros.	Longton
Feb 1	1	270042–50	Minton, Hollins & Co.	Stoke
10	2	270298	W. & J. A. Bailey	Alloa
12	4	270354	Bates, Elliott & Co.	Burslem
15	1	270385	Minton & Co.	Stoke
19	14	270600–1	J. & T. Bevington	Hanley
25	6	270700	Geo. Jones	Stoke
27	4	270751	Thos. Till & Sons	Burslem
27	8	270755	Minton, Hollins & Co.	Stoke
Mar 6	1	271031–2	Minton & Co.	Stoke
6	9	271057	The Brownhills Pottery Co.	Tunstall
26	6	271561–2	Geo. Jones	Stoke
Apr 3	6	271851	Minton & Co.	Stoke
15	4	272091	Taylor, Tunnicliffe & Co.	Hanley
19	2	272206	Minton & Co.	Stoke
23	6	272293	Gelson Bros.	Hanley
28	5	272364–5	Powell & Bishop	Hanley
29	3	272384–5	Geo. Jones	Stoke
May 3	2	272637	Thos. Till & Sons	Burslem
3	7	272642–6	Wm. Brownfield & Son	Cobridge
3	8	272647–8	Minton & Co.	Stoke
6	2	272662	idem	Stoke
12	8	272835	T. C. Brown–Westhead, Moore & Co.	Hanley
14	7	272896–7	Moore Bros.	Longton
16	6	272983	Minton, Hollins & Co.	Stoke
17	4	272988–90	John L. Johnson & Co.	Longton
22	5	273089	Worthington & Son	Hanley
26	7	273158–9	Moore Bros.	Longton
26	8	273160	Soane & Smith	London
29	4	273246	Worthington & Son	Hanley
29	8	273251	Thos. Ford	Hanley

Date	Parcel No.	Patent No.	Factory, Retailer Wholesaler, etc	Place
30	15	273376	T. C. Brown–Westhead, Moore & Co.	Hanley
June 11	4	273662–3	Bates, Elliott & Co.	Burslem
17	3	273736–7	Taylor, Tunnicliffe & Co.	Hanley
19	3	273804	Pinder & Bourne & Co.	Burslem
28	4	274047	Thos. Goode & Co.	London
30	3	274054–5	Minton, Hollins & Co.	Stoke
July 3	9	274162	Minton, Hollins & Co.	Stoke
4	7	274183	T. C. Brown–Westhead, Moore & Co.	Hanley
28	2	274663	Chas. Hobson	Burslem
28	8	274701	John Meir & Sons	Tunstall
29	3	274704	McBirney & Armstrong	Belleek
31	1	274725–6	Mintons	Stoke
Aug 5	2	274804	Baker & Chetwynd	Burslem
14	10	275050	T. C. Brown–Westhead, Moore & Co.	Hanley
25	1	275514–5	Geo. Jones	Stoke
27	1	275600	The Worcester Royal Porcelain Co. Ltd.	Worcester
30	2	275661	T. C. Brown–Westhead, Moore & Co.	Hanley
Sept 2	8	275755	Edge, Malkin & Co.	Burslem
4	3	275816	Mintons	Stoke
10	7	275994	Powell & Bishop	Hanley
15	3	276151	T. C. Brown–Westhead, Moore & Co.	Hanley
16	4	276159	idem	Hanley
17	8	276213	The Worcester Royal Porcelain Co. Ltd.	Worcester
19	4	276338	T. C. Brown-Westhead, Moore & Co.	Hanley
25	8	276517	Harvey, Adams & Co.	Longton
25	10	276522	Jane Beech	Burslem
29	2	276566	Wm. Brownfield & Son	Cobridge

Date	Parcel No.	Patent No.	Factory, Retailer Wholesaler, etc	Place
Oct 4	3	276796–8	Moore Bros.	Longton
4	4	276799	Heath & Blackhurst	Burslem
6	6	276816–7	T. C. Brown–Westhead, Moore & Co.	Hanley
11	6	277136	Mintons	Stoke
13	3	277148–9	Geo. Jones	Stoke
22	6	277385	Mintons	Stoke
Nov 3	3	277844	Hope & Carter	Burslem
3	4	277845–7	Geo. Jones	Stoke
6	6	277969	Wedgwood & Co.	Tunstall
10	7	278169	T. C. Brown-Westhead, Moore & Co.	Hanley
12	3	278185	Worthington & Son	Hanley
Dec 2	6	278769–70	Taylor, Tunnicliffe & Co.	Hanley
4	6	278821	The Old Hall Earthenware Co. Ltd.	Hanley
5	1	278822	Harvey, Adams & Co.	Longton
5	8	278867	Wm. Brownfield & Son	Cobridge
10	12	279180	Geo. Jones & Sons	Stoke
27	7	279437	idem	Stoke
1874				
Jan 1	3	279476–7	Bates, Elliott & Co.	Burslem
10	15	279655–6	Davenports & Co.	London (and Longport)
20	3	279938	Powell & Bishop	Hanley
21	7	279964	W. T. Copeland & Sons	Stoke
23	5	280010	John Meir & Son	Tunstall
30	4	280153–6	Haviland & Co.	Limoges and London
Feb 9	4	280343	The Worcester Royal Porcelain Co. Ltd.	Worcester
9	5	280344	Bodley & Co.	Burslem

APPENDIX B

Date	Parcel No.	Patent No.	Factory, Retailer Wholesaler, etc	Place
11	2	280350	Thos. Booth & Sons	Hanley
14	9	280492	Worthington & Son	Hanley
19	1	280609	Geo. Jones & Sons	Stoke
25	6	280785	Robinson & Leadbeater	Stoke
25	7	280786	Geo. Jones & Sons	Stoke
26	7	280802–4	Minton, Hollins & Co.	Stoke
Mar 2	1	280853	McBirney & Armstrong	Belleek
3	4	280907	Geo. Jones & Sons	Stoke
4	3	280919	Mintons	Stoke
4	8	280925	The Worcester Royal Porcelian Co. Ltd.	Worcester
13	6	281106	J. Dimmock & Co.	Hanley
14	2	281129	Mintons	Stoke
17	5	281190	Powell & Bishop	Hanley
21	5	281301	idem	Hanley
24	4	281319	Mintons	Stoke
27	2	281404	Worthington & Son	Hanley
28	3	281429–30	Geo. Jones & Sons	Stoke
30	1	281437	Worthington & Son	Hanley
Apr 7	4	281639	The Worcester Royal Porcelain Co. Ltd.	Worcester
14	4	281776	A. Bevington	Hanley
15	7	281822	Mintons	Stoke
20	7	281871–80	Minton, Hollins & Co.	Stoke
21	8	281899	Geo. Jones & Sons	Stoke
22	1	281902	Wm. Brownfield & Son	Cobridge
23	8	281954	T. C. Brown–Westhead, Moore & Co.	Hanley
25	2	281984	Geo. Jones & Sons	Stoke
29	7	282088	Ridgway, Sparks & Ridgway	Hanley
29	9	282091	T. Furnival & Son	Cobridge
30	2	282098	Thos. Booth & Sons	Hanley
May 5	3	282134	Bates, Elliott & Co.	Burslem
9	3	282218–9	Geo. Jones & Sons	Stoke

APPENDIX B

Date	Parcel No.	Patent No.	Factory, Retailer Wholesaler, etc	Place
11	2	282249–51	Moore Bros.	Longton
11	3	282252	J. Thomson & Sons	Glasgow
11	4	282253	Holland & Green	Longton
20	11	282497	Bates, Elliott & Co.	Burslem
21	5	282526	Mintons	Stoke
22	8	282555	idem	Stoke
23	4	282567–8	Geo. Jones & Sons	Stoke
June 1	7	282662	The Worcester Royal Porcelain Co. Ltd.	Worcester
6	2	282799–802	Wm. Brownfield & Son	Cobridge
6	5	282806	Chas. Ford	Hanley
16	6	282982	Cockson & Chetwynd	Cobridge
17	7	283041	Edge, Malkin & Co.	Burslem
18	1	283050	Mintons	Stoke
23	3	283201	Williamson & Son	Longton
23	7	283208	The Worcester Royal Porcelain Co. Ltd.	Worcester
25	5	283266–8	Thos. Ford	Hanley
26	4	283275	Pinder, Bourne & Co.	Burslem
July 10	2	283547	Mintons	Stoke
13	6	283570–1	T. C. Brown–Westhead, Moore & Co.	Hanley
27	1	283980	Hulse & Adderley	Longton
30	5	284053	Minton, Hollins & Co.	Stoke
Aug 1	8	284131–5	Mintons	Stoke
1	9	284136	Cockson & Chetwynd	Cobridge
6	7	284204	T. C. Brown–Westhead, Moore & Co.	Hanley
8	2	284254–5	Wm. Brownfield & Son	Cobridge
15	4	284417	Bates, Elliott & Co.	Burlsem
22	6	284562	J. T. Hudden	Longton
28	4	284699–700	Geo. Jones & Sons	Stoke
31	6	284779	T. J. & J. Emberton	Tunstall

APPENDIX B

Date	Parcel No.	Patent No.	Factory, Retailer Wholesaler, etc	Place
Sept 1	3	284791	Thos. Till & Sons	Burslem
3	11	284883	Geo. Adler	Saxony and London
3	12	284884–5	Cockson & Chetwynd	Cobridge
4	3	284897	Mintons	Stoke
5	4	284916–7	The Worcester Royal Porcelain Co. Ltd.	Worcester
5	7	284920	Furnival & Son	Cobridge
7	3	284936–7	Thos. Booth & Sons	Hanley
10	3	285013	Wm. Brownfield & Son	Cobridge
12	1	285181	Mintons	Stoke
15	2	285281	Geo. Jones & Sons	Stoke
16	7	285304	M. Bucholz	London
17	4	285322	R. Britton & Sons	Leeds
30	4	285776	Wm. Brownfield & Son	Cobridge
Oct 2	5	285826–8	Geo. Grainger & Co.	Worcester
3	4	285841–4	Moore Bros.	Longton
6	3	286000	Mintons	Stoke
6	4	286001	Grove & Stark	Longton
10	4	286134	Mintons	Stoke
12	2	286171	Powell & Bishop	Hanley
17	8	286359–60	Bates, Elliott & Co.	Burslem
21	8	286424	Geo. Jones & Sons	Stoke
24	3	286504–5	Robinson & Leadbeater	Stoke
27	1	286530	George Ash	Hanley
28	9	286563	Pinder, Bourne & Co.	Burslem
Nov 2	3	286715	James Edwards & Son	Burslem
3	4	286720–2	W. & E. Corn	Burslem
6	3	286759	Wm. Brownfield & Son	Cobridge
7	4	286774–80	Thos. Ford	Hanley
10	3	286794	Geo. Jones & Sons	Stoke
12	3	286931	Mintons	Stoke
12	12	286942	Bates, Elliott & Co.	Burslem
20	12	287317	F. & R. Pratt & Co.	Fenton

Date	Parcel No.	Patent No.	Factory, Retailer Wholesaler, etc	Place
25	7	287438–9	Minton, Hollins & Co.	Stoke
Dec 1	5	287598	W. T. Copeland & Sons	Stoke
4	6	287638	Thos. Barlow	Longton
5	4	287676	Holmes & Plant	Burslem
7	8	287694–7	T. C. Brown–Westhead, Moore & Co.	Hanley
8	2	287699	Geo. Jones & Sons	Stoke
10	4	287731	Pinder, Bourne & Co.	Burslem
10	11	287752–6	The Worcester Royal Porcelain Co. Ltd.	Worcester
12	3	287776	Geo. Jones & Sons	Stoke
12	5	287785	Port Dundas Pottery Co.	Port Dundas
18	6	287982	Geo. Jones & Sons	Stoke
18	7	287983	Ambrose Bevington	Hanley
18	9	287985	Geo. Grainger & Co.	Worcester
18	11	287990–7	Minton, Hollins & Co.	Stoke
1875				
Jan 2	4	288241–2	T. C. Brown–Westhead, Moore & Co.	Hanley
6	3	288276–8	Minton, Hollins & Co.	Stoke
12	3	288366	The Worcester Royal Porcelain Co. Ltd.	Worcester
16	9	288502	The Brownhills Pottery Co.	Tunstall
18	8	288521	T. C. Brown–Westhead, Moore & Co.	Hanley
20	3	288552	Robinson & Leadbeater	Stoke
20	4	288553–6	Wm. Brownfield & Son	Cobridge
21	2	288682	Geo. Jones & Sons	Stoke
23	9	288755–8	T. C. Brown–Westhead, Moore & Co.	Hanley
28	5	288830	Mintons	Stoke
29	1	288861–2	Worthington & Son	Hanley
Feb 3	7	288972	Chas. Ford	Hanley

Date	Parcel No.	Patent No.	Factory, Retailer Wholesaler, etc	Place
5	5	289076	T. & R. Boote	Burslem
6	2	289083	Moore Bros.	Longton
9	1	289172	Pinder, Bourne & Co.	Burslem
9	2	289173	Geo. Jones & Sons	Stoke
12	6	289280	J. Maddock & Sons	Burslem
15	2	289310	Moore Bros.	Longton
17	7	289334	Mintons	Stoke
23	5	289503	J. Maddock & Sons	Burslem
23	6	289504	Geo. Jones & Sons	Stoke
23	8	289507–8	George Ash	Hanley
24	3	289535	Stephen Clive	Tunstall
Mar 5	2	289769	Wm. Brownfield & Son	Cobridge
12	5	289874–6	Geo. Jones & Sons	Stoke
24	13	290153	Minton, Hollins & Co.	Stoke
24	14	290154–5	T. C. Brown–Westhead, Moore & Co.	Hanley
30	1	290186	Thos. Booth & Sons	Hanley
31	5	290209–10	Wm. Brownfield & Son	Cobridge
Apr 3	7	290259	J. Dimmock & Co.	Hanley
3	9	290261–2	E. F. Bodley & Son	Burslem
7	3	290352	Mintons	Stoke
9	6	290393–4	Wm. Brownfield & Son	Cobridge
10	7	290407–8	Powell & Bishop	Hanley
15	5	290500	R. Malkin	Fenton
17	1	290738	Pinder, Bourne & Co.	Burslem
20	1	290787	J. Dimmock & Co.	Hanley
20	2	290788	Mintons	Stoke
21	5	290812	Stephen Clive	Tunstall
22	3	290841–2	W. P. & G. Phillips	London
22	4	290843–6	Minton, Hollins & Co.	Stoke
May 3	8	290998	Soane & Smith	London
7	7	291109	Geo. Jones & Sons	Stoke
7	8	291110	Burgess & Leigh	Burslem
11	6	291229	Thos. Goode & Co.	London
20	1	291440	Bates, Elliott & Co.	Burslem

Date	Parcel No.	Patent No.	Factory, Retailer Wholesaler, etc	Place
20	3	291444	J. Dimmock & Co.	Hanley
22	1	291458	Holland & Green	Longton
26	6	291518–20	T. C. Brown–Westhead, Moore & Co.	Hanley
28	10	291556	Campbellfield Pottery Co.	Glasgow
28	12	291558	J. Mortlock	London
31	8	291568	Geo. Jones & Sons	Stoke
31	18	291611	Ridgway, Sparks & Ridgway	Hanley
June 2	9	291749–51	Minton, Hollins & Co.	Stoke
5	7	291870–1	W. P. & G. Phillips	London
7	3	291882	W. & T. Adams	Tunstall
8	4	291911	The Worcester Royal Porcelain Co. (Ltd.)	Worcester
10	6	292005	Wm. Brownfield & Son	Cobridge
12	5	292034	Chas. Stevenson	Greenock
12	6	292035	Maddock & Gater	Burslem
12	10	292042	Thos. Furnival & Son	Stoke
15	5	292080	Josiah Wedgwood & Sons	Etruria
19	6	292184	Thos. Till & Sons	Burslem
26	2	292367–70	Geo. Jones & Sons	Stoke
July 5	1	292542	Wm. Brownfield & Son	Cobridge
7	8	292579–80	Moore Bros.	Longton
8	5	292620	idem	Longton
20	4	292985	E. J. D. Bodley	Burslem
23	10	293035	T. C. Brown–Westhead, Moore & Co.	Hanley
27	5	293114	F. W. Grove & J. Stark	Longton
28	7	293129	Minton, Hollins & Co.	Stoke
Aug 19	7	293748	F. W. Grove & J. Stark	Longton
28	6	294038–9	W. P. & G. Phillips	London
Sept 2	3	294147	T. Elsmore & Son	Tunstall
13	2	294434–5	Geo. Jones & Sons	Stoke
14	9	294514	Minton, Hollins & Co.	Stoke
18	2	294571–2	Geo. Jones & Sons	Stoke

Date	Parcel No.	Patent No.	Factory, Retailer Wholesaler, etc	Place
21	1	294595	R. Cochran & Co.	Glasgow
24	2	294657	H. Aynsley & Co.	Longton
25	3	294662	F. W. Grove & J. Stark	Longton
28	6	294768–9	T. C. Brown–Westhead, Moore & Co.	Hanley
30	4	294825–7	John Edwards	Fenton
Oct 2	6	294906	Josiah Wedgwood & Sons	Etruria
6	4	294936	R. Cooke	Hanley
11	4	295001	Powell & Bishop	Hanley
11	10	295014–5	The Brownhills Pottery Co.	Tunstall
16	8	295131	Burgess, Leigh & Co.	Burslem
28	3	295443	Minton, Hollins & Co.	Stoke
30	9	295473–4	W. P. & G. Phillips	London
Nov 5	3	295551–3	Geo. Jones & Sons	Stoke
8	4	295792–8	Minton, Hollins & Co.	Stoke
8	8	295803	W. T. Copeland & Sons	Stoke
12	1	295908	Geo. Jones & Sons	Stoke
12	2	295909	Burgess, Leigh & Co.	Burslem
13	8	295933	The Worcester Royal Porcelain Co. Ltd.	Worcester
Dec 1	2	296475	Wm. Brownfield & Son	Cobridge
1	9	296508	Gelson Bros.	Hanley
3	4	296531	Geo. Jones & Sons	Stoke
6	8	296644	John Meir & Son	Tunstall
10	3	296770	Mintons	Stoke
11	5	296813	F. W. Grove & J. Stark	Longton
11	8	296818	Soane & Smith	London
13	8	296834–49	Minton, Hollins & Co.	Stoke
15	2	296939–40	Mintons China Works	Stoke
15	3	296941–5	Mintons	Stoke
24	4	297217–8	Chas. Ford	Hanley
24	6	297221	Bates, Walker & Co.	Burslem
29	5	297245	Edge, Malkin & Co.	Burslem
29	6	297246–7	T. C. Brown–Westhead, Moore & Co.	Hanley

APPENDIX B

Date	Parcel No.	Patent No.	Factory, Retailer Wholesaler, etc	Place
30	2	297250	Mintons	Stoke
30	8	297276	Mintons, Hollins & Co.	Stoke
1876				
Jan 4	4	297343	Mintons	Stoke
6	2	297471	Moore Bros.	Longton
11	7	297587	E. J. D. Bodley	Burslem
21	13	297791	Bale & Co.	Etruria
22	6	297809–11	Geo. Jones & Sons	Stoke
22	8	297813	Chas. Ford	Hanley
24	1	297817	Mintons	Stoke
24	4	297845	J. Friedrich	London
24	6	297863–4	Bates, Walker & Co.	Burslem
26	2	297977	Edge, Malkin & Co.	Burslem
26	3	297978	Powell & Bishop	Hanley
28	8	298018	James Edwards & Son	Burslem
29	3	298027–9	Wm. Brownfield & Son	Cobridge
Feb 1	2	298049	idem	Cobridge
2	7	298063	Josiah Wedgwood & Sons	Etruria
2	12	298069	Ridgway, Sparks & Ridgway	Hanley
3	5	298077	Powell & Bishop	Hanley
4	6	298103	Mintons	Stoke
4	12	298141–2	The Worcester Royal Porcelain Co. Ltd.	Worcester
8	9	298235	Bates, Walker & Co.	Burslem
19	5	298458	Geo. Jones & Sons	Stoke
21	4	298473	The Worcester Royal Porcelain Co. Ltd.	Worcester
22	3	298480–3	Minton, Hollins & Co.	Stoke
29	9	298693	J. Dimmock & Co.	Hanley
Mar 2	8	298821–4	T. Gelson & Co.	Hanley
2	11	298832	The Brownhills Pottery Co.	Tunstall
10	8	299076–8	Minton, Hollins & Co.	Stoke

Date	Parcel No.	Patent No.	Factory, Retailer Wholesaler, etc	Place
14	5	299177	T. C. Brown–Westhead, Moore & Co.	Hanley
17	5	299236	Mintons	Stoke
18	3	299246	Robinson & Chapman	Longton
23	8	299366	E. J. D. Bodley	Burslem
24	7	299380	Bates, Walker & Co.	Burslem
28	8	299474	W. E. Withinshaw	Burslem
30	4	299497–9	Geo. Jones & Sons	Stoke
Apr 8	6	299773	Bates, Walker & Co.	Burslem
11	4	299819	Thos. Gelson & Co.	Hanley
12	4	299830	Powell & Bishop	Hanley
12	11	299852	J. Dimmock & Co.	Hanley
21	7	300020	Minton, Hollins & Co.	Stoke
21	10	300037–8	Furnival & Son	Cobridge
22	5	300105	The Worcester Royal Porcelain Co. Ltd.	Worcester
27	3	300260	Mintons	Stoke
May 8	7	300421–3	T. C. Brown–Westhead, Moore & Co.	Hanley
10	3	300463	Geo. Jones & Sons	Stoke
11	9	300491	F. & R. Pratt & Co.	Fenton
16	7	300603–4	Mintons	Stoke
22	3	300682	Moore Bros.	Longton
22	4	300683–5	Josiah Wedgwood & Sons	Etruria
23	7	300734–7	Haviland & Co.	Limoges and London
24	3	300746	Mintons	Stoke
25	6	300779	Moore Bros.	Longton
29	8	300809–10	Geo. Jones & Sons	Stoke
June 3	2	301030	Mintons	Stoke
3	5	301035–7	E. J. D. Bodley	Burslem
7	1	301087	Thos. Gelson & Co.	Hanley
8	4	301099	Mintons	Stoke
9	6	301164	W. T. Copeland & Sons	Stoke

APPENDIX B

Date	Parcel No.	Patent No.	Factory, Retailer Wholesaler, etc	Place
15	1	301254	Henry Meir & Son	Tunstall
15	9	301267–9	Minton, Hollins & Co.	Stoke
19	2	301302	Josiah Wedgwood & Sons	Etruria
19	9	301310	J. Holdcroft	Longton
21	4	301330	Mintons	Stoke
22	4	301342	Thos. Gelson & Co.	Hanley
23	5	301402	Mintons	Stoke
26	6	301443–4	Minton, Hollins & Co.	Stoke
28	8	301543	J. Aynsley	Longton
July 1	3	301589–90	Mintons	Stoke
1	4	301591	John Tams	Longton
3	2	301596	Ford & Challinor	Tunstall
5	1	301619	Thos. Till & Sons	Burslem
5	7	301641	W. T. Copeland & Sons	Stoke
10	3	301877	Thos. Gelson & Co.	Hanley
12	2	301926	E. J. D. Bodley	Burslem
18	3	301984	Soane & Smith	London
26	3	302125	Geo. Jones & Sons	Stoke
28	10	302178	Thos. Gelson & Co.	Hanley
28	11	302179	Powell & Bishop	Hanley
31	8	302220	G. Grainger & Co.	Worcester
Aug 8	1	302384	Robinson & Chapman	Longton
25	8	302901	F. & R. Pratt & Co.	Fenton
Sept 5	5	303289–90	Bates & Walker & Co.	Burslem
6	9	303308	Pinder & Bourne & Co.	Burslem
6	10	303309	Wm. Brownfield & Sons	Cobridge
9	8	303455	Worthington & Son	Hanley
9	9	303456–7	T. C. Brown–Westhead, Moore & Co.	Hanley
11	1	303459	E. J. D. Bodley	Burslem
12	6	303522–3	Geo. Jones & Sons	Stoke
18	10	303677	G. L. Ashworth & Bros.	Hanley
20	3	303731–2	Hollinshead & Kirkham	Burslem
22	3	303757	Powell & Bishop	Hanley
26	5	303853	Hope & Carter	Burslem

351

Date	Parcel No.	Patent No.	Factory, Retailer Wholesaler, etc	Place
26	10	303918	T. C. Brown–Westhead, Moore & Co.	Hanley
28	2	303926–7	Moore Bros.	Longton
28	10	303942	Hope & Carter	Burslem
Oct 7	2	304128	Wm. Harrop	Hanley
7	3	304129–31	Wm. Brownfield & Sons	Cobridge
7	4	304132–3	Josiah Wedgwood & Sons	Etruria
7	6	304144–5	Wm. Adams	Tunstall
9	1	304149–50	Geo. Jones & Sons	Stoke
12	8	304321	Ambrose Bevington	Hanley
17	4	304376	T. C. Brown–Westhead, Moore & Co.	Hanley
17	9	304383	Wardle & Co.	Hanley
19	3	304428	Burgess, Leigh & Co.	Burslem
20	2	304454–66	Mintons	Stoke
21	3	304473	Edge, Malkin & Co.	Burslem
23	2	304489	Mintons	Stoke
31	2	304910–4	Wm. Brownfield & Sons	Cobridge
Nov 1	2	304926	Moore Bros.	Longton
7	3	305065	Robert Jones	Hanley
8	3	305080	Geo. Jones & Sons	Stoke
8	9	305090	Wm. Brownfield & Sons	Cobridge
9	10	305150	Belfield & Co.	Preston-pans
11	9	305173	Moore Bros.	Longton
13	3	305181	Mintons	Stoke
14	2	305189	Josiah Wedgwood & Sons	Etruria
14	8	305195	Clementson Bros.	Hanley
17	3	305222	Banks & Thorley	Hanley
18	3	305233	Minton, Hollins & Co.	Stoke
18	7	305264	Minton, Hollins & Co.	Stoke
18	9	305266	The Worcester Royal Porcelain Co. Ltd.	Worcester
23	5	305312	Wm. Adams	Tunstall
24	15	305461–2	Thos. Furnival & Sons	Cobridge

APPENDIX B

Date	Parcel No.	Patent No.	Factory, Retailer Wholesaler, etc	Place
28	2	305510	W. Hudson & Son	Longton
29	11	305568	Thos. Furnival & Sons	Cobridge
Dec 5	2	305684	Wedgwood & Co.	Tunstall
11	2	305829	John Tams	Longton
12	11	305885	The Campbell Brick & Tile Co.	Stoke
14	1	305934	Harvey Adams & Co.	Longton
14	11	305973	J. Dimmock & Co.	Hanley
18	9	306100	James Beech	Longton
20	7	306184	J. & T. Bevington	Hanley
21	2	306202	F. W. Grove & J. Stark	Longton
23	5	306282	Chas. Ford	Hanley
27	15	306341	The Campbell Brick & Tile Co.	Stoke
28	6	306367	Harvey Adams & Co.	Longton
1877				
Jan 4	10	306564	The Campbellfield Pottery Co.	Glasgow
17	5	306953	The Worcester Royal Porcelain Co. Ltd.	Worcester
20	2	307028	F. W. Grove & J. Stark	Longton
24	10	307213	Wm. Brownfield & Sons	Cobridge
25	6	307236	Wood & Co.	Burslem
25	7	307237–9	Geo. Jones & Sons	Stoke
26	3	307258	Mintons	Stoke
26	4	307259	Powell & Bishop	Hanley
Feb 1	6	307432	James Edwards & Son	Burslem
2	7	307495–7	The Worcester Royal Porcelain Co. Ltd.	Worcester
3	4	307506–7	Minton, Hollins & Co.	Stoke
5	2	307525–7	McBirney & Armstrong	Belleek
7	3	307551	Holland & Green	Longton
7	7	307570–2	Wm. Brownfield & Sons	Cobridge
9	7	307603	Robinson & Co.	Longton

APPENDIX B

Date	Parcel No.	Patent No.	Factory, Retailer Wholesaler, etc	Place
9	11	307613	T. C. Brown–Westhead, Moore & Co.	Hanley
12	3	307646	James Beech	Longton
14	16	307782	The Worcester Royal Porcelain Co. Ltd.	Worcester
15	10	307794	Minton, Hollins & Co.	Stoke
16	9	307866	John Rose & Co.	Coalport
19	2	307877	Wm. Brownfield & Sons	Cobridge
20	8	307892	G. Grainger & Co.	Worcester
21	6	307906	Mintons	Stoke
21	9	307909	W. T. Copeland & Sons	Stoke
24	3	307983	Thos. Hughes	Burslem
27	2	308010	Mintons	Stoke
Mar 1	4	308116–21	Hallam, Johnson & Co.	Longton
8	14	308329	W. T. Copeland & Sons	Stoke
10	7	308357	Geo. Jones & Sons	Stoke
14	9	308493	The Campbell Brick & Tile Co.	Stoke
20	3	308650–2	Clementson Bros.	Hanley
20	8	308662	J. Dimmock & Co.	Hanley
22	14	308718	E. J. D. Bodley	Burslem
24	1	308781–2	Powell & Bishop	Hanley
31	7	308916	E. F. Bodley & Co.	Burslem
Apr 3	1	308918	Powell & Bishop	Hanley
4	5	308932	J. Mortlock	London
5	2	308934	Ford, Challinor & Co.	Tunstall
12	11	309233	J. Dimmock & Co.	Hanley
23	4	309617	John Tams	Longton
26	2	309680	J. & T. Bevington	Hanley
26	7	309696	The Worcester Royal Porcelain Co. Ltd.	Worcester
27	10	309746	John Rose & Co.	Coalport
May 2	2	309818–21	Geo. Jones & Sons	Stoke
4	13	309917	The Old Hall Earthenware Co. Ltd.	Hanley

APPENDIX B

Date	Parcel No.	Patent No.	Factory, Retailer Wholesaler, etc	Place
5	4	309922	Josiah Wedgwood & Sons	Etruria
12	7	310034	Thos. Furnival & Sons	Cobridge
16	5	310175	Wm. Brownfield & Sons	Cobridge
18	6	310267	Josiah Wedgwood & Sons	Etruria
22	5	310359–61	Wm. Brownfield & Sons	Cobridge
24	8	310448	T. C. Brown–Westhead, Moore & Co.	Hanley
30	13	310556	T. Furnival & Sons	Cobridge
June 1	2	310599	J. & R. Hammersley	Hanley
5	6	310670	E. J. D. Bodley	Burslem
7	1	310709	idem	Burslem
7	2	310710	Joseph Holdcroft	Longton
8	7	310761–4	Minton, Hollins & Co.	Stoke
9	3	310775–6	Baker & Co.	Fenton
13	2	310909	idem	Fenton
15	7	310972	Ridgway, Sparks & Ridgway	Hanley
19	4	311031	Ford & Challinor	Tunstall
19	6	311033	Murray & Co.	Glasgow
22	3	311141	Walker & Carter	Stoke
22	13	311181–6	Steele & Wood	Stoke
22	14	311187	E. F. Bodley & Co.	Burslem
26	11	311366	T. Furnival & Sons	Cobridge
28	9	311423	idem	Cobridge
29	10	311448–9	Sherwin & Cotton	Hanley
July 2	3	311523	W. T. Copeland & Sons	Stoke
6	2	311626	Mintons	Stoke
7	4	311684	Ridge, Meigh & Co.	Longton
9	2	311711	Minton, Hollins & Co.	Stoke
14	2	311883–4	John Tams	Longton
17	9	312019–21	James Edwards & Son	Burslem
20	7	312062–4	Haviland & Co.	London and Limoges
20	15	312113	Taylor, Tunnicliffe & Co.	Hanley

355

Date	Parcel No.	Patent No.	Factory, Retailer Wholesaler, etc	Place
23	2	312125	John Edwards	Fenton
25	5	312187	Ford, Challinor & Co.	Tunstall
26	6	312311–4	Minton, Hollins & Co.	Stoke
31	1	312421	McBirney & Armstrong	Belleek
31	2	312422	Minton & Hollins & Co.	Stoke
Aug 1	4	312434	Holmes, Stonier & Hollinshead	Hanley
3	14	312521	The Campbell Brick & Tile Co.	Stoke
13	5	312909	Haviland & Co.	London and Limoges
15	7	313009	The Campbell Brick & Tile Co.	Stoke
17	11	313080	Ridgway, Sparks & Ridgway	Stoke
18	6	313099–101	Minton, Hollins & Co.	Stoke
18	7	313102	Furnival & Son	Cobridge
23	6	313280	W. Hudson & Son	Longton
25	2	313324	Wm. Wood & Co.	Burslem
25	3	313325–9	Minton, Hollins & Co.	Stoke
28	9	313381	T. C. Brown–Westhead, Moore & Co.	Hanley
Sept 11	3	314046	G. W. Turner & Sons	Tunstall
19	5	314292	Minton, Hollins & Co.	Stoke
20	3	314385	Josiah Wedgwood & Sons	Etruria
22	7	314470–1	Mintons	Stoke
22	13	314480	Minton, Hollins & Co.	Stoke
25	5	314548	Mintons	Stoke
28	9	314675	J. Holdcroft	Longton
Oct 2	7	314890	Bates, Walker & Co.	Burslem
3	2	314896	Robinson & Leadbeater	Stoke
4	4	314906–7	J. & T. Bevington	Hanley
10	3	315102	John Edwards	Fenton

APPENDIX B

Date	Parcel No.	Patent No.	Factory, Retailer Wholesaler, etc	Place
10	5	315104–5	Wm. Brownfield & Sons	Cobridge
15	2	315271–2	Geo. Jones & Sons	Stoke
16	6	315400–1	Powell & Bishop	Hanley
19	8	315473	Minton, Hollins & Co.	Stoke
19	13	315479	T. C. Brown–Westhead, Moore & Co.	Hanley
24	10	315565	F. W. Grove & J. Stark	Longton
24	14	315574	F. & R. Pratt & Co.	Fenton
30	7	315684	Wedgwood & Co.	Tunstall
31	6	315765	Geo. Jones & Sons	Stoke
Nov 5	4	315918	Powell & Bishop	Hanley
6	11	315954–6	Wm. Brownfield & Sons	Cobridge
7	1	316087–9	E. J. D. Bodley	Burslem
7	2	316090	Mintons	Stoke
7	10	316101	Pinder, Bourne & Co.	Burslem
9	8	316122	Taylor, Tunnicliffe & Co.	Hanley
15	12	316309	T. C. Brown–Westhead, Moore & Co.	Hanley
20	9	316502	James Edwards & Sons	Burslem
21	8	316526	Davenports & Co.	Longport
22	1	316542–3	The Old Hall Earthenware Co. Ltd.	Hanley
22	13	316560	B. & S. Hancock	Stoke
24	7	316605	J. Dimmock & Co.	Hanley
29	3	316723	J. Holdcroft	Longton
Dec 1	5	316763	J. Holdcroft	Longton
1	6	316764	Oakes, Clare & Chadwick	Burslem
5	2	316842	E. J. D. Bodley	Burslem
6	4	316863	Mintons	Stoke
7	14	316912	J. Unwin	Longton
14	1	317112	J. Dimmock & Co.	Hanley
15	10	317203	The Worcester Royal Porcelain Co. Ltd.	Worcester
21	6	317404	Mintons	Stoke

357

Date	Parcel No.	Patent No.	Factory, Retailer Wholesaler, etc	Place
21	10	317410	T. Furnival & Sons	Cobridge
22	5	317427–8	Wm. Brownfield & Sons	Cobridge
29	6	317494	T. C. Brown–Westhead, Moore & Co.	Hanley
1878				
Jan 3	4	317537–9	Minton, Hollins & Co.	Stoke
9	4	317692–4	The Brownhills Pottery Co.	Tunstall
10	12	317733	J. Mortlock & Co.	London
14	1	317756	J. Maddock & Sons	Burslem
14	2	317757	Cotton & Rigby	Burslem
14	3	317758	Wm. Adams	Tunstall
14	6	317763	Minton, Hollins & Co.	Stoke
15	5	317780	Josiah Wedgwood & Sons	Etruria
18	5	317826	Taylor, Tunnicliffe & Co.	Hanley
22	6	317940	J. Dimmock & Co.	Hanley
24	6	318041	W. T. Copeland & Sons	Stoke
25	9	318107–8	Wm. Brownfield & Sons	Cobridge
28	11	318141	T. C. Brown–Westhead, Moore & Co.	Hanley
30	3	318158–9	Geo. Jones	Stoke
30	15	318189–90	The Brownhills Pottery Co.	Tunstall
31	1	318210	B. & S. Hancock	Stoke
Feb 1	4	318239	Geo. Jones & Sons	Stoke
1	11	318265–6	Minton, Hollins & Co.	Stoke
1	16	318275–9	The Derby Crown Porcelain Co. Ltd.	Derby
5	5	318397	The Campbell Brick & Tile Co.	Stoke
9	6	318469	J. Dimmock & Co.	Hanley
11	5	318543–4	T. C. Brown–Westhead, Moore & Co.	Hanley
12	5	318556–63	Derby Crown Porcelain Co. Ltd.	Derby
20	6	318800	Minton, Hollins & Co.	Stoke

APPENDIX B

Date	Parcel No.	Patent No.	Factory, Retailer Wholesaler, etc	Place
20	7	318801	The Worcester Royal Porcelain Co. Ltd.	Worcester
21	10	318821	W. E. Cartlidge	Burslem
22	8	318843	The Campbell Brick & Tile Co.	Stoke
28	3	319041	Dunn, Bennett & Co.	Hanley
Mar 5	2	319190	F. W. Grove & J. Stark	Longton
6	5	319201	Minton, Hollins & Co.	Stoke
7	4	319219	John Edwards	Fenton
9	1	319278–9	The Brownhills Pottery Co.	Tunstall
9	8	319293	Moore Bros.	Longton
9	11	319296	Powell & Bishop	Hanley
11	1	319310–1	Taylor, Tunnicliffe & Co.	Hanley
13	1	319370	Mintons	Stoke
13	7	319387	J. & T. Bevington	Hanley
13	10	319394	W. T. Copeland & Sons	Stoke
15	10	319507	John Rose & Co.	Coalport
23	8	319634–6	Derby Crown Porcelain Co. Ltd.	Derby
25	9	319679	F. J. Emery	Burslem
27	6	319725–6	G. W. Turner & Sons	Tunstall
27	15	319867–72	Minton, Hollins & Co.	Stoke
Apr 2	6	320030	Belfield & Co.	Preston-pans
10	4	320281	Mintons	Stoke
13	9	320373	McBirney & Armstrong	Belleek
17	4	320482	Mintons	Stoke
17	14	320568–9	Ridgway, Sparks & Ridgway	Stoke
20	2	320606	Thos. Furnival & Sons	Cobridge
20	6	320616	The Worcester Royal Porcelain Co. Ltd.	Worcester
24	2	320669	Wm. Brownfield & Sons	Cobridge
27	12	320793	McBirney & Armstrong	Belleek
30	7	320874–5	Josiah Wedgwood & Sons	Etruria

APPENDIX B

Date	Parcel No.	Patent No.	Factory, Retailer Wholesaler, etc	Place
May 3	2	321028	Josiah Wedgwood & Sons	Etruria
3	9	321163	Robinson & Leadbeater	Stoke
8	9	321231–2	Bates & Bennett	Cobridge
14	6	321361	Elsmore & Son	Tunstall
17	12	321575	J. Dimmock & Co.	Hanley
20	9	321632–4	Derby Crown Porcelain Co. Ltd.	Derby
21	11	321693	Banks & Thorley	Hanley
23	3	321704	Josiah Wedgwood & Sons	Etruria
23	4	321705	Moore Bros.	Longton
24	2	321726	Josiah Wedgwood & Sons	Etruria
27	20	322007	E. J. D. Bodley	Burslem
29	9	322039	Minton, Hollins & Co.	Stoke
June 1	5	322130	J. Mortlock & Co.	London
4	9	322168	F. Furnival & Sons	Cobridge
5	14	322223–4	W. T. Copeland & Sons	Stoke
7	1	322309	Geo. Jones & Sons	Stoke
8	8	322390	Wm. Wood & Co.	Burslem
12	10	322471	Harvey Adams & Co.	Longton
13	2	322476	John Tams	Longton
13	3	322477	McBirney & Armstrong	Belleek
19	7	322597–8	E. F. Bodley & Co.	Burslem
21	8	322662	Allen & Green	Fenton
27	7	322931–2	Josiah Wedgwood & Sons	Etruria
29	1	322948	Wood, Son & Co.	Cobridge
July 1	1	322971	Burgess & Leigh	Burslem
3	2	323132	Mintons	Stoke
6	7	323315–20	Joseph Cliff & Sons	Leeds
8	6	323396	Josiah Wedgwood & Sons	Etruria
9	8	323434	Mintons	Stoke
9	9	323435	Josiah Wedgwood & Sons	Etruria
9	10	323436	J. Dimmock & Co.	Hanley
10	14	323508	Bates & Bennett	Cobridge
11	1	323521	Soane & Smith	London
11	11	323596	W. & J. A. Bailey	Alloa

APPENDIX B

Date	Parcel No.	Patent No.	Factory, Retailer Wholesaler, etc	Place
12	4	323604	Josiah Wedgwood & Sons	Etruria
12	13	323626	Samuel Lear	Hanley
12	15	323628	T. C. Brown–Westhead, Moore & Co.	Hanley
15	1	323650–1	Pratt & Simpson	Fenton
17	9	323774–5	Wm. Adams	Tunstall
18	2	323778	Ambrose Bevington	Hanley
20	1	323847	J. Bevington	Hanley
20	6	323893	John Meir & Son	Tunstall
20	11	323910–1	E. J. D. Bodley	Burslem
26	3	324177	Josiah Wedgwood & Sons	Etruria
30	2	324324	idem	Etruria
30	6	324336	Powell, Bishop & Stonier	Hanley
30	12	324347	E. Clarke	Longport
31	8	324383	Mintons	Stoke
31	13	324388	James Edwards & Son	Burslem
Aug 6	3	324576	Moore Bros.	Longton
7	3	324730	Thos. Hughes	Burslem
9	10	324848	Derby Crown Porcelain Co. Ltd.	Derby
9	12	324870–2	Craven, Dunnill & Co. Ltd.	Jackfield
14	4	325029–34	S. H. Sharp	Leeds
16	9	325094	The Campbell Brick & Tile Co.	Stoke
23	1	325278	Moore Bros.	Longton
23	7	325319	J. Dimmock & Co.	Hanley
Sept 3	12	325612	G. & L. Wohlauer	Dresden
5	3	325716	Moore Bros.	Longton
9	5	325992–4	Wm. Brownfield & Sons	Cobridge
10	2	326006	Josiah Wedgwood & Sons	Etruria
12	6	326146	J. Bevington	Hanley
13	5	326155	G. L. Ashworth & Bros.	Hanley

APPENDIX B

Date	Parcel No.	Patent No.	Factory, Retailer Wholesaler, etc	Place
13	16	326198	The Worcester Royal Porcelain Co. Ltd.	Worcester
20	19	326482	R. Wotherspoon & Co.	Glasgow
24	3	326785	T. Bevington	Hanley
28	5	326970–1	Minton, Hollins & Co.	Stoke
30	1	327000	Mintons	Stoke
Oct 2	2	327035	Mintons	Stoke
3	8	327110	J. T. Hudden	Longton
4	8	327227	F. & R. Pratt & Co.	Fenton
5	4	327235	Jones Bros. & Co.	W/hmptn
5	13	327271	The Worcester Royal Porcelain Co. Ltd.	Worcester
8	6	327359	Moore Bros.	Longton
8	7	327360	Bates, Gildea & Walker	Burslem
9	9	327392	Josiah Wedgwood	Etruria
11	8	327556	Minton, Hollins & Co.	Stoke
14	8	327625–6	W. T. Copeland & Sons	Stoke
23	1	328018	The Brownhills Pottery Co.	Tunstall
23	11	328144–5	Pinder & Bourne & Co.	Burslem
24	1	328146	T. Furnival & Sons	Cobridge
24	2	328147	J. Dimmock & Co.	Hanley
24	13	328274	The Worcester Royal Porcelain Co. Ltd.	Worcester
26	4	328320	Wm. Brownfield & Sons	Cobridge
30	3	328436–7	Minton, Hollins & Co.	Stoke
30	5	328439–40	Mintons	Stoke
Nov 1	3	328620	J. Bevington	Hanley
4	1	328699	Edge, Malkin & Co.	Burslem
5	11	328774	H. Burgess	Burslem
5	17	328790–2	E. J. D. Bodley	Burslem
6	3	328795	Samuel Lear	Hanley
13	13	329075	John Rose & Co.	Coalport
15	1	329108	Craven, Dunnill & Co. Ltd.	Jackfield
15	11	329147	F. & R. Pratt & Co.	Fenton
16	5	329157	J. Dimmock & Co.	Hanley

APPENDIX B

Date	Parcel No.	Patent No.	Factory, Retailer Wholesaler, etc	Place
20	13	329378	Cliff & Tomlin	Leeds
23	2	329456	E. & C. Challinor	Fenton
26	14	329673	T. & R. Boote	Burslem
27	9	329709	J. McIntyre & Co.	Burslem
29	14	329782–3	W. & E. Corn	Burslem
Dec 2	7	329901	T. C. Brown–Westhead, Moore & Co.	Hanley
2	8	329902	J. F. Meakin	London
3	9	329922	J. McIntyre & Co.	Burslem
4	2	329939	Wm. Brownfield & Sons	Cobridge
6	3	330061	Mintons	Stoke
7	2	330097	A. Shaw	Burslem
19	8	330485	Thos. Hughes	Burslem
27	13	330677	T. & R. Boote	Burslem
28	4	330687	J. Gaskell, Son & Co.	Burslem
1879				
Jan 7	7	330920	W. T. Copeland & Sons	Stoke
8	11	330965–6	Minton, Hollins & Co.	Stoke
9	8	330997–8	Wm. Brownfield & Sons	Cobridge
14	5	331152	The New Wharf Pottery Co.	Burslem
14	6	331153	The Campbell Brick & Tile Co.	Stoke
16	3	331228	B. & S. Hancock	Stoke
16	13	331342	F. & R. Pratt & Co.	Fenton
20	15	331418–9	Derby Crown Porcelain Co. Ltd.	Derby
22	4	331458	Dunn, Bennett & Co.	Hanley
28	11	331597	W. T. Copeland & Sons	Stoke
29	2	331600	T. Furnival & Sons	Cobridge
29	3	331601	T. Bevington	Hanley
29	15	331677	E. J. D. Bodley	Burslem
1	13	331775	Clementson Bros.	Hanley
3	1	331777	Josiah Wedgwood & Sons	Etruria

Date	Parcel No.	Patent No.	Factory, Retailer Wholesaler, etc	Place
5	7	331892–3	Mintons	Stoke
8	1	332030	Mintons	Stoke
14	4	332251	T. Furnival & Sons	Cobridge
15	2	332266	The Campbell Brick & Tile Co.	Stoke
17	6	332296	McBirney & Armstrong	Belleek
24	2	332606	W. P. Jervis	Stoke
24	3	332607–9	W. & T. Adams	Tunstall
25	4	332642	Mintons	Stoke
28	1	332823	E. Chetwynd	Stoke
28	7	332831	Clementson Bros.	Hanley
Mar 1	1	332837	T. Furnival & Sons	Cobridge
4	4	332938	F. W. Grove & J. Stark	Longton
6	10	333047	Powell, Bishop & Stonier	Hanley
12	4	333210	Edge, Malkin & Co.	Burslem
12	12	333235–6	W. T. Copeland & Sons	Stoke
13	1	333241–4	Wm. Davenport & Co.	Longport
13	14	333301	Clementson Bros.	Hanley
14	9	333319	E. Clarke	Longport
17	2	333368	Powell, Bishop & Stonier	Hanley
18	1	333431	Josiah Wedgwood & Sons	Etruria
19	2	333485	J. Hawthorn	Cobridge
26	17	333751–2	The Worcester Royal Porcelain Co. Ltd.	Worcester
28	6	333801	Clementson Bros.	Hanley
29	4	333813	Beck, Blair & Co.	Longton
Apr 3	9	334030	T. C. Brown–Westhead, Moore & Co.	Hanley
4	12	334052–3	Pinder, Bourne & Co.	Burslem
9	5	334137	H. Alcock & Co.	Cobridge
10	12	334200	T. C. Brown–Westhead, Moore & Co.	Hanley
12	1	334206	The Worcester Royal Porcelain Co. Ltd.	Worcester

APPENDIX B

Date	Parcel No.	Patent No.	Factory, Retailer Wholesaler, etc	Place
15	6	334241–2	T. C. Brown–Westhead, Moore & Co.	Hanley
23	8	334508	T. C. Brown–Westhead, Moore & Co.	Hanley
24	3	334531	Josiah Wedgwood & Sons	Etruria
May 2	5	334803	A. Bevington	Hanley
5	1	334860–1	T. Furnival & Sons	Cobridge
5	6	334897	Bates, Gildea & Walker	Burslem
6	7	334923–5	Sampson Bridgwood & Son	Longton
7	11	334978	The Worcester Royal Porcelain Co. Ltd.	Worcester
9	15	335057	idem	Worcester
13	4	335148–51	Pinder & Bourne & Co.	Burslem
13	8	335167–8	Clementson Bros.	Hanley
14	9	335182	T. C. Brown–Westhead, Moore & Co.	Hanley
14	13	335187–8	E. J. D. Bodley	Burslem
19	1	335308–9	Wm. Brownfield & Sons	Cobridge
21	5	335496	Harvey Adams & Co.	Longton
23	2	335551–2	Sampson Bridgwood & Son	Longton
23	14	335608	Harvey Adams & Co.	Longton
29	2	335715	John Tams	Longton
29	12	335739–40	Pinder, Bourne & Co.	Burslem
30	3	335744	McBirney & Armstrong	Belleek
30	10	335791	J. Dimmock & Co.	Hanley
30	12	335793	F. W. Grove & J. Stark	Longton
31	4	335805	Minton, Hollins & Co.	Stoke
June 10	4	336030	T. Furnival & Sons	Cobridge
11	8	336075	Thos. Till & Sons	Burslem
13	13	336132	T. C. Brown–Westhead, Moore & Co.	Hanley
18	4	336185	F. W. Grove & J. Stark	Longton
24	11	336415	Josiah Wedgwood & Sons	Etruria
25	1	336417	Clementson Bros.	Hanley

APPENDIX B

Date	Parcel No.	Patent No.	Factory, Retailer Wholesaler, etc	Place
26	13	336471–4	Haviland & Co.	Limoges and London
27	11	336496	Shorter & Boulton	Stoke
30	12	336586–7	Birks Bros. & Seddon	Cobridge
July 2	2	336676	Josiah Wedgwood & Sons	Etruria
7	2	336917	J. F. Wileman	Fenton
8	1	336930	Mintons	Stoke
8	16	336967–8	T. C. Brown–Westhead, Moore & Co.	Hanley
9	12	337058	idem	Hanley
10	2	337060	T. Bevington	Hanley
10	3	337061	Moore Bros.	Longton
16	4	337157–8	A. Bevington & Co.	Hanley
16	14	337177	T. C. Brown–Westhead, Moore & Co.	Hanley
25	4	337497	Mintons	Stoke
26	6	337536	Minton, Hollins & Co.	Stoke
31	2	337660	Mintons	Stoke
Aug 2	2	337814	H. M. Williamson & Sons	Longton
5	12	337945–7	J. Mortlock & Co.	London
6	6	337958	Wardle & Co.	Hanley
13	2	338135	F. W. Grove & J. Stark	Longton
22	4	338559	McBirney & Armstrong	Belleek
27	13	338872	Bates, Gildea & Walker	Burslem
Sept 4	6	339193	T. C. Brown–Westhead, Moore & Co.	Hanley
10	13	339373	idem	Hanley
17	4	339685–6	Wm. Brownfield & Sons	Cobridge
18	10	339979	T. C. Brown–Westhead, Moore & Co.	Hanley
26	4	340431	J. T. Hudden	Longton
29	3	340569	Edge, Malkin & Co.	Burslem
Oct 9	6	341137	Bates, Gildea & Walker	Burslem

APPENDIX B

Date	Parcel No.	Patent No.	Factory, Retailer Wholesaler, etc	Place
10	2	341151	T. C. Brown–Westhead, Moore & Co.	Hanley
11	5	341229–30	E. J. D. Bodley	Burslem
15	1	341347	Mintons	Stoke
16	5	341466	J. Roth	London
16	16	341500	Minton, Hollins & Co.	Stoke
17	2	341502	G. L. Ashworth & Bros.	Hanley
18	3	341629	Josiah Wedgwood & Sons	Etruria
23	12	341864	C. Pillivuyt & Co.	London
24	4	341882–3	The Campbell Brick & Tile Co.	Stoke
27	9	341997	E. F. Bodley & Co.	Burslem
29	5	342098	Mintons	Stoke
29	7	342100	Clementson Bros.	Hanley
29	15	342152	F. D. Bradley	Longton
30	4	342158	Mintons	Stoke
Nov 3	12	342396	Minton, Hollins & Co.	Stoke
3	14	342398	Tundley, Rhodes & Procter	Burslem
6	2	342461	Josiah Wedgwood & Sons	Etruria
6	3	342462–3	Moore Bros.	Longton
6	4	342464–72	Burmantofts (Wilcock & Co.)	Leeds
12	11	342769	The Worcester Royal Porcelain Co. Ltd.	Worcester
15	12	342921	C. Ford	Hanley
15	16	342925–7	W. T. Copeland & Sons	Stoke
17	2	342929	Powell, Bishop & Stonier	Hanley
19	5	343017	idem	Hanley
20	4	343070–1	Elsmore & Son	Tunstall
21	6	343148	Mintons	Stoke
21	14	343166	Soane & Smith	London
22	7	343219	The Worcester Royal Porcelain Co. Ltd.	Worcester
28	5	343530	Wm. Brownfield & Sons	Cobridge

APPENDIX B

Date	Parcel No.	Patent No.	Factory, Retailer Wholesaler, etc	Place
28	6	343531	A. Bevington & Co.	Hanley
29	3	343585	Mintons	Stoke
29	4	343586	T. C. Brown–Westhead, Moore & Co.	Hanley
Dec 1	2	343618	J. Holdcroft	Longton
2	4	343652–3	T. C. Brown–Westhead, Moore & Co.	Hanley
2	5	343654	Elsmore & Son	Tunstall
2	17	343716	J. Aynsley & Sons	Longton
6	2	343815–6	T. & R. Boote	Burslem
10	14	344077	Clementson Bros.	Hanley
11	4	344082–4	Moore Bros.	Longton
17	11	344387	Ridgways	Stoke
19	1	344452	Clementson Bros.	Hanley
19	3	344454	Burmantofts (Wilcock & Co.)	Leeds
20	5	344478	Josiah Wedgwood & Sons	Etruria
22	2	344503	Mintons	Stoke
24	2	344568	Sherwin & Cotton	Hanley
1880				
Jan 3	1	344838	Sherwin & Cotton	Hanley
7	3	344961–2	T. Bevington	Hanley
7	4	344963	T. & R. Boote	Burslem
7	5	344964–9	Soane & Smith	London
7	8	344972	Minton, Hollins & Co.	Stoke
8	9	344997	The Old Hall Earthenware Co. Ltd.	Hanley
9	3	345003	Sherwin & Cotton	Hanley
9	12	345045	T. G. Allen	London
13	1	345131	T. C. Brown–Westhead, Moore & Co.	Hanley
14	11	345184–5	The Worcester Royal Porcelain Co. Ltd.	Worcester
16	8	345288	S. Fielding & Co.	Stoke

APPENDIX B

Date	Parcel No.	Patent No.	Factory, Retailer Wholesaler, etc	Place
16	14	345299	Brockwell & Son	London
21	7	345469–71	Pinder, Bourne & Co.	Burslem
22	2	345481	Mintons	Stoke
22	8	345493–4	Minton, Hollins & Co.	Stoke
23	5	345511	Mintons	Stoke
26	11	345719	Wm. Brownfield & Sons	Cobridge
27	13	345798	Wardle & Co.	Hanley
28	3	345801	T. C. Brown–Westhead, Moore & Co.	Hanley
28	4	345802	J. Aynsley & Sons	Longton
28	12	345833	Powell, Bishop & Stonier	Hanley
29	9	345860–1	E. J. D. Bodley	Burslem
30	2	345864	Taylor, Tunnicliffe & Co.	Hanley
Feb 3	11	345952	Powell, Bishop & Stonier	Hanley
9	18	346202	Whittingham, Ford & Riley	Burslem
10	4	346208–10	Mintons	Stoke
11	10	346344	T. Bevington	Hanley
12	4	346360	W. A. Adderley	Longton
12	7	346363	Wm. Brownfield & Sons	Cobridge
14	14	346467	Bates, Gildea & Walker	Burslem
18	12	346594	The Derby Crown Porcelain Co. Ltd.	Derby
24	2	346832	Mintons	Stoke
24	11	346870	Wm. Harrop & Co.	Hanley
25	18	346920	Clementson Bros.	Hanley
25	23	346945	Sherwin & Cotton	Hanley
26	6	346952–3	Minton, Hollins & Co.	Stoke
26	7	346954	Moore Bros.	Longton
Mar 3	6	347138	J. Holdcroft	Longton
4	8	347203	Soane & Smith	London
8	4	347344	T. Furnival & Sons	Cobridge
8	10	347360	W. Harrop & Co.	Hanley
12	4	347476	W. A. Adderley	Longton
16	3	347599	J. F. Wileman & Co.	Fenton
16	11	347645	Sherwin & Cotton	Hanley

Date	Parcel No.	Patent No.	Factory, Retailer Wholesaler, etc	Place
16	12	347646–7	J. Macintyre & Co.	Burslem
17	6	347660	Josiah Wedgwood & Sons	Etruria
18	3	347690–6	Moore Bros.	Longton
22	4	347838	Powell, Bishop & Stonier	Hanley
23	4	347872	Taylor, Tunnicliffe & Co.	Hanley
25	6	348018	Mintons	Stoke
30	4	348110	Sherwin & Cotton	Hanley
31	3	348114	Thos. Peake	Tunstall
Apr 12	6	348606–8	Bates, Gildea & Walker	Burslem
15	11	348761	Ridgways	Stoke
19	11	348911–3	The Worcester Royal Porcelain Co. Ltd.	Worcester
22	11	349025–6	Sherwin & Cotton	Hanley
22	5	349027	W. H. Grindley & Co.	Tunstall
26	1	349221	T. Furnival & Sons	Cobridge
27	11	349239–41	Moore Bros.	Longton
27	13	349318–23	The Worcester Royal Porcelain Co. Ltd.	Worcester
29	4	349340–1	Mintons	Stoke
30	6	349380	T. Furnival & Sons	Cobridge
May 3	3	349438–43	Wm. Brownfield & Sons	Cobridge
5	13	349528	S. Fielding & Co.	Stoke
10	6	349693	Powell, Bishop & Stonier	Hanley
11	15	349791	Soane & Smith	London
13	8	349852–3	Mintons	Stoke
13	15	349869	Minton, Hollins & Co.	Stoke
14	26	349939	Bates, Gildea & Walker	Burslem
25	4	350098	Wm. Brownfield & Sons	Cobridge
26	6	350142	Mintons	Stoke
June 1	4	350251	Mintons	Stoke
2	3	350353	Sherwin & Cotton	Hanley
7	6	350476	J. Dimmock & Co.	Hanley
8	1	350477	Geo. Jones & Sons	Stoke
10	3	350554	Sherwin & Cotton	Hanley
10	4	350555	E. J. D. Bodley	Burslem

Date	Parcel No.	Patent No.	Factory, Retailer Wholesaler, etc	Place
10	12	350613	J. Dimmock & Co.	Hanley
11	3	350616	Josiah Wedgwood & Sons	Etruria
14	12	350842	J. Roth	London
15	4	350848	Buckley, Wood & Co.	Burslem
16	3	350972	Wedgwood & Co.	Tunstall
17	4	351025	Samuel Lear	Hanley
17	15	351058	Ridgways	Stoke
17	16	351059	J. Macintyre & Co.	Burslem
17	20	351063	The Crystal Porcelain Co.	Hanley
17	21	351064	J. Dimmock & Co.	Hanley
19	11	351186	Josiah Wedgwood & Sons	Etruria
19	15	351190	J. Roth	London
22	1	351259	W. H. Grindley & Co.	Tunstall
26	13	351496–7	The Worcester Royal Porcelain Co. Ltd.	Worcester
July 5	11	351866	Westwood & Moore	Brierley Hill
7	4	351909	Sherwin & Cotton	Hanley
7	5	351910	Mintons	Stoke
7	15	351928	F. J. Emery	Burslem
12	4	352094	Mintons	Stoke
13	12	352138	Thos. Barlow	Longton
15	3	352192	Dunn, Bennett & Co.	Hanley
15	4	352193	F. W. Grove & J. Stark	Longton
16	9	352224	Sherwin & Cotton	Hanley
16	10	352225	Moore Bros.	Longton
16	19	352278	S. Fielding & Co.	Stoke
28	2	352872	The Brownhills Pottery Co.	Tunstall
31	8	353079	The Old Hall Earthenware Co. Ltd.	Hanley
Aug 4	3	353108	Pinder, Bourne & Co.	Burslem
11	14	353543	Clementson Bros.	Hanley
14	12	353713–4	Wm. Davenport & Co.	Longport
17	6	353746	Sherwin & Cotton	Hanley
18	3	353818	Josiah Wedgwood & Sons	Etruria

APPENDIX B

Date	Parcel No.	Patent No.	Factory, Retailer Wholesaler, etc	Place
21	2	354026	Sherwin & Cotton	Hanley
21	10	354081	W. A. Adderley	Longton
23	5	354092	Jackson & Gosling	Longton
23	6	354093–4	T. C. Brown–Westhead, Moore & Co.	Hanley
24	10	354154	E. J. D. Bodley	Burslem
Sept 3	3	354639	T. C. Brown–Westhead, Moore & Co.	Hanley
4	7	354766–7	J. Beech & Son	Longton
11	3	355091–100	Wm. Brownfield & Sons	Cobridge
14	6	355169	Mintons	Stoke
15	6	355231	G. L. Ashworth & Bros.	Hanley
15	12	355255–7	Minton, Hollins & Co.	Stoke
23	3	355575	Ambrose Wood	Hanley
25	6	355651–4	Minton, Hollins & Co.	Stoke
27	5	355745–6	John Marshall & Co.	Bo'ness, Scotland
29	3	355947–8	The Brownhills Pottery Co.	Tunstall
30	4	355987	The Worcester Royal Porcelain Co. Ltd.	Worcester
Oct 1	3	356014	Wade & Colclough	Burslem
6	4	356163	Josiah Wedgwood & Sons	Etruria
12	4	356514	Mintons	Stoke
13	5	356532	Josiah Wedgwood & Sons	Etruria
20	10	356970	Burgess & Leigh	Burslem
21	13	357033–5	The Worcester Royal Porcelain Co. Ltd.	Worcester
22	4	357039	E. F. Bodley & Son	Burslem
22	12	357088	J. Aynsley & Sons	Longton
26	13	357298–9	Minton, Hollins & Co.	Stoke
27	5	357305	Taylor, Tunnicliffe & Co.	Hanley
27	20	357429	J. Tams	Longton
27	21	357430	G. Woolliscroft & Son	Etruria
28	2	357466	Sherwin & Cotton	Hanley

Date	Parcel No.	Patent No.	Factory, Retailer Wholesaler, etc	Place
30	6	357560	Jones & Hopkinson	Hanley
Nov 2	2	357609	W. H. Grindley & Co.	Tunstall
4	4	357656-7	W. & T. Adams	Tunstall
4	15	357724-5	Minton, Hollins & Co.	Stoke
9	4	357954	Josiah Wedgwood & Sons	Etruria
10	2	358062-3	Wilcock & Co. (Burmantofts)	Leeds
10	13	358141	Bednall & Heath	Hanley
18	3	358466	S. Radford	Longton
18	14	358500	Mintons	Stoke
19	15	358552	The Crown Derby Porcelain Co. Ltd.	Derby
24	4	358747	F. W. Grove & J. Stark	Longton
24	5	358748	Bates, Gildea & Walker	Burslem
Dec 6	2	359292	Powell, Bishop & Stonier	Hanley
7	10	359321-6	Pinder, Bourne & Co.	Burslem
8	5	359342-3	Wittmann & Roth	London
15	15	359668-71	Wm. Brownfield & Sons	Cobridge
18	2	359784	Bates, Gildea & Walker	Burslem
24	8	359997	T. C. Brown–Westhead, Moore & Co.	Hanley
29	7	360042-4	Doulton & Co.	Lambeth
31	1	360100	The Old Hall Earthenware Co. Ltd.	Hanley
31	4	360103-5	Sherwin & Cotton	Hanley
1881				
Jan 5	7	360326	J. Roth	London
6	2	360331	B. & S. Hancock	Stoke
6	8	360355	F. D. Bradley	Longton
7	13	360484	Sherwin & Cotton	Hanley
12	5	360633	idem	Hanley
14	10	360747	The Worcester Royal Porcelain Co. Ltd.	Worcester
14	18	360799	E. J. D. Bodley	Burslem

Date	Parcel No.	Patent No.	Factory, Retailer Wholesaler, etc	Place
15	4	360806–7	Holmes, Stonier & Hollinshead	Hanley
20	3	360900	Mintons	Stoke
21	11	360954	W. & T. Adams	Tunstall
26	4	361116–7	Minton, Hollins & Co.	Stoke
27	15	361151	The Worcester Royal Porcelain Co. Ltd.	Worcester
28	3	361170	G. Woolliscroft & Son	Hanley
Feb 8	5	361537	F. W. Grove & J. Stark	Longton
8	6	361538–41	Wm. Brownfield & Sons	Cobridge
11	10	361668	F. J. Emery	Burslem
15	6	361748	W. A. Adderley	Longton
16	3	361784	F. D. Bradley	Longton
17	2	361813	Murray & Co.	Glasgow
18	3	361868	S. Radford	Longton
19	15	361927	S. S. Bold	Hanley
21	4	361937	Taylor, Waine & Bates	Longton
24	8	362086	Wm. Harrop & Co.	Hanley
25	14	362166	J. Macintyre & Co.	Burslem
28	9	362242	E. J. D. Bodley	Burslem
Mar 3	5	362423	J. Dimmock & Co.	Hanley
7	11	362545	J. Aynsley & Sons	Longton
8	3	362548	F. W. Grove & J. Stark	Longton
14	1	362815	E. J. D. Bodley	Burslem
17	9	362992	Shorter & Boulton	Stoke
19	4	363026–7	Mintons	Stoke
23	4	363157	Mintons	Stoke
24	2	363206–7	T. S. Pinder	Burslem
24	3	363208	W. A. Adderley	Longton
29	6	363421	T. A. Simpson	Hanley
31	2	363461	J. T. Hudden	Longton
Apr 7	2	363720	Sherwin & Cotton	Hanley
7	9	363732	The Old Hall Earthenware Co. Ltd.	Hanley
8	2	363738	W. Harrop & Co.	Hanley

Date	Parcel No.	Patent No.	Factory, Retailer Wholesaler, etc	Place
8	3	363739	Wedgwood & Co.	Tunstall
8	14	363785	The Worcester Royal Porcelain Co. Ltd.	Worcester
9	5	363793	R. H. Plant & Co.	Longton
11	1	363800	A. Bevington & Co.	Hanley
12	4	363849–50	Mintons	Stoke
14	10	363975	Mintons	Stoke
16	17	364110	J. Marshall & Co.	Bo'ness, Scotland
19	3	364116	Sherwin & Cotton	Hanley
19	5	364118	T. & R. Boote	Burslem
21	4	364172	Sherwin & Cotton	Hanley
21	5	364173–4	E. J. D. Bodley	Burslem
23	7	364238	J. F. Wileman	Fenton
28	12	364488	W. T. Copeland & Sons	Stoke
30	3	364528	Trubshaw, Hand & Co.	Longton
30	4	364529	Josiah Wedgwood & Sons	Etruria
May 3	4	364604	Wm. Wood & Co.	Burslem
3	5	364605	Sherwin & Cotton	Hanley
4	2	364624	idem	Hanley
4	3	364625–7	Wm. Brownfield & Sons	Cobridge
5	2	364648	W. & T. Adams	Tunstall
6	4	364736	R. H. Plant & Co.	Longton
11	3	364941	J. Tams	Longton
13	2	365005	Mintons	Stoke
16	2	365066	Josiah Wedgwood & Sons	Etruria
17	9	365134–5	J. Mortlock & Co.	London
20	11	365206	W. A. Adderley	Longton
21	3	365211	Powell, Bishop & Stonier	Hanley
24	5	365391	G. L. Ashworth & Bros.	Hanley
24	6	365392–3	Mintons	Stoke
24	7	365394	F. J. Emery	Burslem
25	3	365424	Powell, Bishop & Stonier	Hanley
25	9	365442–4	The Worcester Royal Porcelain Co. Ltd.	Worcester

APPENDIX B

Date	Parcel No.	Patent No.	Factory, Retailer Wholesaler, etc	Place
25	10	365445–6	Josiah Wedgwood & Sons	Etruria
26	7	365461	G. Woolliscroft & Son	Hanley
30	1	365539	T. Furnival & Sons	Cobridge
30	2	365540	The Decorative Art Tile Co.	Hanley
June 1	3	365730	Mintons	Stoke
1	13	365793	J. Mortlock & Co.	London
3	4	365827	S. P. Ledward	Cobridge
4	3	365852	T. Furnival & Sons	Cobridge
4	4	365853	The Decorative Art Tile Co.	Hanley
7	3	365875	E. F. Bodley & Son	Burslem
7	4	365876–7	The Decorative Art Tile Co.	Hanley
7	17	365914–6	The Worcester Royal Porcelain Co. Ltd.	Worcester
8	6	365955	The Crystal Porcelain Co.	Hanley
13	1	366015	S. Lear	Hanley
16	8	366078–9	S. Fielding & Co.	Stoke
18	1	366093	Jackson & Gosling	Longton
21	13	366220–2	Birks Bros. & Seddon	Cobridge
21	20	366246	Gildea & Walker	Burslem
July 2	1	366634	McBirney & Armstrong	Belleek
2	5	366643	T. Furnival & Sons	Cobridge
6	7	366809	Josiah Wedgwood & Sons	Etruria
9	10	366922–3	Wardle & Co.	Hanley
14	6	367133–4	T. C. Brown–Westhead, Moore & Co.	Hanley
15	5	367150	Wm. Corbitt & Co.	Rthrham
16	3	367213	Trubshaw, Hand & Co.	Longton
18	4	367249	G. Hall	Worcester
19	2	367259	The Dalehall Brick & Tile Co.	Burslem
25	2	367418	J. H. Davis	Hanley
28	3	367516	McBirney & Armstrong	Belleek

APPENDIX B

Date	Parcel No.	Patent No.	Factory, Retailer Wholesaler, etc	Place
28	4	367517	A. Wood	Hanley
28	14	367538	Ridgways	Stoke
29	2	367542–3	Sherwin & Cotton	Hanley
29	3	367544	Whittmann & Roth	London
30	3	367549	Sampson Bridgwood & Son	Longton
30	4	367550	Sherwin & Cotton	Hanley
30	5	367551	Mintons	Stoke
30	15	367590	W. T. Copeland & Sons	Stoke
Aug 2	1	367608	E. J. D. Bodley	Burslem
5	12	367892–3	Pinder, Bourne & Co.	Burslem
10	13	368044	The Old Hall Earthenware Co. Ltd.	Hanley
20	11	368686	The Worcester Royal Porcelain Co. Ltd.	Worcester
23	3	368802	F. W. Grove & J. Stark	Longton
24	11	368942	T. & R. Boote	Burslem
27	3	369202	S. Lear	Hanley
27	9	369215–8	Gildea & Walker	Burslem
29	7	369248	W. & T. Adams	Tunstall
Sept 2	4	369389	Dale, Page & Goodwin	Longton
3	11	369526	T. A. Simpson	Hanley
6	1	369538	The Derby Crown Porcelain Co. Ltd.	Derby
7	10	369654	Adams & Sleigh	Burslem
9	11	369731	The Worcester Royal Porcelain Co. Ltd.	Worcester
10	12	369778–81	J. Roth	London
16	10	370093	Geo. Jones & Sons	Stoke
22	9	370400	Bold & Michelson	Hanley
23	21	370470–2	Minton, Hollins & Co.	Stoke
27	9	370611	Pinder, Bourne & Co.	Burslem
28	4	370620	E. J. D. Bodley	Burslem
28	13	370633	Gildea & Walker	Burslem
29	3	370636	Geo. Jones & Sons	Stoke
30	3	370702–3	Davenports Ltd.	Longport

APPENDIX B

Date		Parcel No.	Patent No.	Factory, Retailer Wholesaler, etc	Place
	30	15	370725–8	Mintons	Stoke
Oct	4	6	370885	Wm. Brownfield & Sons	Cobridge
	6	5	370998	J. & R. Boote	Burslem
	6	7	371000	The Campbell Brick & Tile Co.	Stoke
	7	27	371098	Mintons	Stoke
	8	3	371102	Adams & Sleigh	Burslem
	11	16	371247	The Worcester Royal Porcelain Co. Ltd.	Worcester
	12	14	371330–1	Mintons	Stoke
	13	3	371337	Adderley & Lawson	Longton
	13	5	371339	T. & R. Boote	Burslem
	20	1	371866	Thos. Begley	Burslem
	20	2	371867	Robinson & Chapman	Longton
	22	1	371959	Mintons	Stoke
	26	8	372138	Mintons	Stoke
	26	16	372171	T. C. Brown–Westhead, Moore & Co.	Hanley
	27	1	372185	Robinson & Chapman	Longton
	29	3	372347	T. & R. Boote	Burslem
	29	4	372348	Wm. Brownfield & Sons	Cobridge
	29	11	372376	Wardle & Co.	Hanley
	29	14	372379	Minton, Hollins & Co.	Stoke
	31	11	372464	T. A. Simpson	Hanley
Nov	2	1	372489–90	T. C. Brown–Westhead, Moore & Co.	Hanley
	3	12	372613	The Worcester Royal Porcelain Co. Ltd.	Worcester
	4	24	372727	idem	Worcester
	8	1	372918	T. & R. Boote	Burslem
	9	6	372979	F. W. Grove & J. Stark	Longton
	9	7	372980–2	E. J. D. Bodley	Burslem
	10	2	372995	Brough & Blackhurst	Longton
	19	3	373541	Sampson Bridgwood & Son	Longton

Date	Parcel No.	Patent No.	Factory, Retailer Wholesaler, etc	Place
19	12	373573	The Worcester Royal Porcelain Co. Ltd.	Worcester
21	1	373575	J. Bevington	Hanley
22	9	373615	J. Tams	Longton
22	17	373647	Ambrose Wood	Hanley
23	13	373707	Shorter & Boulton	Stoke
25	1	373821	Adams & Sleigh	Burslem
25	15	373860	J. Roth	London
29	10	374058	The Worcester Royal Porcelain Co. Ltd.	Worcester
Dec 2	16	374229	J. Roth	London
5	11	374376	John Rose & Co.	Coalport
8	9	374498	Adderley & Lawson	Longton
9	2	374516	E. J. D. Bodley	Burslem
10	7	374579	T. C. Brown–Westhead, Moore & Co.	Hanley
12	12	374628	John Fell	Longton
16	3	374782	Mintons	Stoke
20	9	374948	Bednall & Heath	Hanley
21	3	374955	F. Grosvenor	Glasgow
21	9	374987	The Worcester Royal Porcelain Co. Ltd.	Worcester
24	5	375054	J. Broadhurst	Fenton
1882				
Jan 3	6	375415	Holmes, Plant & Maydew	Burslem
4	2	375426–7	W. T. Copeland & Sons	Stoke
4	7	375439	J. Roth	London
4	9	375444	F. & R. Pratt & Co.	Fenton
7	2	375494	W. H. Grindley & Co.	Tunstall
7	11	375580	Ridgways	Hanley
10	5	375599	S. Lear	Hanley
11	1	375709–12	Minton, Hollins & Co.	Stoke
13	4	375815–6	The Decorative Art Tile Co.	Hanley

Date	Parcel No.	Patent No.	Factory, Retailer Wholesaler, etc	Place
18	10	376032	Robinson & Son	Longton
26	5	376425	J. T. Hudden	Longton
26	16	376443	S. Fielding & Co.	Stoke
27	8	376461	Craven, Dunnill & Co. Ltd.	Jackfield
30	2	376528	Hollinshead & Kirkham	Tunstall
30	3	376529	F. W. Grove & J. Stark	Longton
Feb 1	1	376580	Edge, Malkin & Co.	Burslem
3	4	376672–3	T. C. Brown–Westhead, Moore & Co.	Hanley
4	10	376754	Minton, Hollins & Co.	Stoke
6	4	376764–6	The Campbell Tile Co.	Stoke
7	2	376798	Wm. Mills	Hanley
8	7	376839	Wardle & Co.	Hanley
15	4	377048	F. W. Grove & J. Stark	Longton
16	6	377135–7	Mintons	Stoke
18	5	377273	J. F. Wileman & Co.	Fenton
23	17	377488–9	Minton, Hollins & Co.	Stoke
24	3	377492	Taylor, Tunnicliffe & Co.	Hanley
Mar 1	11	377779	The Worcester Royal Porcelain Co. Ltd.	Worcester
1	12	377780	Minton, Hollins & Co.	Stoke
7	7	378051	idem	Stoke
13	3	378252	J. T. Hudden	Longton
15	3	378337	Powell, Bishop & Stonier	Hanley
15	4	378338	Murray & Co.	Glasgow
20	5	378643	W. A. Adderley	Longton
23	2	378739	W. & T. Adams	Tunstall
23	15	378823	T. A. Simpson	Hanley
27	3	378937	D. Chapman	Longton
27	10	378959	Shorter & Boulton	Stoke
28	12	378988	Ambrose Wood	Hanley
28	16	378993–4	A. Bevington & Co.	Hanley
30	13	379076	John Rose & Co.	Coalport
30	17	379080	S. Fielding & Co.	Stoke
31	3	379088	A. Bevington & Co.	Hanley

APPENDIX B

Date	Parcel No.	Patent No.	Factory, Retailer Wholesaler, etc	Place
Apr 4	2	379212–3	Wm. Brownfield & Sons	Cobridge
11	6	379434	Geo. Jones & Sons	Stoke
11	7	379435–6	Minton, Hollins & Co.	Stoke
21	7	379767	Sampson Bridgwood & Son	Longton
27	14	380072	The New Wharf Pottery Co.	Burslem
May 2	5	380194	G. L. Ashworth & Bros.	Hanley
3	1	380199	S. Radford	Longton
5	2	380401	Wood, Hines & Winkle	Hanley
6	5	380418	Powell, Bishop & Stonier	Hanley
6	6	380419–20	Whittaker, Edge & Co.	Hanley
8	18	380549–50	Davenports Ltd.	Longport
9	3	380553–4	H. Alcock & Co.	Cobridge
9	4	380555	Whittaker, Edge & Co.	Hanley
9	7	380558	Wm. Brownfield & Sons	Cobridge
9	11	380564	Minton, Hollins & Co.	Stoke
10	4	380571–2	John Edwards	Fenton
10	14	380676	S. Fielding & Co.	Stoke
13	6	380789	Geo. Jones & Sons	Stoke
17	2	380869–70	E. J. Bodley	Burslem
24	4	381376	Minton, Hollins & Co.	Stoke
24	21	381434	Doulton & Co.	Burslem
25	11	381480	W. A. Adderley	Longton
27	3	381568	Samuel Lear	Hanley
30	5	381611	W. H. Grindley & Co.	Tunstall
June 5	6	381805	Mintons	Stoke
5	7	381806	Wood, Hines & Winkle	Hanley
9	3	381964	Hall & Read	Burslem
9	4	381965–6	W. A. Adderley	Longton
13	11	382126	A. Shaw & Son	Burslem
13	14	382130–1	Wardle & Co.	Hanley
21	4	382406	Wm. Lowe	Longton
21	5	382407–8	Sampson Bridgwood & Son	Longton
21	11	382472	The Old Hall Earthenware & Co. Ltd	Hanley

Date	Parcel No.	Patent No.	Factory, Retailer Wholesaler, etc	Place
23	1	382593–4	Josiah Wedgwood & Sons	Etruria
23	5	382598	Burgess & Leigh	Burslem
28	2	382721	The Derby Crown Porcelain Co.	Derby
July 1	8	382829	Taylor, Tunnicliffe & Co.	Hanley
3	2	382842	Mintons	Stoke
3	3	382843	E. J. D. Bodley	Burslem
4	3	382859	Wright & Rigby	Hanley
6	4	383020–1	Wm. Brownfield & Sons	Cobridge
14	3	383436–7	Geo. Jones & Sons	Stoke
14	10	383468	Wardle & Co.	Hanley
14	14	383482	Beech & Tellwright	Cobridge
17	8	383549	Wood & Son	Burslem
19	7	383641	Wardle & Co.	Hanley
20	1	383694–6	John Edwards	Fenton
22	8	383802	Geo. Jones & Sons	Stoke
25	3	383855	F. Grosvenor	Glasgow
25	9	383869–71	The Brownhills Pottery Co. Ltd.	Tunstall
26	4	383893	Adderley & Lawson	Longton
28	3	384078	Hawley & Co.	Longton
31	2	384160–1	Sampson Bridgwood & Son	Longton
31	9	384171–2	Mintons	Stoke
Aug 5	4	384353–4	Wm. Brownfield & Sons	Cobridge
10	5	384464	Wright & Rigby	Hanley
21	2	385106	John Tams	Longton
21	8	385129	Adams & Bromley	Hanley
25	2	385411	Mintons	Stoke
26	4	385490	Wm. Wood & Co.	Burslem
28	2	385527	Belfield & Co.	Preston-pans
28	9	385544	Mintons	Stoke
29	12	385623	Wm. Brownfield & Sons	Cobridge
30	14	385693	The Worcester Royal Porcelain Co. Ltd.	Worcester

APPENDIX B

Date	Parcel No.	Patent No.	Factory, Retailer Wholesaler, etc	Place
31	3	385701	A. Bevington & Co.	Hanley
Sept 6	2	385954	Hawley & Co.	Longton
8	5	386085–6	Mintons	Stoke
9	3	386126	Taylor, Tunnicliffe & Co.	Hanley
11	4	386178	Adams & Bromley	Hanley
16	2	386388–9	Hulme & Massey	Longton
19	2	386542	W. H. Grindley & Co.	Tunstall
28	4	387147–8	T. C. Brown–Westhead, Moore & Co.	Hanley
28	22	387229	Bridgett & Bates	Longton
29	2	387231–2	The Brownhills Pottery Co.	Tunstall
Oct 6	2	387598–603	Mintons	Stoke
9	3	387771	W. T. Copeland & Sons	Stoke
9	4	387772	Dean, Capper & Dean	Hanley
11	3	387958–60	Sampson Bridgwood & Son	Longton
11	4	387961	Wood & Son	Burslem
12	17	388200	T. Furnival & Sons	Cobridge
16	4	388296	Wood & Son	Burslem
19	4	388395	Lowe, Ratcliffe & Co.	Longton
31	2	389136	Wm. Lowe	Longton
Nov 1	14	389201	Stonier, Hollinshead & Oliver	Hanley
4	19	389390	The Worcester Royal Porcelain Co. Ltd.	Worcester
8	2	389554	Mintons	Stoke
10	10	389793	Ridgways	Stoke
10	12	389795–7	Pratt & Simpson	Fenton
11	2	389801	Powell, Bishop & Stonier	Hanley
13	1	389893	Edge, Malkin & Co.	Burslem
13	2	389894	Sampson Bridgwood & Son	Longton
14	3	389911–2	Ed. Steel	Hanley
15	7	390004–5	S. Fielding & Co.	Stoke
16	3	390023	Taylor, Tunnicliffe & Co.	Hanley
21	4	390255	J. Holdcroft	Longton

Date	Parcel No.	Patent No.	Factory, Retailer Wholesaler, etc	Place
21	8	390264	Gildea & Walker	Burslem
22	11	390285	S. Fielding & Co.	Stoke
24	19	390588	Minton, Hollins & Co.	Stoke
27	3	390617	H. Alcock & Co.	Cobridge
27	4	390618	The Derby Crown Porcelain Co. Ltd.	Derby
27	5	390619	J. F. Wileman & Co.	Fenton
Dec 2	8	390976	Minton, Hollins & Co.	Stoke
4	7	390985	A. Bevington & Co.	Hanley
6	2	391068–9	T. C. Brown–Westhead, Moore & Co.	Hanley
13	4	391361–2	Mintons	Stoke
13	5	391363–4	Josiah Wedgwood	Etruria
14	6	391409	S. Lear	Hanley
15	3	391460	The Old Hall Earthenware Co. Ltd.	Hanley
18	9	391596	J. Lockett & Co.	Longton
19	3	391620	H. Kennedy	Glasgow
21	4	391768	E. J. D. Bodley	Burslem
21	5	391769	Wood, Hines & Winkle	Hanley
22	2	391818	F. W. Grove & J. Stark	Longton
22	14	391846	Lorenz Hutschenreuther	Bavaria
23	4	391855	J. F. Wileman	Fenton
23	12	391917	The New Wharf Pottery Co.	Burslem
23	14	391922–7	The Worcester Royal Porcelain Co.	Worcester
27	1	391929	The New Wharf Pottery Co.	Burslem
1883				
Jan 2	2	392166	The Derby Crown Porcelain Co. Ltd.	Derby
3	1	392176	Wm. Hines	Longton
3	14	392362	T. Furnival & Sons	Cobridge

384

Date	Parcel No.	Patent No.	Factory, Retailer Wholesaler, etc	Place
3	18	392388–9	John Rose & Co.	Coalport
4	5	392403	T. C. Brown–Westhead, Moore & Co.	Hanley
8	5	392590	W. T. Copeland & Sons	Stoke
8	12	392621	The Worcester Royal Porcelain Co. Ltd.	Worcester
9	3	392626	Powell, Bishop & Stonier	Hanley
9	4	392627	E. F. Bodley & Son	Longport
9	5	392628–30	Hall & Read	Hanley
9	11	392652	Davenports Ltd.	Longport
10	17	392693	Gildea & Walker	Burslem
12	3	392725	Holmes, Plant & Maydew	Burslem
13	6	392760	Moore & Co.	Longton
13	17	392809	T. & R. Boote	Burslem
16	1	392855	Blair & Co.	Longton
17	3	392888	W. H. Grindley & Co.	Tunstall
23	8	393099	E. F. Bodley & Son	Longport
23	10	393102–3	W. T. Copeland & Sons	Stoke
24	1	393107	Sampson Bridgwood & Son	Longton
24	2	393108–9	Wm. Brownfield & Sons	Cobridge
25	3	393177	The Brownhills Pottery Co.	Tunstall
26	8	393258	Wm. Lowe	Longton
27	8	393298	G. W. Turner & Sons	Tunstall
29	6	393310	Wm. Brownfield & Sons	Cobridge
29	7	393311–2	W. H. Grindley & Co.	Tunstall
30	1	393323	E. F. Bodley & Son	Longport
30	12	393362	Wedgwood & Co.	Tunstall
31	14	393413	Minton, Hollins & Co.	Stoke
Feb 1	3	393418	Sampson Bridgwood & Son	Longton
1	17	393474	E. J. D. Bodley	Burslem
2	4	393495	S. Hancock	Stoke
2	17	393539	Wedgwood & Co.	Tunstall
3	3	393548	Mintons	Stoke
5	2	393647	J. Holdcroft	Longton
6	1	393668	Wood, Hines & Winkle	Hanley

APPENDIX B

Date	Parcel No.	Patent No.	Factory, Retailer Wholesaler, etc	Place
7	4	393714	Hawley & Co.	Longton
7	5	393715	Mountford & Thomas	Hanley
9	9	393979	E. J. D. Bodley	Burslem
12	3	394086	Dunn, Bennett & Co.	Hanley
14	3	394185	W. H. Grindley & Co.	Tunstall
15	5	394215	J. H. Davis	Hanley
17	13	394371	G. W. Turner & Sons	Tunstall
19	1	394374	W. A. Adderley	Longton
20	13	394443	Davenports Ltd.	Longport
20	17	394448	Gildea & Walker	Burslem
21	3	394452	Geo. Jones & Sons	Stoke
22	6	394556–61	Hall & Read	Hanley
22	20	394599	The Worcester Royal Porcelain Co. Ltd.	Worcester
22	21	394600	The Old Hall Earthenware Co.	Hanley
24	12	394676	Josiah Wedgwood & Sons	Etruria
24	13	394677	The Worcester Royal Porcelain Co. Ltd.	Worcester
26	6	394687	Williamson & Sons	Longton
28	3	394765	Thos. Till & Sons	Burslem
Mar 8	5	395284	M. Massey	Hanley
8	20	395316–7	E. F. Bodley & Son	Longport
14	3	395560	The Derby Porcelain Co. Ltd.	Derby
15	3	395622	T. Furnival & Sons	Cobridge
16	6	395688	J. Broadhurst	Fenton
17	8	395703	Mintons	Stoke
20	3	395818	E. A. Wood	Hanley
20	4	395819	Josiah Wedgwood & Sons	Etruria
24	3	396056	Sampson Bridgwood & Son	Longton
30	1	396200–1	Mintons	Stoke
30	9	396245	Minton, Hollins & Co.	Stoke
Apr 2	3	396313	T. & E. L. Poulson	Castleford
3	3	396316	E. Warburton	Longton

APPENDIX B

Date	Parcel No.	Patent No.	Factory, Retailer Wholesaler, etc	Place
6	14	396576	G. & J. Hobson	Burslem
10	1	396648	Banks & Thorley	Hanley
19	3	397090	R. H. Plant & Co.	Longton
21	1	397227	J. F. Wileman & Co.	Fenton
24	7	397311	G. L. Ashworth & Bros.	Hanley
25	14	397376	Pratt & Simpson	Fenton
27	17	397512	C. Littler & Co.	Hanley
27	18	397513	J. H. Davis	Hanley
27	19	397514	Powell, Bishop & Stonier	Hanley
May 2	4	397609–11	T. C. Brown–Westhead, Moore & Co.	Hanley
5	4	397751	Whittaker, Edge & Co.	Hanley
7	8	397819	S. Fielding & Co.	Stoke
8	6	397829–30	T. G. & F. Booth	Tunstall
11	5	398059	R. H. Plant & Co.	Longton
16	12	398280	T. A. Simpson	Stoke
22	11	398425	Powell, Bishop & Stonier	Hanley
22	12	398426	Burns, Oates	London
23	7	398436	T. G. & F. Booth	Tunstall
23	8	398437–8	E. A. Wood	Hanley
24	3	398479	The Brownhills Pottery Co.	Tunstall
25	4	398519	W. A. Adderley	Longton
28	2	398577–80	O. G. Blunden	Poling
31	17	398784	Wardle & Co.	Hanley
June 2	9	398849–55	Minton, Hollins & Co.	Stoke
4	8	398877–8	Clementson Bros.	Hanley
8	2	399068	H. Alcock & Co.	Cobridge
9	2	399135–6	Sampson Bridgwood & Son	Longton
9	6	399143	Mintons	Stoke
11	2	399147	F. W. Grove & J. Stark	Longton
11	8	399161	J. Matthews	Westons-s'-Mare
11	9	399162	idem	Westons-s'-Mare

Date	Parcel No.	Patent No.	Factory, Retailer Wholesaler, etc	Place
13	3	399319	Belfield & Co.	Preston-pans
13	7	399336	Pratt & Simpson	Stoke
14	2	399367–70	F. W. Grove & J. Stark	Longton
18	11	399554	John Tams	Longton
18	12	399555–9	Wm. Brownfield & Sons	Cobridge
20	3	399640	T. & R. Boote	Burslem
20	4	399641	Mintons	Stoke
20	16	399675	W. & E. Corn	Burslem
21	22	399822	Wardle & Co.	Hanley
23	4	399875	Josiah Wedgwood & Sons	Etruria
25	5	399891	Ford & Riley	Burslem
25	10	399897–8	Wm. Brownfield & Sons	Cobridge
July 2	4	400146	Edge, Malkin & Co.	Burslem
3	3	400176	J. Aynsley & Sons	Longton
3	4	400177	Moore Bros.	Longton
4	7	400348	Wm. Brownfield & Sons	Cobridge
5	6	400367	F. W. Grove & J. Stark	Longton
5	19	400462	T. Furnival & Sons	Cobridge
5	21	400464	Owen, Raby & Co.	Longport
6	2	400467	Blackhurst & Bourne	Burslem
10	9	400582	Ambrose Wood	Hanley
10	11	400583–4	J. Macintyre & Co.	Burslem
11	1	400596	Josiah Wedgwood & Sons	Etruria
19	4	400941	Davenports Ltd.	Longport
19	21	400994	Geo. Jones & Sons	Stoke
20	11	401035	Hollinshead & Kirkham	Tunstall
21	3	401040	Bridgett & Bates	Longton
23	3	401087	Josiah Wedgwood & Sons	Etruria
26	1	401296	W. A. Adderley	Longton
27	4	401410	T. C. Brown–Westhead, Moore & Co.	Hanley
27	13	401426–7	Wm. Bennett	Hanley
30	10	401553	Wm. Brownfield & Sons	Cobridge
31	3	401593	T. & R. Boote	Burslem

APPENDIX B

Date		Parcel No.	Patent No.	Factory, Retailer Wholesaler, etc	Place
Aug	1	3	401623	Wagstaff & Brunt	Longton
	1	4	401624	Geo. Jones & Sons	Stoke
	1	9	401653	T. C. Brown–Westhead, Moore & Co.	Hanley
	2	3	401663–4	Davenports Ltd.	Longport
	3	17	401769	E. J. Bodley	Burslem
	8	9	401842	J. & E. Ridgway	Stoke
	9	15	401897–9	Haviland & Co.	France and London
	17	5	402346	E. J. D. Bodley	Burslem
	20	8	402514	The Worcester Royal Porcelain Co. Ltd.	Worcester
	22	1	402560–1	The Brownhills Pottery Co.	Tunstall
	23	2	402625–6	Grove & Cope	Hanley
	24	12	402736	Mountford & Thomas	Hanley
	25	11	402839	Wm. Brownfield & Sons	Cobridge
	29	3	402950	J. Aynsley & Sons	Longton
	31	6	403110	W. & E. Corn	Burslem
	31	7	403111	J. F. Wileman & Co.	Fenton
Sept	1	10	403204	S. Fielding & Co.	Stoke
	5	3	403298–9	Wm. Brownfield & Sons	Cobridge
	7	4	403486	The Derby Crown Porcelain Co. Ltd.	Derby
	7	19	403513–4	Powell, Bishop & Stonier	Hanley
	11	4	403665	Josiah Wedgwood & Sons	Etruria
	13	17	403802–3	H. Aynsley & Co.	Longton
	14	1	403805–6	W. & T. Adams	Tunstall
	14	2	403807–9	Mintons	Stoke
	17	14	403978	The Derby Crown Porcelain Co. Ltd.	Derby
	20	12	404171–5	Hall & Read	Hanley
	20	13	404176	The Derby Crown Porcelain Co. Ltd.	Derby

APPENDIX B

Date		Parcel No.	Patent No.	Factory, Retailer Wholesaler, etc	Place
	21	4	404196	T. C. Brown–Westhead, Moore & Co.	Hanley
	24	9	404317	Jones & Hopkinson	Hanley
	25	4	404328	F. W. Grove & J. Stark	Longton
	25	5	404329–30	Sampson Bridgwood & Son	Longton
	27	21	404466	Meigh & Forester	Longton
	28	4	404473	Blair & Co.	Longton
	28	5	404474	E. J. D. Bodley	Burslem
	29	4	404571	Sampson Bridgwood & Son	Longton
Oct	2	15	404643	Mellor, Taylor & Co.	Burslem
	2	22	404652–3	Meigh & Forester	Longton
	4	4	404745	Sampson Bridgwood & Son	Longton
	4	5	404746	Whittaker, Edge & Co.	Hanley
	4	24	404809	The Worcester Royal Porcelain Co. Ltd.	Worcester
	6	2	404870	W. H. Grindley & Co.	Tunstall
	8	1	404900	Hollinson & Goodall	Longton
	8	2	404901–2	T. G. & F. Booth	Tunstall
	8	3	404903–5	Hall & Read	Hanley
	9	9	405016–8	A. Bevington & Co.	Hanley
	11	2	405215	Wittmann & Roth	London
	12	13	405336	Bridgetts & Bates	Longton
	13	3	405341	Wood & Son	Burslem
	13	11	405363–4	Wm. Brownfield & Sons	Cobridge
	17	5	405466	The New Wharf Pottery Co.	Burslem
	17	6	405467–8	Hall & Read	Hanley
	20	3	405724	W. A. Adderley	Longton
	20	4	405725–9	Wm. Brownfield & Sons	Cobridge
	23	6	405855	J. Dimmock & Co.	Hanley
	24	11	405946–8	Minton, Hollins & Co.	Stoke
	25	17	406032–3	Taylor, Tunnicliffe & Co.	Hanley
	26	7	406043	Jones & Hopkinson	Hanley
	27	1	406046	The Brownhills Pottery Co.	Tunstall

APPENDIX B

Date	Parcel No.	Patent No.	Factory, Retailer Wholesaler, etc	Place
30	2	406140	J. Marshall & Co.	Bo'ness, Scotland
30	3	406141	The New Wharf Pottery Co.	Burslem
30	17	406187	J. Robinson	Burslem
Nov 1	1	406223	A. Bevington & Co.	Hanley
1	25	406370	Wood, Hines & Winkle	Hanley
1	26	406371	S. Fielding & Co.	Stoke
1	27	406372	Davenports Ltd.	Longport
2	19	406464–9	The Worcester Royal Porcelain Co. Ltd.	Worcester
5	13	406511	H. Alcock & Co.	Cobridge
6	3	406516	E. & C. Challinor	Fenton
7	2	406561	W. & E. Corn	Burslem
10	9	406781	Taylor, Tunnicliffe & Co.	Hanley
10	10	406782	Wm. Brownfield & Sons	Cobridge
13	10	406875	T. G. & F. Booth	Tunstall
14	3	406893	Stonier, Hollinshead & Oliver	Hanley
15	17	407063	T. Furnival & Sons	Cobridge
17	2	407155	The Derby Crown Porcelain Co. Ltd.	Derby
21	3	407333	F. J. Emery	Burslem
22	3	407385	S. Fielding & Co.	Stoke
23	7	407587–8	Minton, Hollins & Co.	Stoke
24	3	407601	Powell, Bishop & Stonier	Hanley
26	2	407623	W. A. Adderley	Longton
26	3	407624	Sampson Bridgwood & Son	Longton
28	12	407805–10	The Worcester Royal Porcelain Co. Ltd.	Worcester
Dec 1	3	407913	idem	Worcester
3	10	407943	James Wilson	Longton
5	2	408035	Malkin, Edge & Co.	Burslem
5	3	408036	The Derby Crown Porcelain Co. Ltd.	Derby

APPENDIX B

Date	Parcel No.	Patent No.	Factory, Retailer Wholesaler, etc	Place
8	8	408136	J. F. Wileman & Co.	Fenton
14	4	408288	The Brownhills Pottery Co.	Tunstall
15	13	408356	T. G. & F. Booth	Tunstall
15	14	408357	Hollinson & Goodall	Longton
29	4	408849	Powell, Bishop & Stonier	Hanley

Index

Some of the firms listed in Appendix B did not use accepted factory-marks and are therefore omitted from the general index.

394

395

397

400

401

403

410

412

414

416

421

423

424

426